The Mystery of Israel and the Church

A four-volume series

The Mystery of Israel and the Church

The Mystery of Israel and the Church

Volume 1

Figure and Fulfillment

Lawrence Feingold

The Miriam Press

Imprimatur: †Most Reverend Robert J. Hermann
               Auxiliary Bishop of St. Louis
               St. Louis, MO
               April 16, 2008

Copyright © 2010 by Lawrence Feingold
The Miriam Press
4120 West Pine Boulevard
St. Louis, MO 63108
www.hebrewcatholic.org

Cover Design: Kelly Boutross
Cover Art: Mosaic depicting the sacrifice of Isaac from the Cathedral Basilica of St. Louis, MO. Photograph by Mark Abeln. Used with permission.

ISBN: 978-0-939409-03-7

Dedicated to Mary,
Daughter of Zion,
Mother of the Messiah,
Mother of the Church

"Theirs is the sonship and the glory and the covenants and the law and the worship and the promises; theirs are the fathers and from them is the Christ according to the flesh."

Romans 9:4–5

Table of Contents

Foreword

The Mystery of Israel and the Church: Figure and Fulfillment is the first volume in a series that seeks to present Catholic theology with an eye to the great importance of that mystery. Each volume contains the text of a series of lectures presented by Dr. Feingold, with each chapter corresponding to one lecture.

The various series of lectures, sponsored by the Association of Hebrew Catholics (AHC) at the Cathedral Basilica School in Saint Louis, Missouri, have been ongoing since the fall of 2007. We are very grateful for the wonderful gifts given by our Lord to Dr. Feingold and for his great generosity in sharing his gifts, at no cost, with all who have willing hearts and open minds.

Lawrence Feingold expertly weaves together Sacred Scripture, Magisterial teachings, the Church Fathers, St. Thomas Aquinas, Pope John Paul II, Pope Benedict XVI, and many others, along with the teaching that has come from Vatican II. What one especially appreciates about his presentations is his ability to present difficult and abstract material in an intelligible and digestible way. He also presents the story of Israel and her role in salvation history in a magnificent light that enables us to better appreciate all that God has brought to pass through His great fidelity, love, and mercy in fulfilling the promises He made to Israel.

Lawrence Feingold and his wife Marsha, both Hebrew Catholics, entered the Church in 1989. Dr. Feingold studied Philosophy and Theology at the Pontifical University of the Holy Cross in Rome, earning a doctorate in Systematic Theology in 1999. He spent a year studying Biblical Hebrew and Greek at the Studium Biblicum Franciscanum in Jerusalem in 1995–96. He then taught Philosophy and Theology in the House of Formation of Miles Christi in Argentina. Currently he is Assistant Professor of Theology for the Institute of Pastoral Theology of Ave Maria University. In addition to the AHC lectures, Dr. Feingold is also part of the RCIA team at the Cathedral Basilica Parish, has taught at Kenrick-Glennon Seminary, and finds time one evening a week to host a study session in his home on various aspects of the teaching of St. Thomas Aquinas.

In issue 85 of *The Hebrew Catholic*, Dr. Feingold gives his "Account of My Conversion."[1] As he relates his journey to faith in the Messiah and to His Church, Dr. Feingold writes:

---

[1] http://www.hebrewcatholic.org/TheHebrewCatholic/85winter-spring2.html.

So I set out to pray for the first time. I took the train to go to Florence to pray in the Duomo built by Brunelleschi. I was not definitively thinking of Christianity, but nor was I opposed to it. On the way, I was moved to make this prayer: *Teach me to love; teach me to be a light unto others.* I don't know why I prayed like this, but to this day I know of no better prayer.

God so wants us to pray, that if we do so, He pours His grace upon us. After making this prayer, I thought of the words of Psalm 2: *"You are my son; this day I have begotten you."* Although an atheist, I knew the Bible from studying art history and comparative religion. And in this moment of grace I understood that these words were addressed by God the Father to Jesus Christ His Son, and also to me (and all other human beings) *in Christ* the Son.

Not only did our Lord give Dr. Feingold the gift that enabled him to understand who Jesus Christ was and is, but He answered his initial prayer, giving him the grace *to be a light unto others*, a grace to which Dr. Feingold has so faithfully corresponded.

In the concluding paragraphs of his "Account," Dr. Feingold writes:

Many Jews who come to believe in Christ and the Church He founded feel anguish over what is perceived as a betrayal of the Jewish people. My wife and I never experienced this trial. On the contrary, I discovered a great attraction for things Jewish that I never experienced before. I had never learned Hebrew as a child, but I found great joy in learning it as a Christian, so as to pray the Psalms, for example, in the language of the Chosen People. This sense was clarified and stimulated by reading the book *Jewish Identity* by Fr. Elias Friedman, founder of the Association of Hebrew Catholics, which I came across not long after our entrance into the Catholic Church.

In the first years after our conversion, people often asked me why I "chose" Christianity or the Catholic Church, and not Judaism or Buddhism or Protestantism. The question is framed in the language of religious liberalism, as if religion were a matter of our personal sentiments, personal preferences, personal loyalties or choices. The experience of converts is not that we have chosen anything, but that it is God who has chosen to redeem us through the Incarnation and Passion of the Messiah, which is continued and made present in the Catholic Church, and it is God who called us to enter the ark of salvation. We who have been given the grace to hear, through no merit of our own, have the duty to pray for those who have not yet been given that gift.

If these lectures enable readers to grow in their understanding of the mysteries of God, they will find that they will also grow in their appreciation of the Jewish roots of their faith, in gratitude for all that God has done, and in the love of our Lord, *Yeshua haMashiach*.[2] May it be so!

Briefly stated, the mission of the Association of Hebrew Catholics is pastoral and educational: to preserve the identity and heritage of Jews within the Church, helping them to serve the Lord, His Church, and all peoples within the mystery of their irrevocable calling. Those who are interested may write to the AHC, 4120 W Pine Blvd., Saint Louis, MO 63108, for more information and a sample issue of our publication, *The Hebrew Catholic*.

Now we invite you to partake of a feast of the Spirit as you encounter the truths of our faith given by Jesus Christ, preserved by the Church, taught by the Magisterium, and here presented by Dr. Lawrence Feingold. May you be blessed.

David Moss, President
Association of Hebrew Catholics

---

[2] All of the lectures represented by the chapters of this volume, including question-and-answer sessions after each lecture, can be listened to or downloaded to your computer at no cost from the AHC website at http://www.hebrewcatholic.org/Studies/MysteryofIsraelChurch/mysteryofisraela.html.

Preface

This book is the first of a four-volume set that grew out of a lecture series entitled "The Mystery of Israel and the Church," organized by the Association of Hebrew Catholics and held in the fall of 2007 in the Cathedral Basilica of St. Louis. Interest was expressed in bringing these talks to a wider public, without losing their original character as oral presentations. Their principal focus is to bring out the beautiful role of Israel in the history of salvation and the deep ties between Israel and the Church.

It is hoped that this book may deepen the awareness of Catholics (and others) of the luminous teaching of the Second Vatican Council, *Nostra aetate* 4:

> As the sacred synod searches into the mystery of the Church, it remembers the bond that spiritually ties the people of the New Covenant to Abraham's stock.
>
> Thus the Church of Christ acknowledges that, according to God's saving design, the beginnings of her faith and her election are found already among the Patriarchs, Moses, and the prophets. She professes that all who believe in Christ—Abraham's sons according to faith—are included in the same Patriarch's call, and likewise that the salvation of the Church is mysteriously foreshadowed by the chosen people's exodus from the land of bondage. The Church, therefore, cannot forget that she received the revelation of the Old Testament through the people with whom God in His inexpressible mercy concluded the Ancient Covenant. Nor can she forget that she draws sustenance from the root of that well-cultivated olive tree onto which have been grafted the wild shoots, the Gentiles. . . . God holds the Jews most dear for the sake of their Fathers; He does not repent of the gifts He makes or of the calls He issues—such is the witness of the Apostle. In company with the Prophets and the same Apostle, the Church awaits that day, known to God alone, on which all peoples will address the Lord in a single voice and "serve him shoulder to shoulder" (Zeph 3:9).
>
> Since the spiritual patrimony common to Christians and Jews is thus so great, this sacred synod wants to foster and recommend that mutual understanding and respect which is the fruit, above all, of biblical and theological studies as well as of fraternal dialogues.

I would like to thank the President of the Association of Hebrew Catholics, David Moss, and his wife, Kathleen, for organizing and sponsoring the lecture series which were the origin of these volumes.

Special thanks go to Archbishop Burke for welcoming the Association of Hebrew Catholics into the Archdiocese of St. Louis and supporting our work, and to Archbishop Carlson and Bishop Hermann for continuing that support. I also thank our pastor, Msgr. Pins, for his support and for allowing us to use the Cathedral Basilica School for the lecture series. Above all, I would like to thank my wife, Marsha, who is my editor, inspiration, and support, and who spent countless hours improving the text. I also thank everyone else who helped to edit these volumes, and all those who attended the series and contributed with their encouragement and their questions and comments.

I would also like to thank Ave Maria University's Institute for Pastoral Theology. This book and the other volumes in this series have been enriched by my teaching experience with this remarkable program. It is our conviction in the Institute for Pastoral Theology that deeper knowledge of Catholic doctrine, growth in holiness, the life of prayer, and pastoral activity are inseparably united. Greater knowledge of the truths of the faith should help us to love God more faithfully and to lead others to that same truth and love, thereby helping to build up the Church. I pray that a more perfect knowledge of the Catholic faith, including its Jewish roots, may lead the reader to a deeper encounter with the God of Abraham, Isaac, and Jacob—the Triune God glimpsed by these Patriarchs, in whose seed all nations have been blessed (Gen 22:18).

List of Abbreviations

Abbreviation of Sources

ANF   *The Ante-Nicene Fathers*. Peabody, MA: Hendrickson, 1994.

CCC   *Catechism of the Catholic Church*.

D   Denzinger. *The Sources of Catholic Dogma*. Fitzwilliam, NH: Loreto, 2002.

DS   Denzinger-Schönmetzer. *Enchiridion Symbolorum, definitionum et declarationum de rebus fidei et morum* (1965).

PG   *Patrologia graeca*. J.P. Migne, ed. Paris, 1857 ff.

PL   *Patrologia latina*. J.P. Migne, ed. Paris, 1844 ff.

ST   *Summa theologiae of St. Thomas Aquinas*. 2nd ed. Translated by Dominican Fathers of the English Province. London: Burns, Oates, & Washbourne, 1920–1932.

Other Abbreviations

a.   article

ch.   chapter

q.   question

n.   paragraph number

CHAPTER I

The Trinity, the Messiah, and the Election of Israel

Many Jews are surprised to learn that Catholic theology believes firmly in the divine election of Israel for a unique and incomparably noble mission, the greatest role of any nation in history. The modern mind finds it scandalous that God has singled out one people from all the nations of the earth. Furthermore, many secular Jews in recent years also seem ready to renounce the belief of having been uniquely chosen. And this is very understandable, considering the tremendous historical burden of persecution and suffering endured by the Jewish people.

Why did God choose to form a special and absolutely unique covenant with one nation? The brief answer is for the sake of the Messiah. They were chosen to give the Messiah to the world. To Abraham it was promised: "In your seed all nations of the earth will be blessed" (Gen 12:3; 18:18; 22:18; 26:4; 28:14). Orthodox Judaism and Christianity believe this promise refers to the Messiah. They are united in their conviction that the Messiah stands at the center of the meaning of the world, its redemption, and God's plan for humanity.

However, to make this understandable, we have to make a long digression and back up to the beginning of history, and before. In fact, the only way we can properly understand the election of Israel is to ask a second more basic question: Why did God create the world, and man in particular? Let us try to look at this question from God's point of view. Then we shall ask a third question: What is the role of the Messiah in God's plan for mankind? Why did God want to send a Messiah, and what is his connection with every man? To answer we shall have to briefly explain the two fundamental Christian mysteries that pose difficulties to Jews: the Trinity and the Incarnation. Only after having considered these last two questions can we hope to understand our first question of why God chose one people out of all the nations on earth.

Why Did God Create the World?

What is *God's goal* in creating human beings, and in creating the universe? God is an ocean of infinite being, goodness, truth, and beauty. He is the First Cause of all things and thus He must be Himself

1

uncaused, unchanging, eternal, infinitely good, infinitely wise, omnipotent, infinitely just, infinitely merciful. Every perfection that God gives to creatures He must first possess in an unlimited way, for no one can give what he does not have.

Now since this is true, it is obvious that God does not need creation in any way, for He is eternally fulfilled in Himself, being infinite goodness. What could creation add to God that He does not already possess infinitely? Nothing. We do not add anything to God. So why does He create us and the world?

The only answer can be that He creates out of pure goodness, to manifest, share, and communicate that goodness outside of Himself, so that His goodness can be imitated, known, and loved by creatures. Philosophers say that it belongs to the nature of goodness to seek to spread or communicate itself as far as possible. It is not a mechanical necessity, but a communication through love, based on the very power of attraction of the good, which seeks to bring others to it. God creates the world so that His goodness may attract all creatures to Him, and thus they may come to share in that goodness insofar as they can.

Theology and Scripture express this using the notion of *glory* (*kavod*). God creates the world to manifest the glory of His infinite goodness outside of Himself, and thus to attract all things back into union with Him. God can have no other purpose than this. He creates the world, and especially men and angels, to manifest, radiate, and communicate His goodness outside of Himself, which communication leads all things back to Him.[1]

When God revealed Himself on Mt. Sinai, He was clothed in glory, a glory both visible and invisible. It was visible in the cloud, thunder, and fire that accompanied the invisible, and yet more glorious, revelation of the moral law to Israel through Moses. This sensible glory is a sign of the holiness of the moral law.

When God brought the Chosen People out of Israel with an outstretched arm and marvelous prodigies, Miriam and the Israelites sang a hymn to God's glory that was manifested in the miracles, but much more in His mercy to them. Likewise, when King Solomon built the Temple in Jerusalem, the glory of God filled the Temple in a visible way. His glory was revealed invisibly, however, in the manifestation of His mercy in being with His people and being there to hear their prayers.

---

[1] See Vatican I, Dogmatic Constitution *Dei Filius*, ch. 1, canon 5, DS 3025: "If any one shall say that the world was not created for the glory of God, let him be anathema." This glory of God is His *extrinsic glory*.

The notion of glory contains three essential elements: an intrinsic *excellence*, a *manifestation* of that excellence, and an *appreciation* or *praise* of that excellence on the part of others, which is also their participation in it. A genius has no glory if his excellence is kept unknown. Michelangelo, despite his great natural gifts, would have no glory if he made no sculpture; or if having been made, it was never manifested to anyone; or if having been manifested, it was not appreciated by those others. Creation gives glory to God when God's infinite excellence is made known through the cosmos and then is rightly appreciated and praised by man.

The notion of glory, rightly understood, is very different from vainglory. We speak of vainglory when someone seeks to be praised as an end in itself, even though he lacks an intrinsic excellence worthy of praise. Seeking praise for oneself without being the source of some excellence is vain. However, to seek appreciation for intrinsic excellence is not vain, because it is *due* to true goodness to be appreciated, loved, and praised as God's gift.

Now God Himself *is* infinite Goodness that is infinitely glorious in itself, and thus it is not vainglory for God to want Himself, who is infinite Goodness and the source of all good, to be known, shared in, loved, and praised. If goodness is unknown or unappreciated, that is a tragedy for those who do not appreciate it. It does not harm Michelangelo or Beethoven if we do not appreciate their works, but it harms us, because those works are worthy of love and appreciation, and we become perfected by loving what is good. So for God to create the world for the sake of His glory—to manifest and communicate His Goodness and have it loved and imitated—is not vainglory, but love.

God's Intrinsic Glory before the Creation of the World

Let us look more closely at God's glory. Does God have glory independently of creation, or does He need creation to have glory? There is a difficult problem here. On the one hand, God is perfectly glorious in Himself. It would be ridiculous for Him to need creation to have glory, for then in a certain way He would be dependent on us, which would be absurd. However, glory, and beatitude also, as we have said, require a *sharing* and a *communication*. We can grasp from our human experience that possession of the good, without communion, would not make us happy. This is where the ineffable mystery of the Trinity reveals its sublime fittingness.

God can communicate His goodness in two ways: in an infinite and perfect way, or in a finite and hence imperfect way. The finite communication of God's goodness is creation. We know that God has communicated His goodness in a finite way, for here we are. Has He also communicated Himself in an infinite way?

Obviously, an infinite communication would be infinitely more glorious: it would give infinite glory to God. What would this mean? If God communicated Himself infinitely and perfectly, then the recipient of that self-communication of God would receive everything that God is, and thus would also be everything that God is: eternal, all-knowing, omnipotent, Wisdom, Truth, Goodness, Love, Justice, Mercy, etc. He would be the perfect Image of God the Father. This communication would be an eternal and infinite self-giving of God, creating communion within the divinity.

In the Old Testament we find hints of this mystery. In the book of Proverbs 8:22–31, traditionally attributed to King Solomon, there is a mysterious passage about the divine Wisdom, who speaks as follows:

> The Lord possessed me in the beginning of his ways, before he made anything from the beginning. I was set up from eternity, and of old before the earth was made. The depths were not as yet, and I was already conceived, neither had the fountains of waters as yet sprung out. The mountains with their huge bulk had not as yet been established; before the hills I was brought forth: he had not yet made the earth, nor the rivers, nor the poles of the world. When he prepared the heavens, I was present; when with a certain law and compass he enclosed the depths; when he established the sky above, and poised the fountains of waters, when he compassed the sea with its bounds, and set a law to the waters that they should not pass their limits; when he balanced the foundations of the earth, I was with him forming all things, and was delighted every day, playing before him at all times; playing in the world; and my delights were to be with the children of men.[2]

Here we see God's Wisdom, distinct from the Father, delighting in the Father, and in whom the Father delights. Yet He shares in the attributes of the Father, for He is eternal, begotten of the Father before all creation.[3]

---

[2] Douay-Rheims version.

[3] See also Sir 24:3–4: "I came forth from the mouth of the Most High. . . . I dwelt in high places, and my throne was in a pillar of cloud." Another very significant text about Wisdom is from the prophet Baruch 3:31–37, who likewise speaks of the divine Wisdom as distinct from the Father: "No one knows the way to her [Wisdom], or is concerned about the path to her. But he who knows all things knows her, he found her by his understanding. . . . He found the whole way to knowledge, and gave her to Jacob his servant and to Israel whom he loved. Afterward she appeared upon earth and lived among men."

Another text is from the prophet Micah (5:2), who connects the eternal divine Wisdom with the birth of the Messiah in Bethlehem: "And thou, Bethlehem Ephrata, art a little one among the thousands of Judah. Out of thee shall he come forth unto me that is to be the ruler in Israel; and his going forth is *from the beginning, from the days of eternity.*"[4] On the basis of these and other texts, the ancient rabbis recognized that the Messiah pre-existed somehow in God from eternity.[5] We will return to these texts in greater detail in the following chapters.

In this eternal begetting of the divine Wisdom—also spoken of as Word or Son—God is *infinitely glorified,* for He communicates Himself infinitely, and is perfectly comprehended and praised. The Son (divine Wisdom) is not another god, contradicting monotheism, because if God has communicated Himself perfectly and infinitely, then the begotten is not another god, but the same one God, "one in being with the Father." They share the same Godhead. God's Wisdom is not another God, although begotten of Him. The Father and the Son differ only in this: that the Father eternally begets and the Son is eternally begotten.

The Son, receiving the divine Being from the Father as His eternal Word and Wisdom, the fruit of God's infinite knowing of Himself, gives glory to the Father. That glory and love with which the Son loves and glorifies the Father, and vice versa, is itself divine, an impetus of infinite divine love, referred to in the Bible as the Holy Spirit (*ruach ha kodesh*), or the Spirit of God. Spirit here means impetus, wind, or breath of love.

St. Augustine illuminates this great mystery by reflecting on the two spiritual operations of knowing and loving.[6] God is pure Spirit, and He therefore has an eternal operation of knowing all Truth and willing all Good. When we know something, we form in our minds a concept or interior word that represents what we know. Our concepts are limited, vague, and imperfect. Now when God knows Himself, He likewise forms an interior Word that represents what He knows. His interior Word, however, is perfect and infinite, the express Image of the Father,[7] so much so that it is God Himself: the eternal Son.

Likewise, when we love someone, there is engendered in us an impulse of love uniting us to the beloved in an intimate way, through a gift of self. The more perfectly we love someone, the more total is the impetus of love and the resulting gift of oneself. God infinitely loving Himself—the Father loving the Son and the Son loving the Father—

---

[4] Douay-Rheims version.

[5] See Robert Leo Odom, *Israel's Preexistent Messiah* (New York: Israelite Heritage Institute, 1985), 20–23.

[6] See St. Augustine, *The Trinity*, trans. Edmund Hill (Hyde Park, NY: New City Press, 1991).

[7] See Col 1:15.

brings forth the divine Spirit of love—the Holy Spirit—who is God Himself proceeding as Love from the Father and the Son.

The acts by which God knows and loves Himself are infinitely fruitful, infinitely more fruitful than the creation of the world. The communion of the Holy Trinity allows the divine nature to be infinitely glorified in Himself, with the Son glorifying the Father, the Father glorifying the Son, and the Holy Spirit proceeding from the Father and the Son as the glory mutually given.

The communion of the three divine Persons can be obscurely recognized in the very first lines of Genesis, which speak of God the Creator, of His creative Word by which all things were made, and of the "Spirit of God" who "hovered over the waters" (Gen 1:2).

[handwritten margin note: Trinity]

The Glory of God and the Creation of Man

The eternal glory in God is infinite. However, He wills that glory to be manifested outside of Himself, and thus He communicates His goodness to creatures in countless finite ways, creating the natural order.

God created man to give glory to Him by appreciating the beauty of His work and cooperating in it. We do this by expressing our love and gratitude for nature, but much more for the moral law written on the human heart. This is man's natural end: to know and love God through creation and through the practice of the moral law summed up in the commandment of love.

However, God also willed to manifest His glory in a higher way by revealing Himself not just through creation and the natural moral law written on our heart. God revealed Himself to Adam and Eve not just as Creator, but in a more intimate kind of friendship, for Genesis 2 tells us that God walked with them in the Garden. We can deduce from this that Adam and Eve were created in the grace of divine friendship, by which they were *sons* of God and not just creatures of God. They had the initial friendship with God given by sanctifying grace, but not yet the consummated and immutable friendship given by glory in heaven. Their situation was blessed, but they were not yet at their final end—the beatific vision. They were created in a state of trial, as we are also.

God willed for Adam and Eve and for all their descendants including ourselves, a supernatural final end: to see the glory of God face to face, and to praise it, love it, and participate in it for all eternity. We call this the beatific vision. In seeing God we are drawn, as it were, into the eternal life of the blessed Trinity, a divine life of communion and glorification of the divine love. This end gives the maximum glory to God outside of God.

Nevertheless, this end is not due to us, for it infinitely exceeds human nature. It is gratuitous, a work of divine mercy and love. So that we come to duly appreciate this end, God wills that it be achieved as the crown of fidelity in a trial. Beatitude, according to the divine wisdom, is to be the reward of virtue.

The trial of Adam and Eve was simple. They had to keep one precept: not to eat of the tree of the knowledge of good and evil. We should understand this precept to mean that Adam and Eve were not to seek to make themselves masters of the knowledge of good and evil, as if they were morally autonomous, defining the moral law for themselves.[8] It should be noted that Adam had a role of responsibility not only for himself, but for all mankind. He had the power to preserve or destroy the gifts God had given to him and to his descendants through him.

The sin of Adam and Eve entailed doubting the divine goodness, putting themselves into competition with God, and trying to make themselves masters of the moral law. The devil tempted them to be as gods, defining good and evil for themselves.[9] The sin of Adam and Eve was the opposite of the glorification of God, frustrating His work in creation.

The punishment for the sin of Adam and Eve was loss of the gratuitous gifts given to them to be passed to their descendants. They lost the divine friendship in which they were created, the gift of sanctifying grace, the freedom from suffering and death, the infused knowledge, and the dominion over the passions of the body which they had enjoyed in the Garden.

---

[8] See John Paul II, encyclical *Dominum et Vivificantem*, 36: "The 'image of God,' consisting in rationality and freedom, expresses the greatness and dignity of the human subject, who is a person. But this personal subject is also always a creature: in his existence and essence he depends on the Creator. According to the Book of Genesis, 'the tree of the knowledge of good and evil' was to express and constantly remind man of the 'limit' impassable for a created being. God's prohibition is to be understood in this sense: the Creator forbids man and woman to eat of the fruit of the tree of the knowledge of good and evil. The words of the enticement, that is to say the temptation, as formulated in the sacred text, are an inducement to transgress this prohibition—that is to say, to go beyond that 'limit': 'When you eat of it your eyes will be opened, and you will be like God [like gods], knowing good and evil.'

"'Disobedience' means precisely going beyond that limit, which remains impassable to the will and the freedom of man as a created being. For God the Creator is the one definitive source of the moral order in the world created by him. Man cannot decide by himself what is good and what is evil—cannot 'know good and evil, like God.' In the created world God indeed remains the first and sovereign source *for deciding about good and evil*, through the intimate truth of being, which is the reflection *of the Word*, the eternal Son, consubstantial with the Father."

[9] See Gen 3:4–5: "You will not die. For God knows that when you eat of it your eyes will be opened, and you will be like God, knowing good and evil."

Thus with moral evil, physical evil also came into the world of human experience, and in the course of history, personal sins have been multiplied without number.

What is the divine plan for the remedy of the human race and the manifestation of the glory of God? We get a hint of it in the third chapter of Genesis. God speaks to the serpent, who represents Satan, and to Adam and Eve. To the serpent He says: "I will put enmity between you and the woman, and between your seed and her seed; he shall bruise [crush] your head, and you shall bruise his heel" (Gen 3:15). The devil and his cohorts will continually tempt the human race, but there shall be a woman whose seed will crush the head of Satan, and he shall be bruised—that is, suffer—in the process. This is the first mention of the Messiah/Christ in the Bible. We shall return to this cardinal text in the next chapter.

The Incarnation in God's Plan

Here we find a new element in God's eternal plan for the manifestation of His love: a man, born of a woman, will crush sin and the power of Satan, make reparation, and restore the glory of God trampled on by iniquity. In order to understand this, let us try to look at it from God's point of view. What would be the best way to give glory to the divine goodness, given the reality of the opposition of human sin? The glory of God and human sin are in battle. How shall the divine goodness be vindicated, loved, and appreciated by man?

The divine answer is the Incarnation of God the Son. The Son of God, who gives glory to the Father from all eternity before the creation of the world, enters into human history, becoming a son of man, so that the sons of men can become sons of God, enter into the divine friendship, and finally come to see God in heaven. This is the mission of the Messiah. He comes into human history to give glory to the Father, manifest Him to men, and realize the reconciliation of mankind with God.

In order to do this, the Messiah must remove the great obstacle of human sin by making reparation and winning forgiveness for us from the Father. This is what is meant by crushing the head of Satan. Human sin, by opposing God's law and love, offends God and detracts from the manifestation of His goodness. When we offend someone, reparation needs to be made. Yet man is incapable of making proper reparation to God because of the great weakness of his ability to love and the fact that through sin he has lost the right to the divine favor.

Therefore, it was fitting that the Son of God, the Second Person of the Blessed Trinity, become man so as to make reparation for all human sin, accomplishing this through His own suffering and death. Thus reparation would be made by a human being, a descendant of Adam and Eve who, like Adam, would be a new head of the human race and have responsibility for all of mankind. He could suffer for sinners while having a divine dignity and a divine charity that would give that suffering infinite value in the eyes of God, thus meriting the forgiveness of all human sin and the restoration of the divine friendship to all who sincerely seek forgiveness.

In this way the Incarnation would give the greatest possible glory to God that is conceivable, for it would manifest the divine goodness, love, and mercy more than anything else that God could do. "For God so loved the world that He gave His only Son, that whoever believes in Him should not perish, but have eternal life" (Jn 3:16).

In the Incarnation, therefore, divine majesty takes on the humility of a human life in all its stages. The divine power becomes an embryo, an infant in swaddling clothes, a man flogged by Roman soldiers and nailed to a Cross. Majesty takes on humility, power takes on weakness, glory takes on humiliation.[10] Why? For four principal reasons: To satisfy for human sin, to show man the full extent of God's love for man, to give man a perfect model of virtue, and to restore the sons of men to their original dignity as sons of God.

The word "Messiah," which comes from the Hebrew *mashiach*, means "anointed one"—anointed with the Holy Spirit. "Christ" comes from the Greek word for "anointed." The Messiah, or Christ, is a human being whose humanity is to be *anointed* and filled with the divinity, and thus with the divine love. In the Old Testament, anointment was reserved for three roles: (1) the High Priest Aaron and his descendants, (2) the kings of Israel beginning with Saul, and (3) some prophets, as Elijah anointed Elisha as his successor (1 Kings 19:16). In all three cases it indicated the special presence of the Holy Spirit of God in the priest, prophet, or king, to enable them to accomplish their mission to represent God. The Messiah is the Anointed One par excellence who will unite in His Person these three roles, prefigured by the historic prophets, priests, and kings. He is the Prophet, fully revealing God to the world;[11] He is the High Priest, reconciling the world with God; and He is to be the King over the Kingdom of God.[12]

Catholic theology understands this anointing of the humanity of the Messiah with the Holy Spirit as the Incarnation. The Incarnation refers to the fact that the pre-existent Word and Son of God, who glorifies the Father from all eternity, assumed a human nature in the course of

---

[10] See St. Leo the Great, Letter "Lectis dilectionis tuae" to Flavian (Tome of Leo), DS 293 (D 143).

[11] See Deut 18:15–19.

[12] See Ps 72:5.

human history and united it to Himself in the most intimate bond. We refer to this most intimate union of the humanity of the Messiah with His divinity as the *hypostatic union*, which means the union of the divinity and humanity in the one *Person* of the Son of God.

If the plan of God is to reveal the divine glory and crush the head of Satan, at what point in human history should it be realized? The answer is in the center of human history (although not necessarily in the chronological sense). The Incarnation of the Messiah and His Passion and death should be the focal point of human history.

From God's point of view, what preparation would be fitting for such an event—the entrance of God Himself into human history to suffer for the sins of mankind? Obviously, some preparation would have to be made. Mankind would have to be told in advance of God's plan, so that when it was realized, the Son of God would not pass unnoticed, but would be fittingly received.

Judaism as the Preparation for the Incarnation

This preparation was nothing less than the whole history of Judaism from Abraham to Christ, spanning two millennia. Judaism is essentially a divine preparation for the coming of the Messiah.[13] That preparation had many levels and was manifested in every aspect of the Jewish religion: prophecy, doctrine, Torah, liturgy, prayer, penance, etc.

To prepare for this event, God called Abraham out of Mesopotamia two thousand years before the birth of the Messiah, and directed him to go to Canaan and beget a clan that would be as numerous as the stars of heaven and in which all nations would be blessed (Gen 12:3; 18:18; 22:18; 26:4; 28:14). The history of the Jewish people begins with this calling of Abraham and with this promise of the blessing for all nations, which refers to the coming of the Messiah, the Incarnation of God the Son, who is to save all mankind through His Passion. The Jewish people was formed to be the vehicle and transmitter of this blessing.

For if the Son of God were to enter human history as a concrete son of Adam, He would have to become incarnate in a particular people, with a particular language and culture, with a particular religious tradition, nourished in a particular type of piety, with particular forefathers and national heroes, with a particular mother. And in the Incarnation of God, none of this is of secondary importance. God would surely take care to provide for these details in a fitting way.

---

[13] If someone were to claim to be God Incarnate and could show no historical preparation for his advent, then we should not believe him, for God does not fail to prepare adequately for His works.

He did so by preparing a people in which He would be born, beginning with Abraham. This people was endowed with a special religious tradition revealed by God Himself (Judaism), with the great glory of the Ten Commandments written by God, with a special tradition of piety and prayer inspired by Him (that of the Psalms), with special forefathers and national heroes who were great saints, such as Abraham, Moses, and King David, and above all with a Mother special in every way, the Immaculate Virgin, daughter of Zion, full of grace. Catholics believe that this Jewish girl, Mary of Nazareth, was the creature who most loved God, and thus gives Him the most glory outside of God Himself.

The Jewish people is spoken of as the "Chosen People," and Catholics believe that they were chosen for the greatest mission of all time: to prepare for the birth of the Incarnate Son in their bosom, who would reconcile mankind with the Father through His suffering and love, giving us a share in His own Sonship, making us sons and daughters of God.

The Jewish people was most definitely chosen and distinguished with a privilege above all the other nations of the earth. For what privilege could compare with that of God becoming man in one's own nation, race, and culture?

No historical preparation could ever be completely adequate or proportionate to the Incarnation of God Himself, but nevertheless God's actual preparation for the Incarnation of Christ is truly awe-inspiring. He formed a special people for the period of some two thousand years. He nourished them with repeated revelations and astounding miracles. He taught them the sublime truth that there is but one God, almighty, the Creator of heaven and earth. He gave them a Law which declared in writing the commandments written on man's heart. He gave them hope in His coming as Messiah and made of that hope the very center of their national existence. He gave them varied and numerous prophecies about His future coming, as well as about other events of their history. He gave them a beautiful ceremonial law which kept them apart as a people from the time of Abraham until today. He prepared for His coming also by symbolic representations which theologians speak of as Biblical typology. For example, He fed the Jewish people with manna in the desert so as to foreshadow and symbolize the future blessing of the Eucharist. He led them out through the Red Sea so as to symbolize the sacrament of Baptism. He ordained the paschal sacrifice of the lamb to symbolize His own sacrifice on the Cross, the true Lamb of God who takes away the sins of the world.[14]

In other words, God prepared for the Incarnation of the Son of God by revealing Himself to one nation, chosen gratuitously from all the peoples of the earth, to serve as a salvific preparation for that event. For this reason, revealed religion has taken on two distinct forms: Judaism, which is the religion of the preparation for the Messiah, and the Catholic faith, which is the religion of the Incarnation consummated. No other revealed religion is to be expected, because with the Incarnation of God and the redeeming of man in His Passion nothing more is needed, nor can anything greater be conceived, short of heaven.

Other religions are products of man's natural religious sense and imagination. They are attempts of man to reach God. However, Judaism—and its fulfillment in Christianity—is the religion formed by God in which God reaches us, enabling us to reach Him in turn.[15]

Judaism is tremendously noble, for it is the preparation for God's Incarnation, Passion, and Resurrection. In its time it was the one true religion on the earth, the place in which the voice of God Himself could be heard. Moses pointed out this nobility to the people of Israel: "For what other great nation has a god so near to it as the Lord our God is whenever we call to him? And what other great nation has statutes and ordinances as just as this entire law that I am setting before you today?" (Deut 4:7–8). Or again in Psalm 147:19–20: "He (God) declares his

---

[14] See Charles Journet, "The Mysterious Destinies of Israel," in *The Bridge: A Yearbook of Judaeo-Christian Studies*, ed. John Oesterreicher, vol. 2 (New York: Pantheon Books, 1956), 37–38: "If one searches further, one sees, with St. Augustine, that it was not only one or the other in Israel who was prophet of the Messiah but the people as a whole, and that its kingdom was prophetic of the Christian kingdom. Israel was thus chosen to announce the coming of the Christ, to prefigure the world's ransom by His blood, and to foreshow the messianic kingdom, the kingdom of heaven now in the garment of a pilgrim but one day to be vested in glory."

[15] See the Congregation for the Doctrine of the Faith, declaration *Dominus Jesus* 7: "For this reason, the distinction between *theological faith* and *belief* in the other religions, must be *firmly held*. If faith is the acceptance in grace of revealed truth, which 'makes it possible to penetrate the mystery in a way that allows us to understand it coherently,' then belief, in the other religions, is that sum of experience and thought that constitutes the human treasury of wisdom and religious aspiration, which man in his search for truth has conceived and acted upon in his relationship to God and the Absolute. This distinction is not always borne in mind in current theological reflection. Thus, theological faith (the acceptance of the truth revealed by the One and Triune God) is often identified with belief in other religions, which is religious experience still in search of the absolute truth and still lacking assent to God who reveals himself."

word to Jacob, his statutes and ordinances to Israel. He has not dealt thus with any other nation; they do not know his ordinances. Praise the Lord!"[16]

If we look on the religions of the ancient world, the religion of Israel is indeed totally extraordinary. It is the only religion to clearly teach monotheism; the transcendence, omnipotence, and immutability of God; the creation of all things from nothing (*creatio ex nihilo*); the reality and gravity of sin; the moral law in its purity (perfectly formulated in the Ten Commandments); the freedom of the will; the future Resurrection of the dead; the coming of the Redeemer; the expiatory Passion of the Messiah; the future founding of a Church that would encompass all peoples; and the supernatural happiness promised to the just. It is also the only religion, aside from its full flowering in Christianity, to be marked by abundant and astounding prophecies and miracles.

St. Paul speaks of the glory of Judaism in Romans 9:4–5: "They are Israelites, and to them belong the adoption, the glory, the covenants, the giving of the law, the worship, and the promises; to them belong the patriarchs, and from them, according to the flesh, comes the Messiah, who is over all, God blessed forever. Amen."

As St. Paul indicates, everything in Judaism points beyond itself to its culmination in the Incarnation, for which it served and was uniquely chosen. All of Judaism is summarized in John the Baptist, the last of the Jewish prophets, a voice crying in the wilderness to prepare the way for the Lord Himself who is coming. All of Judaism is like the finger of John the Baptist who points out Christ as the Lamb of God. All of Judaism could say, like John the Baptist, that it is not worthy to tie the sandals of the One who comes in the name of the Lord. All Israel could say: "I baptize you with water for repentance, but he who is coming after me is mightier than I, whose sandals I am not worthy to carry; he will baptize you with the Holy Spirit and with fire" (Mt 3:11). And again: "He must increase, but I must decrease" (Jn 3:30).

All the tremendous nobility of Judaism was for the sake of the Messiah, who was to inaugurate a new and everlasting covenant. All of

---

[16] See also 2 Sam 7:23, which contains David's prayer of thanksgiving when God revealed to him that his throne would be established forever in the Messiah who would spring from his loins: "What other nation on earth is like thy people Israel, whom God went to redeem to be his people, making himself a name and doing for them great and terrible things, by driving out before his people a nation and its gods?" But this action of God in conveying Israel through the Red Sea was nothing compared with the work of redeeming mankind through the suffering of the Messiah.

Judaism was essentially *a figure of the One who was to come.* Christ said to the Samaritan woman (Jn 4:21–23):

> Woman, believe me, the hour is coming when neither on this mountain nor in Jerusalem will you worship the Father. You worship what you do not know; we worship what we know, for salvation is from the Jews. But the hour is coming, and now is, when the true worshipers will worship the Father in spirit and truth, for such the Father seeks to worship him.

In this text Christ makes two fundamental affirmations: first, that Judaism was the true religion in comparison with all the other religions of the world (including the sect of the Samaritans which was a kind of adulterated Judaism). Of all the religions of antiquity, only Judaism came from God to prepare human salvation. Second, Christ affirms that this true religion was nevertheless not yet completed, not yet an adoration "in spirit and in truth." It was a divine preparation for the adoration in spirit and in truth which God now asks of the members of His Church, which they can offer through their union with Him in His Mystical Body.

One of the great stumbling blocks for Jews is the existence of Christians unworthy of their name and calling, who do not seem to worship "in spirit and in truth." Who can deny it? God's grace, given first to Jews and then to Christians, does not annul man's free will, which gives us the astounding ability to resist the grace of God and to pervert the greatest gifts. The gifts of God give us the capacity to sanctify ourselves and be reconciled with God, first in Judaism and then in Christianity. In addition to the double commandment of love, sanctification came to Israel through faith in the coming of the Messiah, and in the Church through faith in the Messiah who has already come and died for us. However, the Biblical narrative shows us that the adoption of the Jewish people by God did not render them free from sin. So it should astonish no Jew that the same is true of Christians. Only the Jewish daughter of Zion called to be the mother of the Messiah was free from sin, together with her Son. May she intercede for us that we may adore the Father in spirit and in truth.

CHAPTER 2

Prophecies of the Messiah: Lineage and Mission

John Paul II began his first encyclical, *Redemptor hominis* of 1979, by calling to our attention the centrality of the Incarnation:

> The Redeemer of man, Jesus Christ, is the *centre* of the universe and of history. . . . God entered the history of humanity and, as a man, became an actor in that history, one of the thousands of millions of human beings but at the same time Unique! Through the Incarnation God gave human life the dimension that he intended man to have from his first beginning.

The center of God's plan for history is the Incarnation of God the Son, by which He enters human history in order to redeem it. As we have seen, God prepared for this event by electing and calling the Jewish people, whose life was to center on the expectation of the Messiah, who would be a descendant of Abraham, in whom all nations would be blessed.

A great part of this preparation consisted in a progressive revelation of the mystery of the Incarnation to Israel through manifold and abundant prophecies. Indeed, hundreds of prophecies of the Messiah can be found in the Old Testament. No other figure in history has been the subject of such a quantity of prophecy, spanning 2,000 years. This makes perfect sense when we consider the significance of the event foretold. If God truly wished to become incarnate in history to redeem man, then He certainly would have repeatedly announced the event in solemn form. The fact that there are so many prophecies is in perfect harmony with the unique claim of Christianity. For without Old Testament prophecy, Christ's claim to be the divine Redeemer of mankind would not have been credible.

Most Catholics today are insufficiently acquainted with the prophecies about Christ. This is unfortunate, for knowledge of these prophecies helps greatly to bolster faith in Christ. The Messianic prophecies are one of the most important motives of credibility of the Catholic faith. After all, God took great pains to prepare for the coming of the Messiah by repeated and progressive revelation, century after century.

Consider the testimony of St. Justin Martyr:

> For with what reason should we believe of a crucified man that He is the first-born of the unbegotten God, and Himself will pass judgment on the whole human race, unless we had found testimonies concerning Him published before He came and was born as man, and unless we saw that things had happened accordingly: . . . men of every race persuaded by His teaching through the apostles, and rejecting their old habits.[1]

It is also very interesting to note that these prophecies are preserved by an impartial witness who could never be accused of falsifying them after the event to justify belief in the Messiah. For this witness is that part of Israel which did not become Christian. Thus the prophecies are perfectly protected against any suspicion of self-interest or fraudulent fabrication on the part of Christians.

We shall look here only at a few of the most important prophecies, and trace their features to see what kind of picture they paint, and whether they point to their realization in Jesus Christ as the faith of the Church proclaims.

First Prophecy of the Messiah (Genesis 3:15)

The first mention of the Messiah or Christ presents him as the victor who fights against and triumphs over the devil. This first Messianic prophecy occurs right after the fall of Adam and Eve and on the very threshold of human history. To protect Adam and Eve from despair, God reveals the future coming of a Redeemer, a descendant born of their lineage, who will triumph over the devil. After the sin, God speaks to the three protagonists of that event: the serpent, Eve, and Adam. To the serpent He says (Gen 3:15): "I will put enmity between you and the woman, and between your seed and her seed; he shall bruise [crush] your head, and you shall bruise his heel." Christ the Messiah is the "seed of the woman" who will crush the head of the serpent, which is the devil.

This text is remarkable in many ways. First of all, there is the antiquity of the promise. Humanity was never bereft of Messianic hope, even though the fulfillment of the promise would be delayed by countless centuries. This ancient promise can account for belief in a Redeemer in traditional religious cultures spread across the globe. It is reasonable to believe that Adam and Eve passed their knowledge on to their descendants (such as Seth), who in turn passed it on to their

---

[1] St. Justin, *First Apology*, ch. 53, *ANF* 1:180.

descendants, forming a primeval religious tradition transmitting knowledge of original sin, the promise of heaven and the Messiah, etc.

Secondly, the unnamed Messiah is identified as one who will crush the head of the Tempter who incites to sin. Crushing the head of Satan must mean crushing his power to lead men away from God. The serpent had blasphemed God's glory to Eve, introducing the idea into her mind that God wanted to forbid them the tree of good and evil to keep them down, to keep them from becoming equal with God, as if God were afraid of man and his intellectual capacity.[2] The implication is that God's Law is opposed to man's true interest, welfare, and happiness. This charge, by the way, is hidden in every sin. The very name of Satan (*diabolos* in Greek) means an adversary who accuses. Satan first accuses God to man in the act of temptation, and then he accuses man to God for succumbing to his temptation.

The promised "seed of the woman" is one who will vindicate God's glory and goodness by opposing the serpent. God does not impose His Law on mankind to keep us down, but rather to lift us up to friendship with Him. He has no "interest" in the economy of salvation that He has established other than to communicate His goodness freely to us, for the sake of the glory of the divine love. The "seed of the woman" will crush the head of the serpent by vindicating the divine goodness and mercy; and He will show us that "God so loved the world that He gave His only Son, that whoever believes in Him should not perish, but have eternal life" (Jn 3:16).

Third, the unnamed Messiah will have to do battle with Satan, and be bruised or crushed in the heel. This is an intimation of a battle in which the Messiah will have to suffer and be crushed in His human nature (signified by the "heel") in the very moment in which He crushes Satan's head. Although it is only obscurely present here, in hindsight we can see how the Passion of Christ realizes this figure. Christ crushes the head of Satan precisely by allowing Satan to mortally bruise His human nature and inflict Him with every suffering in the greatest intensity that can be endured.

Finally, it should be noticed that this text gives great importance to an unnamed woman, spoken of simply as "the woman" (*ha isha*), as if she somehow recapitulates her sex. Again, with hindsight it can easily be seen that this is the first Marian text in the Bible. Just as two persons, male and female, were involved in the Fall, likewise two persons are involved in the crushing of the head of the serpent: the woman and her seed. The woman brings forth the Son who will crush Satan's head.

---

[2] See Gen 3:4–5: "You will not die. For God knows that when you eat of it your eyes will be opened, and you will be like God, knowing good and evil."

Furthermore, God says that He is putting enmity between Satan and "the woman," who is the Mother of the Redeemer. To be in enmity with the devil is to be in enmity with sin. Perfect enmity with Satan means that one was never under his dominion through sin. This text could not be understood with regard to Eve, for she was not in enmity with him, but rather succumbed to him. It must be understood of a new Eve who will be without sin, in perpetual diametrical opposition to the serpent.

Just as the original sin was a drama with three players, this text shows us that the Redemption will likewise be a drama with three players. Even though Eve sinned first, the decisive fault for our fallen state lies with Adam, because he was the head of the human family and as head he received grace to be passed on to all his descendants as a sacred trust. Just as the welfare of every family is dependent on the father of the family, so the welfare of the human family was dependent on Adam, the father of that family. Thus St. Paul says that "by one man's disobedience many were made sinners" (Rom 5:19). Nevertheless, Eve decisively helped to prepare for Adam's fall through her doubt in God's goodness and her disobedience.

Thus it is fitting that in the reparation of the original sin, which is promised here in Genesis 3:15, both a new Adam and a new Eve be involved. The new Adam is the seed of the woman, and the new Eve is the mysterious "woman" in perpetual enmity with the serpent. St. Irenaeus, a Father of the Church at the end of the second century, is among the first to suggest this traditional reading: "And thus also it was that the knot of Eve's disobedience was loosed by the obedience of Mary. For what the virgin Eve had bound fast through unbelief, this did the virgin Mary set free through faith."[3] We find this idea also in other early Fathers of the Church.[4] Eve's disobedience to God and disbelief in

---

[3] St. Irenaeus, *Against Heresies*, 3.22.4, *ANF* 1:455. See also 5.19.1, *ANF* 1:547: "For just as the former was led astray by the word of an angel, so that she fled from God when she had transgressed His word; so did the latter, by an angelic communication, receive the glad tidings that she should bear God, being obedient to His word. And if the former did disobey God, yet the latter was persuaded to be obedient to God, in order that the Virgin Mary might become the patroness [*advocata*] of the virgin Eve. And thus, as the human race fell into bondage to death by means of a virgin, so is it rescued by a virgin; virginal disobedience having been balanced in the opposite scale by virginal obedience. For in the same way the sin of the first created man receives amendment by the correction of the First-begotten, and the coming of the serpent is conquered by the harmlessness of the dove, those bonds being unloosed by which we had been fast bound to death."

[4] See St. Justin Martyr, *Dialogue with Trypho*, ch. 100, *ANF* 1:249: "He became man by the Virgin, in order that the disobedience which proceeded from the serpent might receive its destruction in the same manner in which it derived its origin. For Eve, who was a virgin and undefiled, having conceived the word of the

His word is set right by the collaboration of Mary in perfect obedience and faith, expressed in what she said at the Annunciation: "Let it be done unto me according to your word."

It seems that Jesus indirectly alludes to this prophecy when He is dying on the Cross, and His mother is standing at the foot of the Cross with St. John, the "beloved disciple." He says to her: "Woman, behold thy son." And to His beloved disciple, He says: "Son, behold thy mother" (Jn 19:26–27). If ever there were a time when we would have expected Him to speak to His mother with the endearing title of "mother," it would have been then. Why does He call her simply "woman," as if it were somehow her name? Is He being cold to His mother, in this of all moments? The best explanation is that He is alluding to the mysterious prophecy of Genesis 3:15. She is the woman whose seed is at this very moment crushing the serpent's head. In another moment He will cry out, "It is consummated" (Jn 19:30). The redemption of man is accomplished. Furthermore, at this moment, according to the Catholic Tradition, He is making Mary the mother of all His beloved disciples for all time.[5] Thus Mary becomes the new Eve, who in Genesis is the "mother of all the living." Mary becomes the spiritual mother of all those given spiritual life in the Messiah.[6]

---

serpent, brought forth disobedience and death. But the Virgin Mary received faith and joy, when the angel Gabriel announced the good tidings to her that the Spirit of the Lord would come upon her, and the power of the Highest would overshadow her: wherefore also the Holy One begotten of her is the Son of God; and she replied, 'Be it unto me according to thy word.' And by her has He been born."

[5] See Vatican II, Constitution on the Church *Lumen gentium* 62: "This maternity of Mary in the order of grace began with the consent which she gave in faith at the Annunciation and which she sustained without wavering beneath the cross, and lasts until the eternal fulfillment of all the elect." See also, for example, Rupert of Deutz, *In Joannem* 13, PL 169:790, quoted in Luigi Gambero, *Mary in the Middle Ages: The Blessed Virgin Mary in the Thought of Medieval Latin Theologians*, trans. Thomas Buffer (San Francisco: Ignatius Press, 2005), 127: "Because [on Calvary] the Blessed Virgin truly suffered the pangs of a woman in childbirth, and because in her Son's Passion she gave birth to the salvation of us all, she is clearly the Mother of us all. Therefore [Jesus'] statement about this disciple, 'Woman, behold your Son' . . . and likewise to the disciple, 'Behold your mother,' could have been said correctly about any other disciple had he been present."

[6] See, for example, St. Ephrem the Syrian, *Homily on Our Lord* 3.2, in *Selected Prose Works*, trans. Edward Mathews and Joseph Amar (Washington DC: Catholic Univ. of America Press, 1994), 278: "And Eve, who had been mother of all the living, became a fountain of death for all the living. But Mary, the new shoot, sprouted from Eve, the old vine, and new life dwelt in her." See also St. Augustine, *Holy Virginity* 6, in *St. Augustine: Treatises on Marriage and Other Subjects* (New York: Fathers of the Church, Inc., 1955), 149: "She is evidently the mother of us who are

We too become engrafted in her "seed," Jesus the Messiah, and thus we become participants in His crushing the head of the serpent. That is, we become participants in the redemptive power of His Cross. Israel, too, through her faith in the Messiah, is associated with the redemptive value of the Cross of Christ.

"In Your Seed All Nations Will Be Blessed"

Let us pass on to the second great Messianic prophecy. After long ages of silence, God revealed to Abraham that the Messiah would spring from his loins as a *universal blessing*, a blessing for "all the nations of the world" (Gen 12:3, 18:18, 22:18, 26:4; 28:14). The first mention of this blessing occurs right after God calls Abram to leave the land of Ur, the land of his fathers, and go to a land that God will show him:

> And the Lord said to Abram: "Go forth out of thy country, and from thy kindred, and out of thy father's house, and come into the land which I will show thee. And I will make of thee a great nation, and I will bless thee, and magnify thy name, and thou shalt be blessed. I will bless them that bless thee, and curse them that curse thee, and in thee shall all the kindred of the earth be blessed."[7]

The promise is given to him again in Genesis 18:18, in a mysterious passage in which three angels come to visit Abraham and announce that he will have a son even though his wife Sarah has been sterile and, in addition, is now well past the age of childbearing. After giving this promise, the three rise up and walk on to Sodom and Gomorrah to destroy it for the sins of their inhabitants. God says: "Can I hide from Abraham what I am about to do, seeing he shall become a great and mighty nation, and in him all the nations of the earth shall be blessed?"

The promise is repeated a third time after Abraham, in obedience to God's command, takes his son, born after the visit of the angels, to be sacrificed on Mt. Moriah, traditionally identified with Jerusalem. God says:

> I swear by myself, says the Lord, since you have done this and have not withheld your only son, I will indeed bless you, and will surely multiply your descendants as the stars of the heavens, as the sands on the seashore. Your descendants shall possess the gates of

---

His members, because she has co-operated by charity that the faithful, who are members of that Head, might be born in the Church."

[7] Gen 12:1–3, Douay-Rheims version.

their enemies. In your descendants all the nations of the earth shall be blessed, because you have obeyed me.[8]

The promise is renewed to Abraham's son Isaac in Genesis 26:4–5: "And I will multiply your seed like the stars of heaven, and I will give to your posterity all these countries [Canaan], and in your seed shall all the nations of the earth be blessed: because Abraham obeyed my voice."[9]

The promise is repeated yet again to Isaac's son Jacob (who receives the name of Israel), the father of twelve sons who become the twelve tribes of Israel. Sleeping at Bethel, Jacob sees a vision of a ladder stretching from earth to heaven, on which the angels of God are ascending and descending. The Lord is leaning on the top of the ladder, and says to him:

> I am the Lord, the God of Abraham your father and the God of Isaac; the land on which you lie I will give to you and to your descendants; and your descendants shall be like the dust of the earth, and you shall spread abroad to the west and to the east and to the north and to the south; and in you and in your descendants shall all the families of the earth be blessed. Behold, I am with you and will keep you wherever you go, and will bring you back to this land; for I will not leave you until I have done that of which I have spoken to you.[10]

We see in these prophecies that the very existence of the people of Israel is repeatedly connected with the blessing that will be given to all nations in their seed. Four promises are given to them: (1) the land of Canaan will be given to their descendants; (2) they will have descendants as numerous as the stars of the heavens and the sand of the earth; (3) God will bless, assist, and accompany them with His intimate presence; and (4) God will bless all nations in the seed of Abraham, Isaac, and Jacob.

It is quite significant that the very existence and multiplication of the Jewish people is linked with a blessing that is absolutely universal in scope. A particular people is promised a particular land, but this particular blessing is not an end in itself. On the contrary, the promise of Israel's existence and fruitfulness is for the sake of a blessing that transcends all national borders and is for all the nations of the earth. The Messiah is not for Israel alone, but for every nation!

This obviously contradicts the common Jewish idea that pictures the Messiah as merely a national liberator or great military figure. How

---

[8] Gen 22:16–18, Douay-Rheims version.

[9] Douay-Rheims version.

[10] Gen 28:13–15.

would a Jewish military genius, freeing them from the bonds of foreign domination, be a blessing for all the nations on earth?

Lineage and Birth of the Messiah (Gen 49:10)

We have seen that the Messiah is to be a descendant of the line of Abraham, Isaac, and Jacob. However, Jacob has twelve sons. Which of them is to be the forefather of the Messiah? Does Genesis tell us? Indeed, yes. Before he dies, the patriarch Jacob prophetically blesses his twelve sons, and we see from the blessing that the Messiah will be born from Judah, the fourth son. This is surprising, for we might have thought that the Messianic blessing would be given to Joseph, the hero among the sons of Jacob, and the first son of his beloved Rachel; or to Benjamin, the youngest and most humble; or to Reuben, the first of all his sons; but certainly not to the man who sold Joseph into slavery, and begot out of wedlock the child who was to be a forefather of David. Nevertheless, God willed the Messianic blessing to pass through Judah, and revealed this through Jacob's blessing. This text, as is so often the case, is not without obscurity. Now in Egypt, and nearing death, Jacob assembles his sons: "Gather yourselves together that I may tell you the things that shall befall you in the last days" (Gen 49:1).

When he gets to Judah, in Genesis 49:8–11, Jacob says:

> Judah, your brothers shall praise you; your hand shall be on the neck of your enemies; your father's sons shall bow down before you. Judah is a lion's whelp. . . . The scepter shall not depart from Judah, nor the ruler's staff from between his feet, until he comes *to whom it belongs*; and to him shall be the obedience of the peoples. . . .
> He washes his garments in wine and his vesture in the blood of grapes.

According to this prophecy, the kingship in Israel shall be in the tribe of Judah, as shall the Messiah, who is the one to whom the scepter belongs by right. In other words, the Messiah is to be the true king of Israel, from the line of Judah. Furthermore, this text is of great interest with regard to the time of the coming of the Messiah. For the text states that sovereignty will not be completely lost to Judah before the Messiah comes. This sovereignty of Judah, progressively diminished in the centuries before Christ, was finally lost when the Roman procurators began to rule in Palestine after the death of King Herod and the exile of his son Archelaus, about the year 6 AD. A more grievous expression of that loss of sovereignty occurred with the destruction of Jerusalem and of the Temple in the year 70 AD. This loss was carried even further in 132–135 AD with the repression of the second Jewish revolt under a false Messiah, Bar Kochba, after which the Jews were dispersed among the peoples for over eighteen centuries. Therefore, the Messiah must certainly have come before that time.

It is also interesting to note an indirect reference to the Passion of Christ at the end of this prophecy: "He washes his garments in wine and his vesture in the blood of grapes." Although one could read the text as referring to the blood of enemies at the time of David and Solomon, it should rather be read as referring to the blood of Christ, with which He washed His garments in His Passion.

Finally, it should be noticed that the coming of the Messiah is vested with a universal significance and is not purely a Jewish affair, for "to him shall be the obedience of the *peoples*."

The Star of Jacob

The next prophecy of the Messiah came from an unlikely source: a pagan Moabite prophet, Balaam, whose king asked him to curse the Israelites who were passing through his country on their way to Canaan. Oddly enough, Balaam truly receives the word of God, who tells him to bless Israel instead of cursing it. Despite the anger of the king, Balaam persists in blessing, against his own will. He first foretells the greatness of Israel and her conquest of Canaan: "How beautiful are thy tabernacles, O Jacob, and thy tents, O Israel!" He then passes on to a Messianic prophecy, which, as he specifies, concerns a much more distant future:

> I shall see him, but not now: I shall behold him, but not near. A star shall rise out of Jacob and a scepter shall spring up from Israel, and shall strike the chiefs of Moab, and shall waste all the children of Seth. . . . Out of Jacob shall he come that shall rule, and shall destroy the remains of the city.[11]

Again it is interesting to observe how Balaam connects the destiny of Israel with its Messianic culmination. The glory of Israel is ordered to giving rise to the glorious "star of Jacob." Here the Messiah is pictured as a king who will have dominion over the peoples and conquer his enemies. It is easy to see how such a prophecy could lead to a nationalistic interpretation. However, we have to read each prophecy in the light of all the others. If we put the "star of Jacob" together with Genesis 3:15, it is clear that the enemies of the Messiah are Satan and sin.

Secondly, it should be noticed that this prophecy cannot be applied to David, Solomon, or any other Jewish king or hero, for they did not

---

[11] Num 24:17–19, Douay-Rheims version.

conquer all the children of Seth, who was the third son of Adam and Eve after Cain and Abel. It was in the line of Seth that the true religion was passed on from Adam and Eve, and Seth is perhaps used as a figure of the just of all ages.[12] Noah was of the line of Seth according to Genesis 5. Therefore all peoples on the earth today are the children of Seth. The Messiah is thus not simply to rule over one country, such as Israel, but over all the children of Seth.

Clearly, the type of conquest that is truly intended by the divine Author is spiritual. It refers to the conversion of the sons of Seth to the worship of the true God.

Prophecy of Moses

Another prophecy about the Messiah comes from roughly the same time, but given this time by Moses himself in the book of Deuteronomy, in his final sermon before the entrance of the Chosen People into the Promised Land (Deut 18:15–19). In the context of discussing the institution of prophecy, Moses tells the people:

> The Lord your God will raise up for you a prophet like me from among you, from your brethren—him you shall heed. . . . And the Lord said to me . . . I will raise up for them a prophet like you from among their brethren; and I will put my words in his mouth, and he shall speak to them all that I command him. And whoever will not give heed to my words which he shall speak in my name, I myself will require it of him.

Moses speaks here of a "prophet" in the singular. To which prophet does this text refer? It must be the Messiah, for Moses assigns to him the same authority as he received: to legislate for the people in the name of God. A severe penalty is implied for refusing to heed this Prophet. In Acts 3:22–23, St. Peter cites this text as being fulfilled in Jesus, after the miracle of the curing of the lame man shortly after Pentecost.

This prophecy reveals a new aspect of the Messianic mission. We have seen that the Messiah is to be invested with the roles of supreme king, prophet, and priest. This text underlines the prophetic nature of Christ's mission. A prophet is not just one who predicts the future, although he also does that. A prophet is one who speaks in the name of

---

[12] See Gen 4:25–26: "And Adam knew his wife again, and she bore a son and called his name Seth, for she said, 'God has appointed for me another child instead of Abel, for Cain slew him.' To Seth also a son was born, and he called his name Enosh. At that time men began to call upon the name of the Lord." Genesis speaks of the separate lineages of Cain and of Seth in Gen 4–5.

the Lord. It is in this sense that the Messiah will be a great prophet like Moses. He is to be the *new Moses*.

To understand this we have to reflect on the role of Moses in the formation of the Jewish people. He was the mediator of the covenant between God and the people, sealed by the blood of sacrifice at Mount Sinai. Second, he was the mediator in passing God's Law to the people. Third, he saw God "face to face" and spoke to Him intimately. Fourth, he led the people out of bondage to the Promised Land. Fifth, he was said to be the meekest man on earth. The new Moses must fulfill these roles in a superabundant and spiritual way. He will bring in a new covenant between God and man, sealed with the blood of the perfect and eternal sacrifice. He will legislate a more perfect law, as we hear in the Sermon on the Mount and in the Gospels. Obedience will be due to Him as it was to Moses. He will liberate the people from the yoke of bondage, not of physical slavery in Egypt, but of the greater yoke of sin and vice. He will lead the people through the waters of Baptism. He will be a man of perfect prayer and intimacy with the Father, and "meek and humble of heart."

The Messiah: Son of David

After the prophecy of Moses, nothing further was revealed by God about the lineage of the Messiah for about four centuries, when it was further determined in a prophecy made by the prophet Nathan to King David. During these centuries, the Chosen People conquered the Promised Land and were ruled by judges, ending with Samuel, who anointed Saul as king in Israel. Saul was not from the tribe of Judah, but from Benjamin. This does not contradict the prophecy of Jacob, however, for Saul lost the kingship due to infidelity, and it passed to David from the tribe of Judah.

To David it was promised that his offspring would rule on his throne after his death, and that the Messiah would be from his seed (2 Sam 7:14). Again the prophecy is not easy to understand, for it partly concerns David's immediate son, Solomon, but ultimately refers to another descendant, the Messiah/Christ, who will be greater than Solomon. At this time, David has defeated Saul, established his capital in Jerusalem, and built himself a palace, but there is not yet a Temple in Jerusalem. David therefore proposes to the prophet Nathan his plan of building a temple in Jerusalem to house the Tabernacle of the Lord. Nathan at first says: "Go, do all that is in thy heart, because the Lord is with thee" (2 Sam 7:3). However, that night, the word of the Lord came to Nathan telling him to say to David that it would not be for him to build the house of the Lord, but for his son, Solomon:

When your days are fulfilled and you lie down with your fathers, I
will raise up your offspring after you, who shall come forth from
your body, and I will establish his kingdom. He shall build a house
for my name, and I will establish the throne of his kingdom for
ever. I will be his father, and he shall be my son. When he commits
iniquity, I will chasten him with the rod of men, with the stripes of
the sons of men; but I will not take my steadfast love from him, as
I took it from Saul, whom I put away from before you. And your
house and your kingdom shall be made sure for ever before me;
your throne shall be established for ever.[13]

This prophecy could be understood to refer partly to King
Solomon, who built the glorious Temple of the Lord and established a
magnificent earthly kingdom, and whose iniquity (and that of his
descendants) could be punished by God. However, the throne of
Solomon was not eternal, nor was his kingdom established forever.
Either God was grossly exaggerating, or this text refers to another son
to be born of the seed of David, who will *reign forever over Jacob*: the
Messiah. What earthly throne can be firm *forever?* The prophecy applies
strictly only to Christ, who built the spiritual house of the Lord—the
Church—a kingdom which shall last until the end of time, ruled over by
Christ the King and administered through His vicar on earth, the
Pope.[14]

As will be seen below, King Solomon was a figure of the Messiah
precisely because he built the Temple and established a kingdom.
However, the true temple and the true kingdom that last forever are
established by Christ. The true temple of the divinity is His own Body,
and the true kingdom is the kingdom of God which He came to
establish: the Church on earth and in heaven.

The promise that the Messiah will be a son of David continued to
be proclaimed in other prophecies through the centuries. Jeremiah,
some four centuries later, wrote (Jer 23:5):

Behold, the days are coming, says the Lord, when I will raise up for
David a just branch, and a king shall reign and be wise, and shall
execute judgment and justice in the earth. In those days Judah will
be saved, and Israel will dwell confidently, and this is the name that
they shall call him: The Lord our just one.

---

[13] 2 Sam 7:12–16.

[14] The mention of "committing iniquity" in 2 Sam 7:14, in addition to
Solomon, can also be understood as referring to the members of Christ's Mystical
Body.

The Davidic prophecy is found also in two Messianic Psalms (89[15] and 132), in which the promise is repeated of an everlasting throne for the seed of David, confirmed forever.

This prophecy of the Davidic lineage of the Messiah is fulfilled in Jesus Christ, as we can see from the genealogies given in Matthew and Luke. It is interesting to note that Davidic descent could hardly be verified of any Jew after the first or second century AD, for the genealogical records were lost with the destruction of the Temple, the dispersal of the Jewish people, and other catastrophes, and the line of David simply disappeared from documented history with the deaths of the cousins of Jesus. One of these, James the Lesser, ruled as bishop in Jerusalem until his martyrdom in 62 AD. He was succeeded as bishop by other members of the family until the end of the first century. The clan continued to survive in the Jewish-Christian community until perhaps the beginning of the fourth century,[16] after which it seems no credible historical trace of the Davidic line is to be found. None of the false Jewish "messiahs" ever attempted to prove they were of Davidic descent.

The Jews had a great military leader some 160 years before Jesus in the person of Judas Maccabeus, who with tremendous courage and ability saved the Jewish people from the yoke of King Antiochus who had tried to suppress the Jewish Law. However, nobody seems to have proposed that Judas Maccabeus was the Messiah. Why not? Most probably because he was not of the tribe of Judah, and everyone knew that the Messiah had to be a son of David.

King David lived over nine centuries before Jesus Christ. It is quite remarkable that his lineage was preserved through nine centuries despite many attempts to eliminate it by usurpers to the throne. The last attempt to cut off the line of David was made by King Herod himself after the birth of Jesus, in the massacre of the innocents.

Christ the King in Psalm 72

Another prophecy of the Messiah as king in the line of David with an everlasting reign is contained in Psalm 72:

---

[15] Ps 89:35–37: "Once for all I have sworn by my holiness; I will not lie to David. His line shall endure for ever, his throne as long as the sun before me. Like the moon it shall be established for ever; it shall stand firm while the skies endure." See also Ps 132:11–12 and 1 Chr 22:10.

[16] Other members of the extended family of Joseph, Mary, and Jesus continue to appear in Christian records up to the beginning of the fourth century. See Emanuel Testa, *The Faith of the Mother Church: An Essay on the Theology of the Judeo-Christians*, trans. Paul Rotondi (Jerusalem: Franciscan Printing Press, 1992), 128–29.

He shall judge the poor of the people, and he shall save the children of the poor, and he shall humble the oppressor. And he shall continue with the sun, and before the moon, throughout all generations. . . . In his days shall justice spring up, and abundance of peace, till the moon be taken away. And he shall rule from sea to sea, and from the river unto the ends of the earth. . . . The kings of Tharsis and the islands shall offer presents; the kings of the Arabians and of Saba shall bring gifts. And all kings of the earth shall adore him; all nations shall serve him. . . . Let his name be blessed for evermore; his name continueth before the sun. And in him shall all the tribes of the earth be blessed; all nations shall magnify him.[17]

This psalm connects the Messianic prophecy about the son of David with the promise given to Abraham that in his seed all nations will be blessed (see verse 17). The glorious son of David will be an eternal king whose kingdom will be universal in two dimensions: time and space. His rule will extend from sea to sea, which indicates the entire world. The other kings of the earth (of Tarshish, Sheba, Seba, etc.) will not be abolished, but they will give homage to the Messiah King. And his kingdom shall have no end, but continue with the sun and the moon "throughout all generations."

Can we assume this king to be a mere man? Obviously an eternal rule is something proper to God Himself. Who else can be king for all generations? The eternal character of the Messianic kingdom absolutely rules out any merely temporal and political interpretation of the Messianic prophecies.

Catholics recognize several dimensions to this universal rule of Christ. First, Christ's rule is universal through His divine dominion. Second, Christ rules a universal kingdom—the Catholic Church—of which He is the invisible Head, and in which all the kings of the earth are called to give the tribute of praise and adoration. Third, in the Last Judgment, Christ will judge all nations and eternally rule the Church Triumphant in heaven.

The Prophecy of the Virgin Birth (Isaiah 7)

One of the most beautiful Messianic prophecies was given to King Ahaz, one of the unworthy descendants of King David. The history is recounted in Isaiah 7. Ahaz, together with the people, was in great anxiety about an imminent attack from the king of Syria who was allied with the northern kingdom of Israel against Judah. The enemy plan was to put on the throne of Judah a certain son of Tabeel, who was not of

---

[17] Ps 72:4–5, 10–11, 17, Douay-Rheims version (where it is numbered Ps 71).

the Davidic line. Isaiah is instructed to meet the king and tell him not to worry, for "it shall not stand" (Is 7:7). However, Ahaz was also told: "If you will not believe, surely you shall not be established" (Is 7:9). To strengthen his faith he was told to ask for a sign of God. Ahaz declined in false modesty: "I will not ask, and I will not put the Lord to the test" (Is 7:12).

The Lord was not pleased by this, for He wanted to give a glorious sign of His providence regarding the seed of David. At stake was not simply the rule of Ahaz, but the Messianic prophecy given to David that his seed would sit on his throne, confirmed forever. Human plans of arms and politics could not block God's promise.

At this point God spoke to Ahaz through Isaiah: "Hear ye therefore, O house of David: Is it a small thing for you to be grievous to men, that you are grievous to my God also? Therefore the Lord himself shall give you a sign. Behold a virgin shall conceive and bear a son, and his name shall be called Emmanuel" (Is 7:13–14).[18]

As we have seen in almost every case, the prophecy is difficult because it mixes two interrelated levels. Immediate and particular political needs—here Ahaz's concern for the survival of the Davidic dynasty—are woven together with the infinitely more significant issue of the future Messiah to be born of that line.

The prophecy is above all an assurance that the coming of the Messiah will not be blocked by human effort, for it will not be brought about by human effort, but by a unique intervention of God. Thus a further sign is foretold regarding the Messiah: He will be born of a virgin, and shall be called Emmanuel, which means "God with us." The Messiah will be God's presence among men, within human history. This is realized in the Incarnation.

Many scholars and rabbis object here that the word in the Hebrew text *(almah)* that we translate as "virgin" simply means a "young woman." The fact is that this word occurs rarely in the Bible and always signifies a young *still unmarried* woman.[19] When the Bible was translated from Hebrew into Greek two centuries before Christ in the *Septuagint* translation, the learned Jewish translators of the Bible translated *almah* as "virgin": *parthenos*. This translation had enormous prestige in the ancient Jewish world and was used throughout the Diaspora. This shows that the common understanding of the Jewish people in the centuries immediately before Christ was that the Messiah was indeed to be born of a virgin.

---

[18] Douay-Rheims version.

[19] See Gen 24:43 (referring to Rebecca, before she was betrothed to Isaac); Ex 2:8 (referring to Moses' young unmarried sister).

Furthermore, if *almah* were to be translated not as "virgin," but simply as a "young woman," what kind of sign would that be? A young woman will bear a child. What would be miraculous or awe-inspiring about that? However, that a virgin bear a son is indeed a unique sign fitting for the role of the Messiah, who is to be "God with us." The Virgin Birth is a worthy sign that the Messiah is from God, and not the effort of man. He comes from above, and not simply from human agency.

"To Us a Son Is Given"

The Messiah's coming into the world is further developed in Isaiah 9 and 11. Isaiah 9:6–7 is familiar to Christians from the Christmas liturgy:

> For to us a child is born, to us a son is given; and the government will be upon his shoulder, and his name will be called "Wonderful Counselor, Mighty God, Everlasting Father, Prince of Peace." Of the increase of his government and of peace there will be no end, upon the throne of David, and over his kingdom, to establish it, and to uphold it with justice and with righteousness from this time forth and for evermore. The zeal of the Lord of hosts will do this.

In ancient Judaism, a name reveals the essence of the one named. The names given to the Messiah in different prophecies indicate the essence of who He is. For example, the name that God gave to Himself in Exodus 3:14 signifies His essence to be *He who is*: the infinite fullness of Being, and the source of all created being.

Here the Messiah is presented as a "Son given to us." The meaning is not only that a son of Israel is given to us, but also that the *Son of God* is given to Israel and mankind. He is given a name with five remarkable attributes: "Wonderful, Counselor, Mighty God, Everlasting Father, Prince of Peace." Some modern Jewish translations simply give this name in transliteration from the Hebrew: "Pele-joez-el-gibbor-abi-ad-sar-shalom."[20] This misses the point. It is not an arbitrary name devoid of significance, but indicates *who* this mysterious son *is*.

The first thing we notice is that the Messianic son is given titles proper to God. What does it mean that the Messiah is called the Prince of Peace, Everlasting Father, and above all, "Mighty God"? We can

---

[20] See *The Holy Scriptures according to the Masoretic Text: A New Translation with the Aid of Previous Versions and with Constant Consultation of Jewish Authorities* (Philadelphia: The Jewish Publication Society of America, 1955). See also *The Jewish Study Bible* (New York, Oxford Univ. Press, 2004), whose translation seems forced by the desire to avoid giving divine attributes to the Messiah: "He has been named 'The Mighty God is planning grace; The Eternal Father, a peaceable ruler.'"

connect the title "Prince of Peace" with Daniel 9 and Genesis 3:15: He is Prince of Peace because He creates peace between God and man by crushing sin and introducing righteousness. To be "Everlasting Father," or "Father of the world to come" (as translated in the Douay-Rheims version), would likewise mean that the Messiah introduces mankind into the Messianic kingdom, which culminates in the kingdom of heaven, an everlasting kingdom over which the Messiah will rule without end. But what about "mighty God"? The literal meaning of the text is that the Messiah—the son who is given to us—is somehow "mighty God" born into human history as a descendant of David. The fact that He is called "Counselor" indicates a mysterious connection with the figure of the divine Wisdom in Proverbs 8:22–31 who pre-existed with God the Father, "counseling" with Him with regard to the creation of the world. For what mere mortal can be said to counsel the Lord? Such a blasphemy is vigorously rejected by other texts of Scripture.[21]

The Spirit of the Lord Rests on the Messiah

Another stupendous prophecy that further develops Isaiah 9:5–6 is given in Isaiah 11:1–5, which is familiar to Christians from the sacrament of Confirmation:

> And there shall come forth a rod out of the root of Jesse, and a flower shall rise up out of his root. And the spirit of the Lord shall rest upon him: the spirit of wisdom, and of understanding, the spirit of counsel, and of fortitude, the spirit of knowledge, and of godliness. And he shall be filled with the spirit of the fear of the Lord. He shall not judge according to the sight of the eyes, nor reprove according to the hearing of the ears. But he shall judge the poor with justice, and shall reprove with equity for the meek of the earth. . . . And justice shall be the girdle of his loins: and faith the girdle of his reins.[22]

The "shoot from the stump of Jesse" refers to the Messiah who will descend from David, for Jesse was the father of King David. The key characteristic given to the Messiah is that He shall be uniquely filled with the Spirit of the Lord, that same Spirit which was said to hover over the face of the deep in Genesis 1:2. The ancient rabbis explicitly make this connection. A text of the Midrash says of Genesis 1:2: "'And the spirit

---

21 See Is 40:13; Wis 9:13, cited in Rom 11:34.
22 Douay Rheims version.

of God moved,' words which identify the king Messiah, of whom it is said: 'And the spirit of the Lord shall rest upon him' (Is 11:2)."[23]

The Spirit of the Lord is manifested in seven gifts, which are familiar to the Christian tradition as the seven gifts of the Holy Spirit: wisdom, understanding, counsel, fortitude, knowledge, piety, and fear of the Lord. The Messiah will *incarnate* these gifts, in the sense that His actions will manifest these gifts of the Holy Spirit in a maximum and super-eminent way. One ancient rabbi says that this "teaches that He loaded him with good deeds and suffering as a mill [is laden]."[24]

This text of Isaiah 11 is very significant for identifying the figure of the Messiah. Not only must He be born of the root of Jesse, but He must have the Spirit of the Lord *rest upon him*. Other prophets received the Spirit of the Lord in various measures, but always in a transient way. They prophesied at some times, but not others; and like David, they were not exempt from losing the Holy Spirit through sin. The Messiah will have the Spirit of the Lord *resting* on Him, which implies an abiding state, in which His human soul is imbued with the Spirit of the Lord. This is His true "anointing." That is, the Messiah will be recognized by a superabundant gift of wisdom, understanding, counsel, fortitude, knowledge, piety, and the fear of the Lord. These divine gifts enable Him to judge the world rightly, as we see in the second half of the prophecy.

The Birth of the Messiah in Bethlehem

So far we have seen that prophecy has narrowed down the lineage of the Messiah to the line of David, and that it was to be a miraculous birth from a virgin mother. Can we learn anything of the place of birth?

We know from the Gospel of Matthew that when the three magi from the Orient came to Jerusalem looking for the newborn Messiah, the chief priests and scribes in Jerusalem told Herod that the Messiah was to be born in Bethlehem, an insignificant town that was the birthplace of David. How did they know? This prophecy is given in Micah, a contemporary of Isaiah from the end of the eighth century before Christ, who prophesied (Mic 5:2): "'But you, O Bethlehem Ephrathah, who are little to be among the clans of Judah, from you shall

---

[23] *Pesikta Rabbati: Discourses for Feasts, Fasts, and Special Sabbaths*, trans. William G. Braude (New Haven: Yale Univ. Press, 1968), 2:642–43, piska 33.6. See also *Midrash Rabbah* (London: Soncino Press, 1961), 1:17 (on Genesis, ch. 2, section 4): "'And the spirit of God hovered:' this alludes to the spirit of Messiah, as you read, 'And the spirit of the Lord shall rest upon him.'" Cited in Robert Leo Odom, *Israel's Pre-Existent Messiah*, 29.

[24] *Babylonian Talmud*, Tractate Shabbat 93b. Quoted in Odom, *Israel's Pre-Existent Messiah*, 27. See also Raphael Patai, *The Messiah Texts* (Detroit: Wayne State Univ. Press, 1979), 28–29.

come forth for me one who is to be ruler in Israel, and his going forth is *from the beginning, from the days of eternity.*"[25]

This was a very specific prophecy, for Bethlehem was a small town. St. Justin Martyr, in his *First Apology* written in the mid-second century, mentions that the birth of Jesus in Bethlehem could still be ascertained from documents existing at that time: the "registers of the taxing made under Cyrenius, your first procurator in Judaea."[26]

This prophecy also alludes to the dual nature and birth of Christ: born in history in Bethlehem, and begotten from the Father from all eternity. The Messiah exists eternally before His earthly birth in Bethlehem. We should connect this passage with the text of Proverbs 8:22–31, which speaks of the pre-existent and eternal Wisdom of God, who is distinct from God the Father and yet rejoices to be with the sons of men.

By the way, the idea that the Messiah exists with God the Father from before the creation of the world is an ancient Jewish idea attested to also in a non-Biblical source written a century and a half before Christ, the *First Book of Enoch*. This interesting work speaks of the Messiah as a "son of man," who "shall be a light unto the nations, and hope for the troubled of heart. And all those who dwell on the earth shall fall down before him, and worship and praise and bless and sing to the Lord of Spirits. It is for this that he has been chosen and hidden before Him, even before the creation of the world and for evermore."[27]

Time of the Coming of the Messiah (Daniel 9:24–27)

The prophets have thus indicated the lineage and birthplace of the Messiah, but what about the time? First of all, it must take place before the extinction of the line of David, for the Messiah is to be his descendant. As we have seen, the last known representatives of the Davidic family were members of the extended family of Jesus (cousins and their descendants), some of whom appear in ecclesiastical records until the beginning of the fourth century AD. Secondly, the Messiah was predicted to come before the complete loss of sovereignty of the tribe of Judah, according to Genesis 49:10: "The scepter shall not depart from Judah, nor the ruler's staff from between his feet, until he comes to whom it belongs (i.e., the Messiah); and to him shall be the obedience

---

[25] For Mic 5:2b I have followed the Douay-Rheims version, in harmony with the *Nova Vulgata*.

[26] St. Justin Martyr, *First Apology*, ch. 34.

[27] 1 Enoch 48:4–6. See also 46:1–3; 62:7–9; quoted in Raphael Patai, *The Messiah Texts*, 18–19. These texts are inspired by Dan 7.

of the peoples." The destruction of Jerusalem in the year 70 AD put the final stroke to the utter loss of Judean sovereignty.

Finally, a more specific indication of the time of the coming of the Messiah was given by the prophet Daniel in a very significant although enigmatic prophecy in Daniel 9. This prophecy is set during the Babylonian exile of the Jewish people in the sixth century BC. Daniel is praying for forgiveness for the sins of his people and contemplating the duration of the exile, which was to be seventy years, as foretold by the prophet Jeremiah.[28] The angel Gabriel bears a message of consolation to Daniel which, surprisingly, does not speak of the seventy years until the end of the exile, but rather tells of a much greater consolation concerning the coming of the Messiah. Gabriel tells him that seventy *weeks of years* have been ordained from the decree to restore Jerusalem until the coming of the Messiah, at which time iniquity would be forgiven and "abolished":

> Seventy weeks are decreed upon thy people and upon thy holy city, that transgression may be finished, and sin may have an end, and iniquity may be abolished; and everlasting justice may be brought; and vision and prophecy may be fulfilled; and the Saint of saints [holy of holies] may be anointed. Know therefore and take notice: from the going forth of the word to build up Jerusalem again, unto Christ [Messiah], the prince, there shall be seven weeks, and sixty-two weeks; and the street [moat] shall be built again, and the walls, in straitness of times. And after sixty-two weeks Christ [the Messiah] shall be slain, and the people that shall deny him shall not be his. And a people with their leader that shall come, shall destroy the city, and the sanctuary: and the end thereof shall be waste, and after the end of the war the appointed desolation.[29]

This extraordinary text contains several very important elements: (1) the time-frame for the coming of the Messiah; (2) the Messiah will be "cut off" or slain;[30] (3) the Messiah will somehow "abolish" iniquity and bring in "everlasting justice"; (4) the death of the Messiah will be

---

[28] This is mentioned in Dan 9:2 and alludes to Jer 25:11–12: "This whole land shall become a ruin and a waste, and these nations shall serve the king of Babylon seventy years. Then after seventy years are completed, I will punish the king of Babylon and that nation, the land of the Chaldeans, for their iniquity, says the Lord, making the land an everlasting waste." See also Jer 29:10: "For thus says the Lord: When seventy years are completed for Babylon, I will visit you, and I will fulfill to you my promise and bring you back to this place."

[29] Dan 9:24–27, Douay-Rheims version.

[30] Another prophetic text indicating that the Messiah will be slain is Zech 12:10.

followed by the destruction of the city and the sanctuary at the hands of another people.

The decree mentioned here to mark the beginning of the seventy weeks seems to be the edict to rebuild the walls of Jerusalem given in the mid-fifth century BC under King Artaxerxes I, at the time of Ezra and Nehemiah (Neh 2:7–8; Ezra 7). Sixty-nine weeks of years (that is, roughly 490 years) after this decree is the time given by Daniel for the coming of the Messiah and the Atonement. This takes us very close to the year 30 AD, the probable date of the Crucifixion. By the way, we need not seek an exact correspondence in dates, but a time-frame.

St. Jerome, in his commentary on Daniel 9, reports that the interpretation of the chronology indicated in the seventy weeks had been the subject of a lively discussion prior to his time, and instead of settling the question, he puts forth the principal views of his predecessors. The first view given is that of Julius Africanus, who, in accordance with Nehemiah 2, establishes the beginning of the seventy weeks with the decree of Artaxerxes in the twentieth year of his reign (445 BC):

> There is no doubt but what it constitutes a prediction of Christ's advent, for He appeared to the world at the end of seventy weeks. After Him . . . sin reached its end and iniquity was destroyed. An eternal righteousness also was proclaimed which overcame the mere righteousness of the law; and the vision and the prophecy were fulfilled, inasmuch as the Law and the Prophets endured until the time of John the Baptist (Lk 16), and then the Saint of saints was anointed. . . . Now the angel himself specified seventy weeks of years, that is to say, four hundred and ninety years from the issuing of the word that the petition be granted and that Jerusalem be rebuilt. The specified interval began in the twentieth year of Artaxerxes, King of the Persians; for it was his cupbearer, Nehemiah [Neh 1], who . . . petitioned the king and obtained his request that Jerusalem be rebuilt. And this was the word or decree which granted permission for the construction of the city and its encompassment with walls; for up until that time it had lain open to the incursions of the surrounding nations.[31]

A second possibility is to put the beginning of the seventy weeks at the decree of Artaxerxes mentioned in Ezra 7:12–26, issued about thirteen years earlier, in 458 BC. However, this is not properly a decree

---

[31] *Jerome's Commentary on Daniel*, trans. Gleason L. Archer, Jr. (Grand Rapids, MI: Baker Book House, 1958), 95–96, in which St. Jerome cites Africanus' work *Tempora (Chronology)*. Africanus lived from c. 160 to c. 240 AD, and is known as the father of Christian chronography.

to rebuild Jerusalem, as was the later decree mentioned in Nehemiah 2, and thus it does not directly relate to the prophecy of the "going forth of the word to restore and build Jerusalem" mentioned in Daniel 9:25.

A third possible interpretation for dating the beginning of the seventy weeks in Daniel 9:25—the "word to build up Jerusalem again"—would be the edict of Cyrus in 538 BC, permitting the rebuilding of the Temple in Jerusalem.[32] However, this earlier edict did not concern the city itself, which was not properly rebuilt until the time of Nehemiah and Artaxerxes I, who issued the edict authorizing timber for reconstructing the gates and walls of Jerusalem, as we read in Nehemiah 2:7–8. Thus it seems much better to hold that the computation of the seventy weeks should begin with Artaxerxes I.

It is very probable that this text of Daniel, together with Genesis 49:10, was the reason that a very high pitch of Messianic expectation existed at the time of Jesus. Several other false messiahs had appeared shortly before, as we know from the speech of Rabbi Gamaliel in Acts 5:34–37, and others appeared afterwards (such as the well-known Bar Kochba), always in the role of political agitators and zealots for Jewish independence.

The most important thing in this text, however, is its spiritual dimension. The Messiah comes not to inaugurate a kingdom on earth in Jerusalem. On the contrary, He will be slain and afterwards Jerusalem will be burnt together with the Temple. He comes rather to abolish sin and iniquity and introduce eternal justice. In other words, He comes to reconcile man with God and to obtain the forgiveness of all sins. Daniel does not explain how the Messiah will do this, but some clarification is given in Isaiah 53, which will be discussed in the following chapter.

In summary, the Messianic texts that we have looked at pinpoint the coming into the world of the Messiah in a very precise way. God has chosen a particular lineage through Abraham, Isaac, Jacob, Judah, and David. His advent will occur in Bethlehem almost five hundred years after the rebuilding of Jerusalem following the Babylonian exile. The Messiah will be born of a virgin, although "his going forth is from the beginning" (Mic 5:2) and He is to be "God with us." He is to be a new Moses and a new David. He will inaugurate a universal kingdom that will last forever; in Him all nations will be blessed. He will abolish iniquity, crush the head of the ancient serpent, and introduce perfect righteousness. He will be slain, and some time thereafter, Jerusalem and the Temple will be burnt and destroyed by another people and prince.

---

[32] This decree of Cyrus is quoted in Ezra 1:2–4; 6:1–12.

The Messiah Is to Be Son of Man and Son of God

In addition to the lineage of the Messiah and the time of His coming, prophecy also indicated something still more mysterious. The Messiah was to be both son of man and Son of God.

The Messiah is given the title "son of man" in Daniel 7:13: "Behold, with the clouds of heaven there came one like a son of man," to whom is given "power, and glory, and a kingdom; and all peoples, tribes and tongues shall serve him." As we know, "son of man" was the title by which Jesus frequently referred to Himself, clearly alluding to the prophecy of Daniel. In Hebrew, the expression "son of an x" means that the thing is a member of species x. "Son of man" means that someone is a member of mankind. To say "*the* son of man" is the same as to say "*the* man," the *new Adam*.

The Messiah is to be also the Son of God. This can be seen in several texts, such as Psalm 2, a Messianic psalm, in which we read: "I will tell of the decree of the Lord: He said to me, 'You are my son, today I have begotten you. Ask of me, and I will make the nations your heritage, and the ends of the earth your possession'" (Ps 2:7–8).[33]

In the Hebrew mentality, if the expression is taken in the full and proper sense of the word, "the son of God" must share in the divine nature. When Caiaphas asked Jesus if He was the "son of the Blessed," in order to accuse Him of the supreme blasphemy (Mk 14:61), the expression is clearly being understood in this proper sense. The Scriptures also sometimes use the expression in a broader sense in which the members of the People of God are said to be (adopted) "sons of God,"[34] by which a mysterious *participation* in the divine nature is

---

[33] See also 2 Sam 7:12–14: "When your days are fulfilled and you lie down with your fathers, I will raise up your offspring after you. . . .. *I will be his father, and he shall be my son.*" As mentioned above, this text has a reference also to Solomon, who is a figure of Christ. However, the whole meaning cannot refer to Solomon, for the throne of David was not established forever in Solomon, but in Christ.

Another beautiful prophecy is Wis 2:13, 18–19. The enemies of the Messiah (righteous man) say: "He professes to have knowledge of God, and calls himself a child of the Lord. . . . If the righteous man is God's son, he will help him, and will deliver him from the hand of his adversaries. Let us test him with insult and torture, that we may find out how gentle he is, and make trial of his forbearance."

[34] Ps 82:6 uses the expression in the sense of adopted sonship through grace: "I say, 'You are gods, sons of the Most High, all of you; nevertheless, you shall die like men.'" Jesus refers to this text in Jn 10:34–36, after He is accused of making Himself God. He adduces this text to show the distinction between divine filiation as applied to the members of the People of God and the unique sense in which it applies to Him. If all Israelites are said to be sons of God, should it not be true in a higher sense of the one sent by God into the world: "Is it not written in your law, 'I said, you are gods?' If he called them gods to whom the word of God came (and

indicated. Catholic theology explains this as the gift of divine filiation which we receive through sanctifying grace given in Baptism, by which the faithful come to be adopted sons of God in Christ. Christ alone, however, is the natural Son of God, eternally begotten of the Father.

In these two titles, Son of God and Son of man, we see revealed the doctrine of the Incarnation, and we also have a hint of the Trinity. Christ is the Son of man and the Son of God (in the proper sense and not by adoption) in that He has two natures united in one Person: He is true man and true God, perfect man and perfect God.

He is the Son of God insofar as He is the second Person of the Blessed Trinity, God from God, light from light, true God from true God. This doctrine of the Trinity was not explicitly revealed in the Old Testament, but it was mysteriously hinted at in speaking of the Messiah as "Son of God." Perhaps the prophets themselves did not fully grasp what this meant.

In addition to the title, Son of God, the Messianic prophecies speak of the Messiah several times directly as *God*. In the prophecy of the Virgin Birth, He is given the name "Emmanuel," which means "God with us." The literal interpretation of this Messianic title points to the fundamental meaning of the Incarnation: Christ is God visiting His people. In Isaiah 9, as seen above, the same "child" of the Virgin is given a divine title: "Wonderful, Counselor, *God the Mighty*, the Father of the world to come, the Prince of Peace." [35]

In Psalm 109:1, the Messiah is spoken of as "Lord," given the same title as God the Father: "The Lord says to my Lord, 'Sit at my right hand until I make your enemies your footstool.'" The expression of "sitting at the right hand" of the Lord refers to a full participation in the governing power of God the Father, which is received by the Messiah in His humanity.

Even aside from these individual texts, however, the whole nature of the Messianic hope shows that such hope could never be fulfilled by a mere man.

---

scripture cannot be broken), do you say of him whom the Father consecrated and sent into the world, 'You are blaspheming,' because I said, 'I am the Son of God?'" See Jn 1:12–13 for the notion of adopted divine sonship through Baptism.

[35] Douay-Rheims version.

CHAPTER 3

Prophecies of the Suffering Servant

We have seen that the prophecies of the Old Testament pinpoint the coming of the Messiah by indicating His lineage and family as that of Abraham, Isaac, Jacob, Judah, and David; His birthplace as Bethlehem; and the time of His coming as about 490 years after the decree for the rebuilding of Jerusalem, which occurred about 450 BC.

We have also seen that the Messiah will be a blessing for all nations, and that His task is to crush the head of the ancient serpent, which means that He will crush iniquity. Nevertheless, He will be bruised in the process. The prophecy in Daniel 9 develops this by connecting the coming of the Messiah with an absolutely transcendent purpose: "that transgression may be finished, and sin may have an end, and iniquity may be abolished; and everlasting justice may be brought; and vision and prophecy may be fulfilled."

How is this to be accomplished? How can a slain Messiah (Dan 9:26) finish transgression, abolish iniquity, and introduce everlasting righteousness? Furthermore, in what sense can sin be said to be crushed and righteousness introduced in the very course of human history, a history marked by continual sin? It cannot mean that temporal human history will no longer be permeated with human sin. It can only mean that sin is crushed spiritually. What does this mean? The answer is given to us in Isaiah's prophecies of the Suffering Servant.

The book of Isaiah is extremely rich in Messianic prophecies. To simplify, we can divide them into three groups: prophecies concerning the birth and coming of the Messiah (especially Is 7, 9, and 11); prophecies concerning the "suffering servant" (Is 42, 49, 50, 53); and those concerning the fruits of the Messiah's coming and the conversion of the Gentiles (especially Is 60–61). This last we shall reserve for the next chapter.

The Suffering Servant (1) (Isaiah 42:1-7)

The middle section of the book of Isaiah contains four canticles concerning a mysterious "suffering servant of the Lord," which explain the mission of the Messiah with great precision, revealing a very different aspect than that of the Messianic child of the earlier chapters. The first of these texts is Isaiah 42:1–7:

> Behold my servant, whom I uphold, my chosen, in whom my soul delights; I have put my Spirit upon him, he will bring forth justice to the nations. He will not cry or lift up his voice, or make it heard in the street; a bruised reed he will not break, and a dimly burning wick he will not quench; he will faithfully bring forth justice. He will not fail or be discouraged till he has established justice in the earth; and the coastlands wait for his law. Thus says God, the Lord, who created the heavens and stretched them out, who spread forth the earth and what comes from it, who gives breath to the people upon it and spirit to those who walk in it: "I am the Lord, I have called you in righteousness, I have taken you by the hand and kept you; I have given you as a covenant to the people, a light to the nations, to open the eyes that are blind, to bring out the prisoners from the dungeon, from the prison those who sit in darkness."

Three important points are found in this prophecy. First, the Messiah is to be a unique and elect servant of the Lord in whom the Father delights, and who receives the very Spirit of the Lord, as we see also in Isaiah 11. Just as Israel was elected out of the nations of the earth to bear a blessing, so the Messiah is elected by God out of all mankind. As in Isaiah 11:3, the Spirit of the Lord enables him to judge the nations. However, the Messiah's teaching and judgment will be marked by a spirit of meekness and mercy. "A bruised reed he will not break, and a dimly burning wick he will not quench." What does this mean? The bruised reed should be understood as referring to the sinner, who is bruised by sin and the experience of his own misery, but not yet hardened by sin. The same idea is conveyed by the dimly burning wick: it is about to be snuffed out but is not yet completely dead. The Messiah will be marked by a predilection for the sinner who is not completely dead to the reality of his sin, but has some awareness of and sorrow for it. This prophecy is perfectly verified in the New Testament accounts of Jesus' dealings with sinners, such as tax-collectors guilty of extortion, women caught in adultery, etc.

Second, the Messiah is said to be "given for a covenant with the people," referring to Israel. He shall inaugurate a new Covenant between God and His people. To understand this, we must look elsewhere in the prophets for other texts on the new Covenant to be established by the Messiah.[1]

---

[1] See Jer 31:31–33; Ez 36:25–27; and Dan 9:27.

Third, the Messiah's mission is universal and includes the Gentiles. The Father has given Him to be a light unto the Gentiles: *lumen gentium.* In the New Testament (Lk 2:32), St. Simeon quotes these words in his canticle of thanksgiving when he encounters the child Jesus being presented in the Temple forty days after His birth, and likewise speaks of the double role of the Messiah to be at once "light for revelation to the Gentiles" and "glory to thy people Israel."

The Suffering Servant (2) (Isaiah 49:1–9)

The second canticle further develops the ideas that the Messiah will establish a covenant with the people and be a light to the Gentiles. It also introduces the idea that the Messiah will suffer, for he will be "deeply despised" and "abhorred by the nations":

> The Lord called me from the womb, from the body of my mother he named my name. . . . But I said, "I have labored in vain, I have spent my strength for nothing and vanity. . ." And now the Lord says, who formed me from the womb to be his servant, to bring Jacob back to him, and that Israel might be gathered to him, . . . : "It is too light a thing that you should be my servant to raise up the tribes of Jacob and to restore the preserved of Israel; I will give you as a light to the nations, that my salvation may reach to the end of the earth." Thus says the Lord, the Redeemer of Israel and his Holy One, to one deeply despised, abhorred by the nations, the servant of rulers: "Kings shall see and arise; princes, and they shall prostrate themselves. . ." Thus says the Lord: "In a time of favor I have answered you, in a day of salvation I have helped you; I have kept you and given you as a covenant to the people, to establish the land, to apportion the desolate heritages; saying to the prisoners, 'Come forth,' to those who are in darkness, 'Appear.'"

The Messiah is presented here as called from his mother's womb to glorify the Father. This means that he is called to restore the honor of God trampled by the weight of human sin. He enters into dialogue with God and says that He has labored in vain, for he will not enjoy earthly success, but will apparently fail in his mission "to bring back Jacob unto him," and to gather Israel to the Lord. In other words, the mission of the Messiah will not have full success among the children of Jacob; in that regard it will seem that he has been sent in vain. Only a remnant of Israel will be converted.

The answer is given to him that it is too small a thing for him solely to raise up the tribes of Jacob and convert the remnant of Israel. As in Isaiah 42, his mission extends to the Gentiles, to whom he is to be the *light* and God's salvation to the ends of the earth. In other words, the apparent failure of the Messiah to gather Israel is not to be considered a failure, for he is to bear great fruit in the extension of the light of revelation and salvation to the Gentiles. As will be seen below (chapter 10), this theme is further developed with great pathos in the New Testament by St. Paul in Romans 9–11.

Isaiah 49:9 seems to extend the mission still further, to include the release of those imprisoned in death—those who are bound in darkness. This can indicate either the bonds and darkness of death in *sheol* (the Jewish name for the underworld) or the bonds of spiritual death which is sin. We know that Christ releases mankind from both bonds. We believe that the gates of heaven were opened after Jesus died on the Cross, and that Jesus immediately descended to *sheol*—the bosom of Abraham—and released the just souls retained there. This is referred to in the Christian tradition as the "Harrowing of hell," the liberation from the limbo of *sheol* of all the souls that died before Good Friday in a state of grace. The full redemption of the body, however, must await the Messiah's Second Coming.

The Suffering Servant (3) (Isaiah 50)

The canticles of the Suffering Servant of the Lord continue in Isaiah 50:5–7, deepening the note of rejection that the servant will undergo:

> The Lord God has opened my ear, and I was not rebellious, I turned not backward. I gave my back to the smiters, and my cheeks to those who pulled out the beard; I hid not my face from shame and spitting. For the Lord God helps me; therefore I have not been confounded; therefore I have set my face like a flint, and I know that I shall not be put to shame.

The reference to the Lord opening his ear means that the suffering servant of the Lord will be marked by a spirit of absolute obedience to the will of the Father, even to the point of utter humiliation and death.[2] He will be spit upon, beaten, and treated with ignominy.[3] However, he shall continue to be meek, his face unmoved, trusting absolutely in the Lord.

The Suffering Servant (4) (Isaiah 53)

The note of failure, rejection, and public humiliation of the Suffering Servant culminates in the famous text of Isaiah 53:2–12, which has been called the fifth Gospel:

---

[2] See Phil 2:6–11.

[3] For the realization of this prophecy in the Passion of Christ, see Mt 26:67–68; Mk 14:65; Lk 22:63–65.

He had no form or comeliness that we should look at him, and no beauty that we should desire him. He was despised and rejected by men; a man of sorrows, and acquainted with grief; and as one from whom men hide their faces he was despised, and we esteemed him not. Surely he has borne our griefs and carried our sorrows; yet we esteemed him stricken, smitten by God, and afflicted. But he was wounded for our transgressions, he was bruised for our iniquities; upon him was the chastisement that made us whole, and with his stripes we are healed. All we like sheep have gone astray; we have turned every one to his own way; and the Lord has laid on him the iniquity of us all.

He was oppressed, and he was afflicted, yet he opened not his mouth; like a lamb that is led to the slaughter, and like a sheep that before its shearers is dumb, so he opened not his mouth. By oppression and judgment he was taken away; and as for his generation, who considered that he was cut off out of the land of the living, stricken for the transgression of my people? And they made his grave with the wicked and with a rich man in his death, although he had done no violence, and there was no deceit in his mouth.

Yet it was the will of the Lord to bruise him; he has put him to grief; when he makes himself an offering for sin, he shall see his offspring. . . . The will of the Lord shall prosper in his hand; he shall see the fruit of the travail of his soul and be satisfied; by his knowledge shall the righteous one, my servant, make many to be accounted righteous; and he shall bear their iniquities. Therefore I will divide him a portion with the great, and he shall divide the spoil with the strong; because he poured out his soul to death, and was numbered with the transgressors; yet he bore the sin of many, and made intercession for the transgressors.

The rejection and humiliation seen in Isaiah 49 and 50 is now magnified and explained. The suffering servant is not esteemed, but rather despised and afflicted, to such an extent that he is said to be "a man of sorrows, acquainted with grief." He recapitulates in his person all human suffering, to such an extent that it defines him. Nevertheless, this suffering is voluntarily undertaken as expiation for the sins of all of us: "He was wounded for our transgressions, he was bruised for our iniquities; upon him was the chastisement that made us whole, and with his stripes we are healed."

What does it mean that "with his stripes we are healed"? The suffering servant freely offers his torment as a perfect holocaust to satisfy for the sins of the world. This idea of holocaust is reinforced in the next verse where he is compared to a sheep led to the slaughter, which is the prophetic source of John the Baptist's identification of

Jesus as the "lamb of God who takes away the sins of the world." His wounds can also be understood as a reference to Genesis 3:15, in which the "seed of the woman" is bruised on the heel by the serpent, as he crushes the serpent's head.

And as the lamb is led to the slaughter in silence and meekness, so will the suffering servant be in his passion as he is "cut off out of the land of the living," being "numbered with the transgressors." In other words, he will die the death of a malefactor in meekness and patience, praying precisely for the transgressors responsible for his death. Of course, the transgressors are ultimately all those for whose sins he is bruised: that is, all men.

However, precisely through this death, "he will justify many," and "bear their iniquities." As a result of his death he will be given "very many" and "divide the spoils of the rich." What does this mean? What can be given to a dead man, and how can he divide spoils? To divide the spoils of the strong means to conquer. Again the conquest must be a spiritual one. He will conquer the souls of many for the kingdom of God through the redemption worked by his expiatory death.[4]

A Jew (or any non-Christian) who reads the text of Isaiah 53 sincerely and without prejudice cannot help but wonder whether this suffering servant is not a prophetic image of Jesus Christ in His Passion. And it is not just a prophecy of a future event—the Passion of Christ— but also of its precise theological significance as an *expiatory sacrifice* for the forgiveness of sins, all sins. How extraordinary that the most precise statement of the expiatory value of the death of Christ should be contained in the Old Testament, in a text written centuries before His birth, and preserved and revered by those who deny that it speaks of Him!

A celebrated Jewish convert to Catholicism, the former Chief Rabbi of Rome, Israel Zolli, said that for about half a century he lived with the

---

[4] Christ applied this image of dividing the spoils of the strong man to Himself. In Mt 12:29, Christ said: "Or how can one enter a strong man's house and plunder his goods, unless he first binds the strong man? Then indeed he may plunder his house." This verse was applied to the Harrowing of hell already in the second century in a homily by Melito of Sardis (died c. 190) who has Jesus say: "I am the one who trampled hell, bound the strong one, and snatched away people and took them up to heaven on high." See Melito of Sardis, *On the Pasch* 102, in the Liturgy of Hours, Office of Readings for Holy Saturday. Christ bound the strong man—the devil—in dying on the Cross. He then despoiled the devil and plundered his house through opening the gates of heaven to all the souls of the just who had awaited the Redemption. See St. Thomas Aquinas, *The Aquinas Catechism: A Simple Explanation of the Catholic Faith by the Church's Greatest Theologian* (Manchester, NH: Sophia Institute Press, 2000), 48–49: "For this reason He descended into hell, deprived the devil of his own, bound him, and carried off his spoils."

doubt as to whether this text of Isaiah 53 was fulfilled in Christ. The doubt came into his mind (at the age of eight!) when he saw the crucifix hanging in the home of one of his childhood school companions (a Catholic), after having read the canticles of the Suffering Servant in Isaiah at school. In his autobiography he describes this encounter with the crucifix:

> Sometimes—I did not know why—I would raise my eyes to that crucifix and gaze for a long time at the figure hanging there. This contemplation, if I may call it that . . . , was not done without a stirring of my spirit. Why was this man crucified? I asked myself. Was he a bad man? . . . This crucified one, moreover, awakened in me a sense of great compassion. I had the same strong impression of his innocence as of his pain . . . he agonized. . . .
>
> No. He, Jesus, that man—now he was "He" for me, with a capital H—He was not bad; He could not have been in any way wicked. Perhaps He was, or perhaps He was not, the "Servant of God" whose canticles we read at school. Perhaps He was, or perhaps He was not, that sufferer of whom the master told us briefly: "It is King Hezekiah, or the people of Israel." I did not know. But of one thing I was certain: He was good.
>
> But then, why did they crucify Him? In the book of Isaiah there are four canticles—42:1–7; 49:1–5; 50:4–9; 52:13–53:12—which present to us an innocent man, purer than any other in the world. He is stricken and humiliated, exhausted by so much suffering; he dies in silence as in silence he suffered. Then the crowd seems to recover from its fury: "Why have we tormented and put to death Him who bore our sins?"[5]

Israel Zolli finally obtained complete certainty in 1944, after the liberation of Rome, while celebrating the feast of Yom Kippur (Feast of Expiation) in the synagogue in Rome. He was baptized some months later in February 1945 at the age of 64, with his wife, and followed by his daughter shortly thereafter. For his baptismal name he took Eugenio, the name of Pius XII. Not surprisingly, he was ostracized from the Jewish community, although he was a very well-known Biblical scholar and had guided the Roman synagogue with heroism in its period of greatest trial.

Psalm 22

Another great prophecy of the Passion of our Lord is contained in Psalm 22, where King David speaks in the person of Christ:

---

 [5] Eugenio Zolli, *Before the Dawn* (New York: Sheed and Ward, 1954), 24–25.

My God, my God, why hast thou forsaken me? . . . But I am a worm, and no man, scorned by men and despised by the people. All who see me mock at me, they make mouths at me, they wag their heads. He committed his cause to the Lord, let him deliver him, let him rescue him, for he delights in him! . . . I am poured out like water, and all my bones are out of joint; my heart is like wax, it is melted within my breast; . . . a company of evildoers encircle me; they have pierced my hands and feet—I can count all my bones—they stare and gloat over me; they divide my garments among them, and for my clothing they cast lots.[6]

While He was dying on the Cross, Jesus cried out the first words of this Psalm, showing us—if there was any doubt—that it was being fulfilled in Him. The mysterious first line reveals to us an interior desolation and hidden anguish of the Messiah, which overshadows even the other sufferings that follow. The Messiah will seem to all (even to Himself) to have been abandoned by God His Father. His humiliation is such that He will seem to be a worm rather than a man, the reproach of all, the butt of a thousand blasphemous jokes. In the midst of His sufferings, onlookers will scorn Him by saying that if he were really the Son of God in whom the Father delights, let Him come and save him.

The Gospels show us an identical picture, as we see in Matthew 27:39–42:

And those who passed by derided him, wagging their heads and saying, ". . . If you are the Son of God, come down from the cross." So also the chief priests, with the scribes and elders, mocked him, saying, "He saved others; he cannot save himself. He is the King of Israel; let him come down now from the cross, and we will believe in him."

Furthermore, the nature of the suffering seems to correspond strikingly with Roman crucifixion. His bones are out of joint; he suffers thirst; his hands and feet are pierced;[7] all his bones are exposed as he is stripped of his clothing, which is divided among the executioners.

Wisdom 2:12–20

In the second century before Christ, a final magnificent prophecy is given of the persecution and rejection of Christ in Wisdom 2:12–20.

---

[6] Ps 22:1–18.

[7] In the Hebrew Masoretic text this verse (Ps 22:17) reads: "like a lion at my hands and feet." However, the Greek translation from the third century BC (the Septuagint) reads "dug a hole in my hands and feet," which seems to be a better reading.

The passage is put in the mouths of the persecutors of the Just One. They say:

> Let us beset the just one, because he is obnoxious to us; he sets himself against our doings, reproaches us for transgressions of the Law and divulges against us the sins of our way of life. He boasts that he has the knowledge of God and *calls himself the son of God.* He is become a censurer of our thoughts. He is grievous unto us, even to behold, for his life is not like other men's, and his ways are very different. We are esteemed by him as triflers and he abstains from our ways as from filthiness, and he prefers the latter end of the just, and *glories that he has God for his father.* Let us see then if his words be true, and let us prove what shall happen to him, and we shall know what his end shall be. For *if he be the true son of God, he will defend him,* and will deliver him from the hands of his enemies. *Let us examine him by outrages and tortures, that we may know his meekness and try his patience. Let us condemn him to a most shameful death,* for according to his own words, God will take care of him.[8]

Although not directly identified as the Messiah, the identification is solid, for the text speaks of the persecution of a Just One who "boasts that he has the knowledge of God and *calls himself the son of God.*" As seen above, other Messianic texts speak of the Messiah as son of God, such as Psalm 2:7[9] and 2 Samuel 7:14.[10]

This text repeats the motif mentioned in Psalm 22:9, in which the Messiah is mocked for having been abandoned by God, whom he claimed to be his Father. Furthermore, this prophecy gives wounded pride as the motive of persecution. The Just One is persecuted because he upholds the sanctity of the Law of God and condemns sin.

Psalm 118

Another detail of Messianic suffering is found in Psalm 118:22–23, a text quoted by Jesus in the week before His Passion:[11] "The stone which the builders rejected; the same is become the head of the corner. This is the Lord's doing and it is wonderful in our eyes."[12] This beautiful Psalm also contains the famous Messianic phrase: "Blessed is he who comes in the name of the Lord" (Ps 118:26).

---

[8] Douay-Rheims version.

[9] "I will tell of the decree of the Lord: He said to me, 'You are my son, today I have begotten you.'"

[10] "I will be his father, and he shall be my son."

[11] See Mt 21:42.

[12] See also Is 28:16.

The stone is clearly the Messiah, who will be the cornerstone of the Messianic kingdom. What does it mean that he will be rejected by the builders? The builders are those who have the responsibility to be judges over the people of God: the high priests and other members of the Sanhedrin. The Messiah, therefore, will not only be "cut off, and shall have nothing" (Dan 9:26), "cut off from the land of the living" (Is 53:9), and "reputed with the wicked" (Is 53:12), but He will be rejected precisely by the authorities responsible for building up the kingdom of God: the high priests. Yet it is this very rejection by the authorities of His people that will make Him the cornerstone of the Messianic covenant, through the miraculous work of God.

The Suffering of the Messiah in the Rabbinical Tradition

Many great Jewish rabbis, reflecting on the canticles of the Suffering Servant, recognized that the Messiah will undergo immense redemptive suffering. There is a large collection of medieval rabbinic tales of the Suffering Messiah. One well-known Jewish author describes this tradition as follows:

> The Messiah . . . must spend his entire life, from the moment of his creation until the time of his advent many centuries or even millennia later, in a state of constant and acute suffering. Despised and afflicted with unhealing wounds, he sits in the gates of Great Rome and winds and unwinds the bandages of his festering sores; as a Midrash expresses it, "pains have adopted him." According to one of the most moving, and at the same time psychologically most meaningful, of all Messiah legends, God, when He created the Messiah, gave him the choice whether or not to accept the sufferings for the sins of Israel. And the Messiah answered: "I accept it with joy, so that not a single soul of Israel should perish."[13] In the later, Zoharic formulation of this legend, the Messiah himself summons all the diseases, pains, and sufferings of Israel to come upon him, in order thus to ease the anguish of Israel, which otherwise would be unbearable.[14]

---

[13] *Pesikta Rabbati: Discourses for Feasts, Fasts, and Special Sabbaths*, 2:679 (piska 36.1): "The Messiah will say: Master of the universe, with joy in my soul and gladness in my heart I take this suffering upon myself, provided that not one person in Israel perish; that not only those who are alive be saved in my days, but that also those who are dead, who died from the days of Adam up to the time of redemption; and that not only these be saved in my days, but also those who died as abortions. . . . Such are the things I desire, and for these I am ready to take upon myself [whatever Thou decreest]." This text was composed c. 845 AD.

[14] Raphael Patai, *The Messiah Texts*, 104.

The rabbinic legends of the suffering Messiah, following Isaiah 53 and Psalm 22, conceive the Messiah as suffering immensely to atone for the sins of every man who ever lived. The Midrash (*Pesikta Rabbati*) describes the sufferings of the Messiah in a dialogue with the Father:

> During the seven-year period preceding the coming of the son of David, iron beams will be brought and loaded upon his neck until the Messiah's body is bent low. Then he will cry and weep, and his voice will rise up to the very height of heaven, and he will say to God: Master of the universe, how much can my strength endure? How much can my spirit endure? How much my breath before it ceases? How much can my limbs suffer? Am I not flesh-and-blood?
>
> It was because of the ordeal of the son of David that David wept, saying "My strength is dried up like a potsherd" (Ps 22:16). During the ordeal of the son of David, the Holy One, blessed be He, will say to him: "Ephraim, My true Messiah, long ago, ever since the six days of creation, thou didst take this ordeal upon thyself. At this moment, thy pain is like My pain."[15]

Various elements of this remarkable text deserve notice. First, the rabbinical understanding of the sufferings of the Messiah is coupled here with the notion of the pre-existent Messiah, who undertakes to suffer atonement for Israel from the beginning of creation. Secondly, the suffering of the Messiah is equated here with a mysterious suffering of compassion in the heart of God Himself. Finally, how can one refrain from comparing the suffering of the Messiah as depicted here (and in similar texts) with the suffering of Jesus as delineated in the Gospels?

The Passion of Jesus Compared to Isaiah 53

Despite brilliant and astounding insights into the expiatory suffering of the Messiah, the rabbinical tradition still fell short in the attempt to grasp the full extent of the dignity that the Messiah would have to possess in order to expiate for the sins of mankind. What would the Messianic sufferings have to be like to atone for every human sin? Could a mere man atone for the sins of mankind? Would not the Messiah have to be not only suffering man, but also "mighty God" and "son of God" as is said of the Messiah in Isaiah 9:4 and Psalm 2:7, in order for his suffering to have the value to atone for the sins of all men of all times? Would this suffering not have to be a "superhuman" suffering, human and superhuman at the same time?

---

[15] *Pesikta Rabbati: Discourses for Feasts, Fasts, and Special Sabbaths*, 2:681 (piska 36.2).

Furthermore, if the Messiah has to atone for every human sin, would his suffering not look just like what we find narrated in the Gospels in the Passion of Jesus? If seen in this context, it becomes clear that the *Passion of Christ has a quintessentially Jewish spirit: it perfectly corresponds with the prophetical accounts and traditions of the suffering Messiah,* although it goes far beyond even the most audacious speculations of the great rabbis.

Jesus endured tremendous dishonor and humiliation in public, and in the largest public that could be had in Israel: Jerusalem during the solemnity of the Passover when all the pilgrims from the Jewish world who could afford the trip were present in the Holy City. Perhaps there were hundreds of thousands of pilgrims there.

This humiliation was accentuated by the fickleness of the crowd, who condemned and rejected Him just five days after offering Him a triumphal entry into Jerusalem. The glory so recently received served only to augment, by contrast, the humiliation of His rejection by the mob. He was humiliated by being sold for only thirty pieces of silver,[16] the price of a common slave.[17] He was humiliated by being betrayed with a kiss, as if He were taken in by Judas' hypocrisy. He was condemned by the Sanhedrin as a blasphemer, false prophet, and religious imposter, and condemned to death for the greatest of all conceivable crimes: making Himself God although being a mere man, usurping the divine honor as if He were Satan or the Antichrist.

The humiliation was heightened further by the fact that Barabbas, a murderer and leader of sedition (see Mk 15:7), was *chosen over Jesus.* When brought before Herod, King of Galilee, and his court, Jesus was treated as a lunatic, a buffoon, and a circus spectacle for the performance of miracles (see Lk 23:8–11). He was then mocked as a false king by being given a crown of thorns, a red mantle, and a stick as scepter. He was ridiculed by his executioners, spit at, blindfolded and struck, mocked as a false prophet and asked to prophesy as to who struck the blow.

He was condemned to be executed in the most ignominious way known—crucifixion—after being scourged nearly to death. And this crucifixion was between two common criminals, as if Christ were just one more common thief. He was stripped of His clothes, which were divided by the executioners. According to the Roman usage, victims were entirely stripped. He would have been covered only by His own Blood.[18] He was humiliated through poverty: He died with *nothing of His*

---

[16] This is also mentioned prophetically in Zech 11:12–13.

[17] Ex 21:32.

[18] The image on the Shroud apparently shows Him *entirely naked*, as was the custom in Roman crucifixion. Artistic representations rightly do not dare reveal this ultimate humiliation, an offense against all sense of modesty.

own, except the instruments of His torture. Not even His grave was His own.

Interior Suffering of Jesus in His Passion

The interior suffering of Christ reached its height in Gethsemane, where it caused Him to sweat blood. Doctors say that such a hemorrhage (called *hematidrosis*) can occur from severe mental anguish.[19] What was the cause of this anguish?

In Gethsemane Christ clearly willed to suffer the *severest of temptations*. Although we do not see the Tempter directly as in the Temptations after His Baptism, the prayer of Christ in the Garden reveals this trial. We can imagine the Devil tempting Christ with (1) the magnitude of the physical sufferings that He would go through, with all the terrible details; (2) the enormity of human sin in all its hideous disorder, for which He was to offer Himself, including the sins of the members of the Church, sins of sacrilege and scandal, especially of those who received most and who should have been most faithful: priests, bishops, and religious; and still more, (3) the thought of the ingratitude of so many of those for whom He was to suffer and shed His Blood, the futility of His Sacrifice for so many men who would not correspond to the grace of redemption, and whose souls would be lost despite the price of His Blood.

Christ made Himself victim for all human sin. He took upon Himself the most tremendous of all humiliations—prostrating Himself before God His Father as if He were the culpable party, as if all these sins were His, though He was without stain. This is the greatest secret of the Passion of Christ, the *secret sanctuary of Christ's anguish* which we cannot penetrate and can only dimly imagine.

Christ took on Himself the penalty for all human sin. The greatest form of that penalty is interior: "sorrow even unto death" (see Mt 26:38), contrition and remorse, a rending of the heart for having offended God, and an experience of the rupture of man's relationship with God, separation from God, abandonment by God. Could Christ who was without sin feel this extreme of sorrow? Yes, for He made Himself one with sinful mankind, not in committing sin, but in satisfying for it, paying its penalty. For this reason St. Thomas Aquinas says that Christ suffered more in His soul than the contrition felt by any

---

[19] See Dr. Leoncio Garza-Valdés, *The DNA of God? Newly Discovered Secrets of the Shroud of Turin* (New York: Berkley Books, 1999), Appendix A, 105: "Blood sweat (hematidrosis) has been reported by several medical doctors in cases of severe mental anguish."

man;[20] indeed it was surely greater than the *combined sorrow* of contrition of all men who ever lived or will live, put together. For He felt the pains of contrition *for all the sins of all humanity*, and He alone felt the sorrow of contrition *as it should be felt,* as by one who knows perfectly what sin is, and who knows intimately the goodness of God offended by sin, for contrition grows in proportion to charity and wisdom. As Isaiah foretold (Is 53:4): *"Surely He hath borne our infirmities and carried our sorrows."*

My God, My God, Why Hast Thou Forsaken Me?

The full extent of this interior sorrow of contrition for the sins of all men is manifested to us in the mysterious words of Christ on the Cross: "My God, my God, why hast thou forsaken me?" (Mt 27:46). How was He forsaken? In two ways: in the exterior and the interior man. First, He was abandoned in the sense of suffering all the physical effects of abandonment. When parents abandon a child, they no longer take care of him, they no longer protect him from death, they no longer comfort him with their presence and with signs of their love, they no longer see to his well-being. This was precisely what happened to Christ in His Passion.

However, it would be wrong to limit the abandonment of Christ to this; the words of Psalm 22 that Jesus cried out on the Cross have a deeper meaning. He was abandoned interiorly by losing all spiritual consolation and receiving *all spiritual desolation*. God allows some of His most beloved saints to experience a taste of this most bitter chalice, which has been described as the "dark night of the soul" by St. John of the Cross. Most recently it has been revealed that Bl. Teresa of Calcutta suffered from this terrible interior desolation for fifty years, from the beginning of her work with the poorest of the poor. But saints like Bl. Teresa received only a taste of what Christ drank to the bottom of the cup.

How could Christ have suffered *total desolation?* Normally, the presence of God in our will and intellect produces consolation; and the vision of God produces complete beatitude, a beatitude which should also be sensible, passing to the emotions as well, since normally what we consider with our intellect and determine with our will arouses corresponding feelings. Now Christ enjoyed the vision of God in His human soul. How then, could He suffer desolation, seeing before His mind's eye, as He did, the glory of God?

St. Thomas explains that this complete spiritual desolation of Jesus in Gethsemane and on the Cross was miraculous, in the sense that the natural laws of the spiritual life were suspended. Christ alone among

---

[20] St. Thomas Aquinas, *ST* III, q. 46, a. 6, ad 4.

men had perfect dominion over His emotional state. We accept consolation or desolation as God wills to send them to us. Jesus, on the contrary, could choose desolation, despite His vision of God, by preventing any consideration—any act of the soul—that could alleviate sorrow, and focusing all the forces of His soul on everything that could produce emotions of sorrow and desolation: His impending suffering, the ingratitude of men, the malice of the most terrible sins, the weight of all human sins, compassion for all human suffering caused by sin and scandal, all of our failings one by one, all the souls that would be lost through the centuries, despite His sacrifice on the Cross.

St. Paul says that Christ "loved me and gave himself for me" (Gal 2:20). Each one of us can say this precisely because Christ enjoyed the vision of God in His Passion.[21] Only in the divine vision can all men be seen at once,[22] at one glance, with all of our sins and failure to respond to grace, with all our ingratitude, known in all its concreteness, *as it will be known in the Last Judgment*. However, here it was not known as by the Judge of all sins, but *by the Victim for all sins*. Our sins were perfectly known and considered by Christ in His Passion, not to judge them, *but to suffer for them*, as much as perfect man—the Son of Man—could suffer.

What other figure in history can so justly be said to be a "man of sorrows, acquainted with grief"? Perhaps other men could have suffered physically something comparable to Jesus. However, it is the interior suffering of Jesus revealed in the Garden of Gethsemane that makes Him the *man of sorrows* for all men and for all times. What other figure of history has ever been depicted in the act of suffering interiorly, to the point of sweating blood, for the iniquity of every individual human being?

It was precisely that interior suffering which Jesus experienced in the Garden of Gethsemane, and then the interior abandonment on the Cross, that makes the suffering of Christ so intimately fulfill the Messianic prophecies of the Suffering Servant in Isaiah 53. Suffering abounds on every page of human history. However, the Passion of Christ shows us not only the man of sorrows, but the fact that the whole mountain of suffering that He has undertaken is essentially *sorrow*

---

[21] See the *Catechism of the Catholic Church* 478: "Jesus knew and loved us each and all during his life, his agony and his Passion, and gave himself up for each one of us: 'The Son of God . . . loved me and gave himself for me.' He has loved us all with a human heart."

[22] See Pius XII, encyclical *Mystici Corporis* 75 (1943): "In the crib, on the Cross, in the unending glory of the Father, Christ has all the members of the Church present before Him and united to Him in a much clearer and more loving manner than that of a mother who clasps her child to her breast, or than that with which a man knows and loves himself."

over all human sin. This is *Messianic suffering.* No other suffering could be conceived or imagined more worthy of the Messiah.

Many people object that the idea of a crucified Messiah is a contradiction and an absurdity. However, it is precisely the Passion that shows the truth of Jesus' Messianic mission and identity as Suffering Servant, "by whose bruises we are healed." As Jesus foretold: "And I, when I am lifted up from the earth, will draw all men to myself" (Jn 12:32).

CHAPTER 4

Prophecies of the Messianic Kingdom

One of the main features of the Messianic prophecies concerns a universal kingdom of peace to be established by the Messiah, to whom all nations shall give homage. After we look at these prophecies, the inevitable question will be raised: Has this kingdom been realized? There is no doubt that this aspect of the Messianic prophecies has been a major stumbling block to Jews for the past two millennia with regard to the Messianic identity of Jesus. If the Messiah has come, as we Christians believe, where is the kingdom of peace and the restoration of Israel?

We see this objection on the pages of the New Testament, and it continues unabated to our own day. Karl Stern, a Jew from Germany and a neurologist who became Catholic in 1943, recounts how for many years he would dismiss the claims of Jesus by citing a Hasidic tale related by Martin Buber: "A rabbi who happened to be in Jerusalem heard the great trumpets blow, and there was a rumor that the Messiah had come. The Rabbi opened the window, looked around and said only, 'I see no change.'"[1]

If the world has not changed in a significant way in accordance with the Messianic prophecies, then Jesus could not have been the Messiah. *A Messiah who leaves no decisive impact on the world is no Messiah.* But has there really been no change in the world? What has happened to the pagan idols that dominated the world in 30 AD? How have they fallen? How has so much of the world come to invoke the God of Abraham, Isaac, and Jacob?[2]

---

[1] Karl Stern, *The Pillar of Fire* (New Hope, KY: Urbi et orbi/Remnant of Israel, 2000), 165.

[2] See the response to this objection by Hilaire Duesberg, "The Trial of the Messiah," in *The Bridge: A Yearbook of Judaeo-Christian Studies*, ed. J. Oesterreicher, vol. 1 (New York: Pantheon Books, 1955), 241: "An old rabbi leaning out of his window muses: 'The Messiah has come? I see no change.' But Rabbi, remember the countryside we saw from Jerusalem two thousand years ago. Fifteen leagues away, in every direction, the gods of the nations flaunted their might. As the prophets had foretold, they were swept away. Was this thanks to Jews who remained simply Jews or thanks to Jews who had become Christians? Is this no change? Let us praise God for it."

The same objection manifested in the above-mentioned Hasidic tale has been expressed in a more intellectual way by a great Jewish scholar, Gershom Scholem, who was an expert on the Messianic idea in Judaism. He wrote:

> Judaism, in all of its forms and manifestations, has always maintained a concept of redemption as an event which takes place publicly, on the stage of history and within the community. It is an occurrence which takes place in the visible world and which cannot be conceived apart from such a visible appearance. In contrast, Christianity conceives of redemption as an event in the spiritual and unseen realm, an event which is reflected in the soul, in the private world of each individual, and which effects an inner transformation which need not correspond to anything outside.[3]

If Scholem were correct about Christianity, then he would be right to prefer the Jewish conception of the Messiah and the Messianic age. If Christianity were *exclusively something inward*, then it would not fulfill the expectations of the Messianic prophecies which speak of a Messianic *kingdom*, which is obviously a social and public historical reality. However, does not Christianity speak of a public and visible Messianic kingdom which we call the Church? This is not something purely inward, but lives in history. Scholem's understanding of Christianity is not Catholic but radically Protestant, for the Protestants tend to conceive of the Church as something essentially invisible, whereas Catholics recognize it to be something simultaneously visible and invisible, like the two natures of Jesus Christ. The real question is whether the kingdom spoken of in Biblical prophecy can be identified with the Church founded by Jesus Christ.

The Dream of Nebuchadnezzar (Daniel 2)

Daniel 2:31–45 recounts the prophetic dream of King Nebuchadnezzar, in which he saw a colossal statue made of gold, silver, bronze, and iron, indicating four successive world empires, destroyed by a stone not cut by human hands which destroyed the statue and grew into a mountain. The king commanded his wise men and diviners to interpret the dream. However, in order to test the truth of the interpretation, he insisted that they tell him the dream itself first—which he had not revealed to them—and then its interpretation. Needless to say, they were all unable to do this, despite the king's threats, and so were put to death. The same test was also reserved for the Jewish exiles in Babylon famed for

---

[3] Gershom Scholem, *The Messianic Idea in Judaism and Other Essays on Jewish Spirituality* (New York: Schocken Books, 1995), 1–2.

wisdom, such as Daniel. To Daniel, however, God revealed the dream and its interpretation, which he then tells to the king.

The colossal statue made of four different metals in Nebuchadnezzar's dream corresponded to four world empires which would succeed one another. Nebuchadnezzar himself, king of the Babylonian empire, is the head of gold. It would be followed by three other world empires, of which the last would be "strong as iron, because iron breaks to pieces and shatters all things; and like iron which crushes, it shall break and crush all these" (Dan 2:40). Nevertheless, the last world empire would have an internal weakness represented by feet and toes partly of iron and partly of clay. Intermarriage would not sufficiently bond the peoples of this empire.

Daniel does not identify these empires, but the identification is fairly clear. The second empire of silver is that which conquered Babylon: the Persians and the Medes, under King Cyrus. It was under this empire that the Jews were allowed to return to Jerusalem and rebuild the Temple and the walls of the city, although they remained under Persian rule. The third great empire, "which shall rule over all the earth," was that conquered by Alexander the Great, but divided after his early death into competing parts.

The fourth great world empire, represented in the dream by the iron legs, is the Roman Empire. This fourth empire is represented by iron to indicate its strength and crushing power. Just as iron is far stronger than gold, silver, or bronze, so the Roman Empire far exceeded the other empires in crushing strength and in duration, lasting over six centuries.[4]

The legs of iron have feet and toes partly of clay and partly of iron. This section is a little more difficult to interpret. The fact that the iron has become mixed with clay shows that the later period of the Roman empire would not be as strong as the earlier (perhaps primarily because conquered Germanic tribes were relied on to perform the basic activities of farming and military service).[5] Furthermore, the two legs and the toes indicate that the Empire would become divided. Indeed, Rome suffered from terrible civil wars, in the first century BC and then again in the

---

[4] St. Jerome gives this interpretation of the four empires in his commentary on Dan 2, in *Jerome's Commentary on Daniel*, 31–32.

[5] See St. Jerome, *Jerome's Commentary on Daniel*, 32: "Now the fourth empire, which clearly refers to the Romans, is the iron empire which breaks in pieces and overcomes all others. But its feet and toes are partly of iron and partly of earthenware, a fact most clearly demonstrated at the present time. For just as there was at the first nothing stronger or hardier than the Roman realm, so also in these last days there is nothing more feeble, since we require the assistance of barbarian tribes both in our civil wars and against foreign nations."

third and fourth centuries AD, resulting in its division into East and West.

Finally, Daniel relates that during the time of the fourth world empire, another kingdom would arise that would take the place of the earlier empires and fill the entire earth, being still more universal than its predecessors:

> As you looked, a stone was cut out by no human hand, and it smote the image on its feet of iron and clay, and broke them in pieces; then the iron, the clay, the bronze, the silver, and the gold, all together were broken in pieces, and became like the chaff of the summer threshing floors; and the wind carried them away, so that not a trace of them could be found. But the stone that struck the image became a great mountain and filled the whole earth.[6]

The stone refers to the Messiah and His Kingdom. The fact that it is cut without human hands indicates the divine origin of both the kingdom and the rock itself, which will shatter the statue.[7] The fact that it struck the statue in the feet shows that this new Kingdom of divine origin begins in the time of the fourth world empire: Rome. As we know, Christ was born during the reign of Caesar Augustus, the first emperor of Rome, and died under the emperor Tiberius.

The stone that struck the statue then "became a great mountain, and filled the whole earth" (Dan 2:35). This refers to the kingdom established by the Messiah, which He founded on the rock of Peter. We see its initial rapid growth in the Acts of the Apostles, especially through the preaching of Peter and Paul and the other Apostles.

After the martyrdom of the Apostles, they were succeeded by bishops instructed and ordained by them, and the Christians steadily multiplied despite tremendous persecution. At the end of the second century, St. Irenaeus speaks of this continuous growth of the Church amid terrible persecution as a sign of its divine origin.[8] A century after St. Irenaeus, the emperor Constantine won a decisive battle in 313 AD after a dream in which he was told that he would have victory under the sign of the Cross. In gratitude, he legalized Christianity, greatly furthering its expansion. His successors made Christianity the religion of the State.

---

[6] Dan 2:34–35.

[7] See St. Jerome, *Jerome's Commentary on Daniel*, 32: "However, at the final period of all these empires of gold and silver and bronze and iron, a rock (namely, the Lord and Savior) was cut off without hands, that is, without copulation or human seed and by birth from a virgin's womb; and after all the empires had been crushed, He became a great mountain and filled the whole earth."

[8] St. Irenaeus, *Against Heresies* 3.3.3.

The subsequent collapse of the Roman Empire in the West actually strengthened the Papacy, since it was thus freed from the control of a strong local secular power. The Church was then enriched by the invading Germanic tribes, who were gradually converted, and it spread further east, to the Slavic peoples and to Russia. In the sixteenth century the Americas were evangelized, as was India, the Far East, and Africa. In sum, the Catholic Church is indeed a universal kingdom which has spread to all parts of the earth, speaking all languages and including members of all races and nations.

After predicting the time of the origin of the Messianic kingdom and its universal character, Daniel 2:44 makes the prophecy that that kingdom "will never be destroyed, nor shall its sovereignty be left to another people. It shall break in pieces all these kingdoms and bring them to an end, and it shall stand for ever." For almost two thousand years this prophecy, repeated by Christ,[9] has been fulfilled in the Catholic Church, while the Church has watched earthly kingdoms and great dynasties rise and fall, one after another, including those who sought to destroy her (Napoleon, Hitler, Stalin, etc.).

Just as these four empires were universal in scope (according to the possibilities of those times), so also the Church which replaces them is to be a universal kingdom, signified in the very name, "Catholic"; she will be a mountain filling the whole earth.

Of course, it is a spiritual rather than a temporal kingdom, founded by the power of God, and not by arms or human power. This is signified in the fact that the rock was not cut by human hands from the mountain. The rock signifies Christ, the cornerstone, and also Peter, the rock on which the Church is founded. When Pilate asked Christ whether He was a king, He answered: "My kingdom is not of this world. If my kingdom were of this world, my servants would certainly strive that I should not be delivered to the Jews: but now my kingdom is not from here" (Jn 18:36). This does not mean that the kingdom of Christ is something purely spiritual, but that it does not come from merely human agency. It is a supernatural kingdom based on purely supernatural means and directed to purely supernatural ends. The supernatural means are principally the seven sacraments established by Christ and the preaching of the Word of the Gospel; the ends are holiness, union with God, and the glory of God.

Dream of Daniel (Daniel 7)

The four great empires and the kingdom of the Messiah reappear in Daniel 7 in another dream—this time dreamt by Daniel himself. He sees

---

[9] Mt 16:18.

four great beasts that successively appear: a lion, a bear, a leopard, and a fourth beast with no name, "terrible and wonderful, and exceeding strong," with "great iron teeth." The last beast has ten horns. These four beasts apparently correspond to the four empires in Daniel 2.[10]

After this vision, the scene changes, and Daniel sees the heavenly court of the eternal God—the Ancient of Days—to whom myriads of angels minister. Before Him comes "one like the son of man":

> I saw in the night visions, and behold, with the clouds of heaven there came one like a son of man, and he came to the Ancient of Days and was presented before him. And to him was given dominion and glory and kingdom, that all peoples, nations, and languages should serve him; his dominion is an everlasting dominion, which shall not pass away, and his kingdom one that shall not be destroyed.[11]

Who is this "son of man"? We know that Christ made a direct reference to this text when He was questioned by Caiaphas before the Sanhedrin on the eve of His Passion. Caiaphas asked Him, in the name of the living God, if He was the Christ (Messiah), the Son of God. He responded affirmatively: "You say that I am."[12] The text continues: "'But I tell you, hereafter you will see the Son of man seated at the right hand of Power, and coming on the clouds of heaven.' Then the High Priest rent his garments, and said, 'He has uttered blasphemy'" (Mt 26:63–65). Christ was referring to His Second Coming at the end of history.

This affirmation of Christ brought on His Passion. However, it is one thing for Christ to say that the text of Daniel applies to Him, and another to realize the further prophecy contained in the text of Daniel: "All peoples, tribes, and tongues shall serve him. His power is an everlasting power that shall not be taken away, and his kingdom shall not be destroyed." We today see that this prophecy is fulfilled, and that this fulfillment has been progressing for twenty centuries.

In harmony with Jewish belief according to which the Messianic kingdom on earth is to be followed by the world to come (*olam ha-ba*),[13] Christians believe that the Kingdom of the Messiah has two principal stages: the Church Militant on earth, and the Church Triumphant in

---

[10] See St. Jerome, *Jerome's Commentary on Daniel*, 72–76.

[11] Dan 7:13–14.

[12] As we see several times in the Gospels, this is an idiomatic way of affirming the truth of the question, corresponding to our expression, "it is as you say." Mark (14:62) translates the idiom for his Gentile audience, telling us that Jesus says: "I am."

[13] See, for example, Babylonian Talmud, Tractate Sanhedrin, folio 99a.

heaven.[14] In both, all nations and tongues serve Christ, to the glory of God the Father. However, here on earth that service is incomplete and mixed with constant rebellion and infidelity. We have to wait for the Second Coming of the Messiah for the complete manifestation of His triumph, in which there shall no longer be any infidelity, but only the pure glorification of God by all His elect.

The Messiah introduces both stages of His Church with two "comings." The first coming of Christ in the middle of history was to found the Church on earth through the merits of His Passion and death. The Second Coming will bring about the Resurrection of the dead, the Last Judgment, and the heavenly kingdom in the world to come.

The title "Son of man" that Jesus frequently gives to Himself in the Gospels clearly refers to this Messianic text (Dan 7:13–14). It is a veiled way to refer to His Messianic dignity, which also emphasizes His true humanity.

In Jerusalem in the days before His Passion, Christ also refers to this text while teaching about the end times. After revealing various signs of the final stages of those times, He describes the coming of the Son of man "on the clouds of heaven with power and great glory; and he will send out his angels with a loud trumpet call, and they will gather his elect from the four winds" (Mt 24:30–31). He is clearly referring to this text of Daniel, and telling us that it refers to His Second Coming.

"Out of Zion Shall Go Forth the Law" (Isaiah 2:2–4)

Another beautiful prophecy of the Messianic kingdom is given in Isaiah 2:2–4:

> It shall come to pass in the latter days that the mountain of the house of the Lord shall be established as the highest of the mountains, and shall be raised above the hills; and *all the nations shall flow to it*, and *many peoples shall come*, and say: "Come, let us go up to the mountain of the Lord, to the house of the God of Jacob; that he may teach us his ways and that we may walk in his paths." For out of Zion shall go forth the law, and the word of the Lord from Jerusalem. He shall judge between the nations, and shall decide for many peoples; and they shall beat their swords into plowshares, and their spears into pruning hooks.

This prophecy does not directly mention the Messiah, but rather describes what He will achieve. In the "latter days," which refers to the Messianic age, the glory of the "house of the God of Jacob" will be

---

[14] The souls expiating their sins in Purgatory are also members of the Church: the Church Suffering.

established on the highest of mountains, which means above all other things in the sight of all nations, who shall flow to the house of the Lord, "that he may teach us his ways and that we may walk in his paths." The law of God shall go out from Mt. Zion in Jerusalem, and shall become the law of the nations, teaching peace.

This is fulfilled in the Church founded by Christ, to which the nations have flowed through the course of twenty centuries to worship the God of Jacob and revere the Ten Commandments revealed on Mt. Sinai.

"Light to the Nations" (Isaiah 49)

Isaiah 49, one of the canticles of the Suffering Servant, speaks of the Messiah as the light to the nations, given so that the salvation of God "may reach the end of the earth":

> And now the Lord says, who formed me from the womb to be his servant, to bring Jacob back to him, and that Israel might be gathered to him . . . : "It is too light a thing that you should be my servant to raise up the tribes of Jacob and to restore the preserved of Israel; I will give you as a *light to the nations*, that my salvation may reach to the end of the earth. . . . Kings shall see and arise; princes, and they shall prostrate themselves. . . . And I will make all my mountains a way, and my highways shall be raised up. Lo, these shall come from afar, and lo, these from the north and from the west, and these from the land of Syene."[15]

We see this prophecy accomplished in the Catholic Church, in which the peoples from north, south, east, and west have become united in the worship of the God of Israel and her Messiah.

Another beautiful Messianic text, Isaiah 60:1–11, further develops the reference in Isaiah 49 to the Messiah as the light to the Gentiles:

> Arise, shine; for your light has come, and the glory of the Lord has risen upon you. For behold, darkness shall cover the earth, and thick darkness the peoples; but the Lord will arise upon you, and his glory will be seen upon you. And nations shall come to your light, and kings to the brightness of your rising. Lift up your eyes all around, and see; they all gather together, they come to you; your sons shall come from afar; . . . the wealth of the nations shall come to you. A multitude of camels shall cover you; . . . all those from Sheba shall come. They shall bring gold and frankincense, and shall bring good news, the praises of the Lord. . . . Foreigners shall build

---

[15] Is 49:5–12.

up your walls, and their kings shall minister to you. . . . Your gates shall be open continually; day and night they shall not be shut; that men may bring to you the wealth of the nations, with their kings led in procession.

At the coming of the Messiah, the nations will be in great darkness, but the glory of the Lord will arise on Zion (in the person of the Messiah), and the nations will come to the light of the revelation made to Israel. They shall come into the Church, which is the fullness of Israel, and shall bring their wealth with them. This refers not so much to their gold as to their cultural patrimony. They shall bring it to enrich the universal Church and to give worship to God. The gates of the Church will be continually open through the centuries to receive the peoples into her bosom through her missionary activity.

This prophecy of Christ as an eternal ruler of a universal Kingdom is confirmed also in Psalm 72:4–17:

And he shall continue with the sun. . . . In his days shall justice spring up, and abundance of peace, till the moon be taken away. And he shall rule from sea to sea, and from the river unto the ends of the earth. Before him the Ethiopians shall fall down, and his enemies shall lick the ground. The kings of Tharsis and the islands shall offer presents; the kings of the Arabians and of Saba shall bring gifts. And all kings of the earth shall adore him; all nations shall serve him. . . . And in him shall all the tribes of the earth be blessed; all nations shall magnify him.[16]

Prophecies Concerning a New Covenant

In Jeremiah and Ezekiel we are told that the Messiah will inaugurate a new Law and a new Covenant, written not on tablets of stone, but on men's hearts. This prophecy concerns the gift of sanctifying grace and the gifts of the Holy Spirit in Baptism and Confirmation, by which the law of God is written in our hearts through the ministry of the Church.

This prophecy of a New Covenant is given in Jeremiah 31:31–33:

Behold, the days are coming, says the Lord, when I will make a *new covenant* with the house of Israel and the house of Judah, not like the covenant which I made with their fathers when I took them by the hand to bring them out of the land of Egypt, my covenant which they broke, though I was their husband, says the Lord. But this is the covenant which I will make with the house of Israel after those days, says the Lord: I will put my law within them, and I will write it upon their hearts; and I will be their God, and they shall be

---

[16] Douay Rheims translation (numbered as Ps 71).

my people. And no longer shall each man teach his neighbor and each his brother, saying, "Know the Lord," for they shall all know me, from the least of them to the greatest, says the Lord; for I will forgive their iniquity, and I will remember their sin no more.

The New Covenant is compared to the covenant established with Israel on Mt. Sinai, but is promised to be superior. The Old Covenant was given to Israel upon tablets of stone. The New Covenant is said here to consist in the forgiveness of sins, and the writing of God's law on our hearts, which occurs through the gift of grace and charity by means of the sacraments. Just as the Old Covenant established Israel as the People of God, so the New Covenant spoken of by Jeremiah must establish a new People of God, which is the Catholic Church.

A similar prophecy is given in Ez 36:24–27:

For I will take you from among the Gentiles, and will gather you together out of all the countries, and will bring you into your own land. And I will pour upon you clean water, and you shall be cleansed from all your filthiness, and I will cleanse you from all your idols. And I will give you a new heart, and put a new spirit within you, and I will take away the stony heart out of your flesh, and will give you a heart of flesh. And I will put my spirit in the midst of you, and I will cause you to walk in my commandments, and to keep my judgments, and do them.

This text refers to the interior cleansing worked by the sacrament of Baptism. The members of the new Israel, taken now from all nations, are incorporated into the People of God, the Church, by means of the water of Baptism, which removes the stain of Original Sin and of all personal sins. Baptism confers the inestimable gift of sanctifying grace and infused charity, which enable those who receive it to follow the Law of God consistently, as long as they cooperate with that grace. The reference to being brought back "into your own land" seems to principally signify incorporation into the People of God, which is the Body of Christ, the Church, spoken of by St. Paul as the "Jerusalem which is above . . . , which is our mother" (Gal 4:26).

A brief but very significant prophecy concerning the Messianic age is given in Malachi 1:11. According to this text, the Messianic age will be marked by the fact that a fitting sacrifice is offered to God throughout the world, *among the Gentiles*: "For from the rising of the sun to its setting my name is great among the nations, and in every place incense is offered to my name, and a pure offering; for my name is great among the nations, says the Lord of hosts." This prophecy is realized in the sacrifice of the Mass, by which the pure offering of the Suffering

Servant (as described in Isaiah 53) is offered up every day and every hour, in all the Catholic churches of the world.

The Kingdom of God as Proclaimed by Jesus in the Gospels

Let us now look at the proclamation of the Messianic Kingdom in the four Gospels. The earliest mention of it occurs in the Annunciation, in which the angel Gabriel announces to Mary that "the Lord God shall give unto him the throne of David his father; and he shall reign in the house of Jacob forever, and of his kingdom there shall be no end" (Lk 1:32–33). This is in perfect harmony with the prophets.

When Jesus begins His public ministry some thirty years later, He starts with the proclamation that the Kingdom of God is at hand, calling people to conversion (Mt 4:17). He compares the kingdom of God to a mustard seed planted in the field, which is the least of all seeds, but which becomes a tree such that the birds can make their nests in its branches (Mt 13:31–32). Likewise, He compares it to yeast mixed in the dough till it is all leavened (Mt 13:33). In other words, the kingdom of God will have a development of slow, continual, and organic expansion in history.

The Kingdom will include not only the righteous, but also sinners. This is shown to us in the parable of the field sown with good seed by the Messiah, but also sown with weeds by the devil. The full separation of the good seed and the weeds cannot take place until the harvest at the end of the world (Mt 13:37–43). Likewise, the Kingdom is compared to a net that captures good fish and bad. At the end of the world they will be separated (Mt 13:47–50).

The Kingdom is governed by the principles given in the Sermon on the Mount. In that discourse, Jesus presupposes the moral law given by Moses and brings it to a higher ideal of holiness that goes beyond the strength of unaided human nature, but which is possible through the aid of the gifts of the Holy Spirit.

Furthermore, this Kingdom will be distinct from a political kingdom. It can exist under Caesar, or any other monarch. This is declared when Jesus is asked if taxes should be paid to Caesar, and He gives the simple and luminous answer: "Render unto Caesar what is Caesar's, and unto God what is God's" (Mt 22:21). The Kingdom of God exists to render unto God the glory that is due to Him, and so to save our souls and seek for sanctity, in a society dedicated to that purpose. To be a citizen of the Kingdom of God—the Church—does not mean that we are not also citizens of a temporal society as well, subject to its temporal authority.

The Kingdom also has a hierarchical structure which ensures its continuous growth. This key aspect of the Kingdom is manifested to us in the crucial text of Matthew 16:18–19. Jesus has just asked the disciples who men say that He is, and who they think that He is. As we know, Peter answers: "You are the Christ, the Son of the living God." Christ responds: "Blessed are you Simon, son of Jonah! For flesh and blood has not revealed this to you, but my Father who is in heaven." Christ then in turn tells Simon bar-Jonah who he is—he has now become *Cephas*, which is Aramaic for "rock"; in Greek this name translates literally as *Petros*, and as *Petrus* in Latin. Our English "Peter" is a derivation from the Greek and Latin: "And I tell you, you are Peter, and on this rock I will build my Church, and the gates of hell shall not prevail against it. I will give you the keys of the kingdom of heaven, and whatever you bind on earth shall be bound in heaven, and whatever you loose on earth shall be loosed in heaven."

In this text Jesus uses the word "Church" (*ekklēsia*), which literally means "convocation." The Church is the society of those who respond to the call to enter the Kingdom preached by Jesus and founded by Him as a supernatural society in this world.

This Church will be built by Christ on a foundation which He declares to be none other than Peter the rock. To this Kingdom/Church He promises that it shall never fail, in accordance with the Messianic prophecies of an eternal kingdom. This is what is meant by saying that the gates of hell shall not prevail over it.

The authority in this Kingdom is represented by the "keys of the kingdom of heaven." The keys to a city were a traditional symbol of the power given to a viceroy or vicar to open and shut the gates of the city and to govern it in peace and war.[17] These keys are then connected by Jesus to a loosing and binding that refers to the power to forgive sins and to declare the true contents of Revelation, which Christ entrusts to Peter.

Here we have a magnificent prophecy that we can test today, almost two thousand years later. Has this Church/Kingdom survived the vicissitudes of time? Has it stood the test of Roman persecution, barbarian invasion, Muslim threat, rebellion from within, the armies of Napoleon, Stalin, and Hitler, the forces of Western secularism, etc.?

Is there still a kingdom on earth built on Peter, claiming the authority to bind and unbind in the name of Jesus Christ? Has it spread as leaven in the dough and as the mustard seed growing into a tree?

Here we have the most astounding combination of prophecy and realization. We have a series of Old Testament prophecies about the Messiah, son of David, founding an eternal kingdom that would come

---

[17] See Is 22:22: "And I will place on his shoulder the key of the house of David; he shall open, and none shall shut; and he shall shut, and none shall open."

to rule over the Gentiles, over the ends of the earth. We have One who claimed to be that son of David, son of Man, son of God, who claimed to found that kingdom which the gates of hell shall not overcome. And today, two thousand years later, we still see that Church/Kingdom, governing over a billion souls, including all nations and tongues! And this has occurred with an uninterrupted series of 264 successors of that Peter, placed by Jesus to be the rock with the power to bind and unbind, to forgive and to teach.

Perhaps Pharaohs or kings or Caesars or caliphs hoped that they would found an eternal kingdom, but none of them exist today.

Some False Messiahs

It is interesting to compare Jesus Christ with false messiahs in Jewish history to see who better fulfilled the prophecies. We know from the Acts of the Apostles that there were some who claimed to be the messiah before Jesus. The great rabbi Gamaliel mentions them in his well-known discourse (Acts 5:35–39):

> Men of Israel, take care what you do with these men. For before these days Theudas arose, claiming to be somebody, and a number of men, about four hundred, joined him; but he was slain and all who followed him were dispersed and came to nothing. After him Judas the Galilean arose in the days of the census and drew away some of the people after him; he also perished, and all who followed him were scattered. So in the present case I tell you, keep away from these men and let them alone; for if this plan or this undertaking is of men, it will fail; but if it is of God, you will not be able to overthrow them. You might even be found opposing God!

The two most well-known examples of false messiahs after Jesus are Shimon Ben-Kosiba (known as Bar Kochba—"the Son of the Star") and Sabbetai Zevi (1626–1676).

Shimon Ben-Kosiba was the military head of an uprising against Roman rule in 132 AD (under the Emperor Hadrian), which ended in utter defeat and the slaughter of half a million Jews. He was the epitome of a temporal messiah, whose claim to fame rested on his military exploits. This was what most of the Jewish people seemed to expect in the Messiah, but it does not match any of the features drawn by the prophets.

Sabbetai Zevi was a Jew from Turkey who fostered the belief that he was the Messiah, and he soon had very many followers. He imbibed kabbalistic or esoteric Jewish thought, and manifested a pronounced manic-depressive personality disorder, in which bouts of depression were followed by periods of messianic exultation.[18] The Ottoman authorities were concerned about the messianic fervor, and offered the would-be Messiah the choice of conversion to Islam or death. To the amazement of his followers, this false messiah actually converted to Islam, accepting the honorary title of "Keeper of the Palace Gates" and a sizeable pension. However, many of his supporters were not deterred either by his apostasy or his subsequent death, and sects of his followers continued up until the twentieth century.

The Jewish Understanding of the Messiah: Maimonides

How does the most authoritative Jewish tradition interpret the character of the Messianic kingdom? It is difficult to answer because there are many interpretations of the Messianic prophecies by the great rabbis. Moses Maimonides, who was most highly respected not only by the subsequent Jewish tradition but also by St. Thomas Aquinas, summarized Jewish belief in the Messianic kingdom as follows:

> King Messiah will arise in the future and will restore the kingship of David to its ancient condition, to its rule as it was at first. And he will rebuild the Temple and gather the exiled of Israel. And in his days all the laws will return as they were in the past. And they will offer up sacrifices, and will observe the Sabbatical years and the jubilee years with regard to all the commandments stated in the Torah. And he who does not believe in him, or he who does not await his coming, denies not only the prophets, but also the Torah and Moses our Master. . . .
>
> And think not that the Messiah must perform signs and portents and bring about new things in the world, or that he will resuscitate the dead, or the like. Not so. . . .
>
> And if there should arise from the House of David a king who studies the Torah and occupies himself with the commandments as his father David had, according to the written and the oral Torah; and if he forces all Israel to follow the Torah and observe its rules; and if he fights the wars of the Lord—then he must be presumed to be the Messiah. And if he succeeds in his acts, and rebuilds the Temple in its place, and gathers the exiled of Israel—then he certainly is the Messiah. And he will repair the whole world to serve the Lord together, as it is written: "For then will I turn to the peoples a pure language that they may all call upon the name of the Lord to serve Him with one consent" (Zeph 3:9).

---

[18] See Gershom Scholem, *Major Trends in Jewish Mysticism* (New York: Schocken Books, 1961), 290: "What is known of his character . . . hardly lacks a single trait of manic-depressive psychosis as described in the standard handbooks of psychiatry."

It should not come to one's mind that in the days of the Messiah anything in the customary order of the world will be annulled, or that there will be something new in the order of Creation. For the world will continue in its path. And that which Isaiah said, "The wolf shall dwell with the lamb, and the leopard shall lie down with the kid" (Is 11:6), is but an allegory and a riddle. . . . And likewise, all the similar things said about the Messiah are but allegories. And in the days of the Messiah it will become known to everybody what thing the allegory signified and to what thing it alluded.

. . . And there are those among the sages who say that prior to the coming of the Messiah will come Elijah. But all these things and their likes, no man can know how they will be until they will be. For they are indistinct in the writings of the prophets. Neither do the sages have a tradition about these things. It is, rather, a matter of interpretation of the Biblical verses. Therefore there is a disagreement among them regarding these matters. . . .

The sages and the prophets yearned for the days of the Messiah not in order that they should rule over the whole world, and not in order that they should lord it over the idolaters, and not in order that the nations should elevate them, and not in order that they should eat and drink and rejoice; but in order that they should devote themselves to the Torah and its wisdom, and that there be nobody to oppress them and to negate, so that they should merit life in the World to Come.[19]

Let us summarize the main points. Maimonides distinguishes the Messianic age from the world to come and the Resurrection of the dead. He was right in saying that the Messianic age will not involve changes in the laws of nature, as will happen in the world to come. The Messianic age precedes the Resurrection and the world to come, and does not yet involve "new heavens and a new earth" (2 Pt 3:13).

Second, he says that the Messianic age involves a restoration of the Kingdom of David as it was formerly. Here, however, Maimonides' interpretation falls short. The Messianic Kingdom continues the line of David, but on a higher level than that of David: it is a spiritual society, not a temporal kingdom. However, Maimonides rightly said that one should not desire the Messianic age for its temporal advantages.

Third, he states that the Messianic age will not involve a fundamental change in the Law of God and the offering of sacrifice. Here too Maimonides' vision falls short of the truth. It is true that Jesus said that He did not "come to abolish the Law and the prophets, but to

---

[19] Maimonides, *Yad haHazaqa*, Shoftim, Hilkhot M'lakhim 11–12, quoted in Raphael Patai, *The Messiah Texts*, 323–26.

fulfill them" (Mt 5:17). The gift of the Holy Spirit through the sacraments makes possible a holy fulfillment of the moral law given in the Law of Moses. The offering of sacrifice continues, but the mode of offering has changed for the better! The ceremonial aspect of the Law of Moses, with its sacrifices, is fulfilled in a far higher way in the sacrifice of the Church—the Eucharist—which is the sacrifice of the Messiah Himself, by whose bruises we are healed.

Fourth, Maimonides held that the Messiah would rebuild the Temple and gather the exiles of Israel into one kingdom. Christians also hold this, but give it a spiritual interpretation. Jesus said that the true Temple of the Lord was His Body, which would be destroyed in His Passion, but rebuilt in His Resurrection. It is now made present in the entire world through the Eucharist. We are joined to the temple of His Mystical Body by being incorporated into Him through the sacrament of Baptism. Thus in this sense the Messiah is continually building the true Temple of the Lord all over the world, as new members are incorporated and as they allow themselves to be sanctified through the sacraments and correspondence to grace.

The exiles who are incorporated into this Body include both Jews and Gentiles. It is interesting to recall that the ten lost tribes of Israel were assimilated into the Gentiles after their deportation to Assyria. Thus some of the Gentiles who entered the Church would have descended from the lost tribes of Israel, fulfilling the prophecies of their return.[20]

Finally, Maimonides rightly pointed out that the Messianic prophecies contain allegories that are difficult to interpret, and which can only rightly be interpreted after the advent of the Messiah. This caution was extremely wise.

Objection: The Messiah Has Not Brought Universal Peace

Jews rightly question how Christ can be the true Messiah if the nations have not beaten "their swords into plowshares, and their spears into pruning hooks." Wars continue and have grown worse than ever, marking the twentieth century as the most brutal of all.

This crucial question requires a nuanced response. On the one hand, the fullness of peace to be brought by the Messiah can only be perfectly fulfilled in the Church Triumphant in heaven in the world to come, in which all the enemies of the Kingdom of God will be eliminated.

---

[20] See Hos 1:10: "Yet the number of the people of Israel shall be like the sand of the sea, which can be neither measured nor numbered; and in the place where it was said to them, 'You are not my people,' it shall be said to them, 'Sons of the living God.'"

Here in the Church Militant on earth, the law of God teaches us to overcome the root of discord, which lies in human vice and injustice. Furthermore, this law is not simply engraved on tablets of stone, but etched on the human heart through sanctifying grace and the gifts of the Holy Spirit, as prophesied by Jeremiah and Ezekiel. This comes to us through the seven sacraments of the New Law of Christ.

However, the sacraments do not function in a mechanical way, disregarding human freedom. They require our good dispositions and our cooperation. The sacraments, the Gospel, and the teaching authority of the Church make possible the attainment of sanctity for all who sincerely seek it. However, grace may be resisted by the hardness of the human heart. Thus in the bosom of the Church countless scandals occur. The Church Militant will always be in conflict with "the world," both outside of her and within the lives of her members and in so-called Christian societies.

The Church is truly holy, as we profess in the Creed, and she is the recipient of the peace of the Lord which passes all understanding. Yet the sanctity of the Church does not exclude the presence of sin and sinners in her midst. For members of the Church do not always live in accord with the sanctity of Christ and the grace of the Holy Spirit by which the Church is animated. In the Church, there are *living members*, who are in a state of sanctifying grace, and *dead members*, who are in a state of mortal sin, despite their baptism and their outward profession of the Catholic faith. The sanctity of the Church and the beatitude of the peacemakers are manifested only by the living members, and especially by those who not only live in a state of grace, but who excel in holiness. Such holy members have never been lacking in the history of the Church, as can be seen in the beatification and canonization of the saints.

On the Importance of the Prophecies

The messianic prophecies form a great motive of credibility through their multiplicity and diversity. Pascal stresses their cumulative value:

> If a single man had written a book foretelling the time and manner of Jesus' coming and Jesus had come in conformity with these prophecies, this would carry infinite weight. But there is much more here. There is a succession of men over a period of four thousand years, coming consistently and invariably one after the other, to foretell the same coming; there is an entire people proclaiming it, existing for four thousand years to testify in a body to the certainty they feel about it, from which they cannot be

deflected by whatever threats and persecutions they may suffer. This is of a quite different order of importance.[21]

Not only do the messianic prophecies stem from a succession of many different prophets, they also speak of disparate and seemingly irreconcilable aspects of the Messiah and His mission, who, for example, is to suffer and be slain and yet rule forever over an eternal kingdom that will include all nations. The fact that such apparently contrasting prophecies come together perfectly in Jesus Christ, gives to the prophecies a supernatural weight.[22] As Pascal observes, "It takes boldness to foretell the same thing in so many ways."[23]

Furthermore, the prophecies concerning the formation of the Church are fulfilled in a reality that is before our eyes today. No one can say that the realization of these prophecies perhaps did not really occur, as perhaps one could in the case of prophecies that were fulfilled long ago but whose evidence no longer remains, as in the division of the vestments of Christ (Ps 22:18). Here we ourselves are witnesses of their realization. For this reason, the formation, miraculous expansion, and continuity of the Catholic Church in history is a great sign of its being truly founded by the Messiah, and thus by God.[24]

Perhaps this is the most impressive aspect of the prophecies. Who could have imagined, in the centuries before Christ, that the pagan nations would come to believe in one God, the God of Israel, and become incorporated into one *spiritual kingdom*—the new Israel—and share the faith of Israel in the Jewish Messiah? Who could imagine that this spiritual kingdom, to be augmented continually by the incorporation of the Gentiles, would last until the end of time, and be universal in scope? This is a prophecy of enormous magnitude.

---

[21] Pascal, *Pensées*, section 1, series 24, n. 332, trans. A. J. Krailsheimer (New York: Penguin Classics, 1966), 129.

[22] See Charles Journet, "The Mysterious Destinies of Israel," in *The Bridge: A Yearbook of Judaeo-Christian Studies*, ed. John Oesterreicher, 2:51: "Saying that the contents of the prophecies surpassed the prophets' knowledge of them is the same as saying that the realization of the prophecies was itself a revelation, indeed the greatest of all. Jesus alone could explain the past and give Israel's history its full significance; He alone could put at one what had seemed disparate. He did so when he brought together in his own person the scattered traits of the promised Messiah, and when he announced that the messianic kingdom of glory and power and majesty would begin as a kingdom crucified."

[23] Pascal, *Pensées*, section 1, series 24, n. 336, p. 130.

[24] See the First Vatican Council, Dogmatic Constitution *Dei Filius*, ch. 3, no. 12: "The Church herself by reason of her astonishing propagation, her outstanding holiness and her inexhaustible fertility in every kind of goodness, by her Catholic unity and her unconquerable stability, is a kind of great and perpetual motive of credibility and an incontrovertible evidence of her own divine mission."

CHAPTER 5

Biblical Typology: The Old Testament Prefigures the New

In this and the following two chapters we shall look at how certain events of the Old Testament prefigure the principal events of the New. This is called Biblical "typology," in that Old Testament events are "types" or figures of truths taught in the New Testament. These Old Testament events have a meaning that goes beyond the purely historical level: they are a kind of "prophecy" of future salvific events concerning the Messiah and the founding of the Church. Or to put it another way, they are a kind of divine foreshadowing of future events.

Normal history books do not contain foreshadowing of distant future events after the time of the historian. The Bible can do this because its primary author is God, who sees all of history, past and future, in His eternal present.

Inspiration of the Bible

Before looking at how the Old Testament prefigures the New, it may be useful to briefly explain the teaching of the Church concerning the divine authorship of the Bible, which is a dogma of faith. We find it expressed most recently in the Second Vatican Council's Dogmatic Constitution on Divine Revelation, *Dei Verbum* 11:

> Those divinely revealed realities which are contained and presented in Sacred Scripture have been committed to writing under the inspiration of the Holy Spirit. For holy mother Church, relying on the belief of the Apostles (see Jn 20:31; 2 Tim 3:16; 2 Pt 1:19–20, 3:15–16), holds that the books of both the Old and New Testaments in their entirety, with all their parts, are sacred and canonical because written under the inspiration of the Holy Spirit, they have God as their author and have been handed on as such to the Church herself. In composing the sacred books, God chose men and while employed by Him they made use of their powers and abilities, so that with Him acting in them and through them, they, as true authors, consigned to writing everything and only those things which He wanted.

The Catholic faith teaches that God is the primary and principal author of the Bible, and therefore the Bible is rightly said to be the *Word of God* in an exclusive sense. It is God's Word because God inspired its composition in such a way that the human author wrote *exactly what God wished him and inspired him to write, and only that and nothing more.*

Biblical inspiration is not to be confused with artistic inspiration. Despite the beauty and "inspiration" of a Beethoven symphony, we have no assurance that God directly approved of and personally inspired every note. However, in Sacred Scripture, because God has directly inspired the sacred writers, the entire work is to be attributed directly to God as its principal author.

The Catholic faith firmly believes and professes that "inspiration," in the strict theological sense, is not present in the Koran or any book other than those contained in the Old and New Testaments. Indeed, we believe that no other book, until the end of the world, will ever again be inspired in this strict sense. It is the *exclusive property of the Bible.*

Another and more perfect way of describing the mystery of Biblical inspiration is to see the human writers of the various books of the Bible as living and thinking *instruments* in the hands of God.[1] Philosophers speak of instrumental causality when an agent produces an effect by means of an instrument. In fact, almost all human production makes use of instruments. The instrumental cause acts as a kind of *servant* of the agent or principal cause, and the effect is produced through the cooperation of the instrumental cause under the direction of the principal cause. A paintbrush in the hands of a painter, a chisel in the hands of a sculptor, a pen in the hands of a writer, a violin in the hands of a violinist, an orchestra under the direction of a conductor or composer, are examples of instrumental causes. The canvas is painted by the paintbrush under the direction of the hand, eye, mind, and will of the artist. In this way the paintbrush produces an effect that it could never have achieved without this superior direction and impulse stemming from the artist's mind. The effect transcends the power of the instrumental cause taken alone, and manifests the power of the principal cause that moves and directs the instrumental cause. Therefore, the effect is most properly attributed to the principal cause which is the artist, and only secondarily to the paintbrush, chisel, pen, violin, or orchestra.

---

[1] See Benedict XV, encyclical *Spiritus Paraclitus* 8 (1920): "This partnership of God and man in the production of a work in common Jerome illustrates by the case of a workman who uses instruments for the production of his work; for he says that whatsoever the sacred authors say 'is the word of God, and not their own; and what the Lord says by their mouths He says, as it were, by means of an instrument' (*Tract. de Ps.*, 88)."

Applying this analogy to the case of the inspiration of Sacred Scripture, the human authors of the books of the Bible served as *living and free instruments* for the composition of the sacred books under the mysterious direction of God, as if they were intelligent paintbrushes or chisels moved by the hands of the Supreme Artist. In this way they were enabled to produce an effect which infinitely transcends the capacity of any human author acting by his own powers alone. Thus the effect is properly attributed to God, the principal author, just as a painting by Raphael is attributed more properly to Raphael than to his paintbrush!

The difference between these two cases, however, is that paintbrushes are not intelligent or free, and the human authors of Scripture were certainly intelligent and free in the use of all their capacities, like any other author. However, like the paintbrush or pen, the human authors wrote only what the divine Author directed them to, as He inspired their minds and wills. If this were not the case, then we could not call the Scriptures the Word of God. The divine authorship of Scripture is thus made possible because the instrumental causes—the sacred writers—were acting under the direct impulse and direction of God, through the effect of His efficacious grace acting on their rational powers. It is in virtue of the divine impulse which moved the sacred writer like a living and rational paintbrush or chisel, that Sacred Scripture is truly the Word of God.

It should be observed that when an artist or craftsman makes a work, the choice of tools or instruments is not arbitrary. Even though the principal cause is the artist, nevertheless the instruments are chosen for their aptness to the task at hand, and their particular contribution can generally be seen in the effect that is produced. The sculptor uses different types of chisels for different purposes, and the composer uses different instruments in making a symphony to produce different types of effects.

In a similar way, God has chosen various sacred authors, with differing experience, knowledge, temperament, and literary ability, to be his instruments in the composition of Holy Scripture. The different instruments have been chosen for their ability to be moved by God to achieve the particular effect that He has planned from all eternity for that particular part of Scripture.

This explains why the different books of Scripture show different literary styles and levels of culture.[2] It is true that the principal Author is

---

[2] See Pius XII, encyclical *Divino afflante Spiritu* 35 (1943): "The inspired writer, in composing the sacred book, is the living and reasonable instrument of the Holy Spirit. . . . Impelled by the divine motion, he so uses his faculties and powers, that from the book composed by him all may easily infer 'the special character of each one and, as it were, his personal traits.'"

one and the same, but the instruments are distinct, although each one is surely appropriate for the effect that God intended.

Since God is the primary Author of Scripture, it follows that Scripture, correctly interpreted, must be held to be without error, for such error would have to be imputed to God Himself. This universal belief of the Church, referred to as the inerrancy of the Bible, is restated in Vatican II, *Dei Verbum* 11:

> Therefore, since everything asserted by the inspired authors or sacred writers must be held to be asserted by the Holy Spirit, it follows that the books of Scripture must be acknowledged as teaching solidly, faithfully and without error that truth which God wanted put into sacred writings for the sake of salvation. Therefore "all Scripture is divinely inspired and has its use for teaching the truth and refuting error, for reformation of manners and discipline in right living, so that the man who belongs to God may be efficient and equipped for good work of every kind" (2 Tim 3:16–17).[3]

Biblical Typology: The "Spiritual Sense" of the Old Testament

The fact that God is the principal author of the Bible gives the Bible unique properties. One of these properties is its prophetic aspect, and another very important property is what is known as *Biblical typology*. As mentioned above, the Bible not only contains prophetic texts, but at times even the *events themselves are prophetic*, in that they were ordained by God as *symbols of future salvific events*. The key principle used in the interpretation of the Old Testament by the Church's liturgy and Tradition is the idea that the *Old Testament symbolically represents in a sensible way spiritual realities which are fully revealed in the New Testament*. This symbolic sense, however, in no way detracts from the historical sense or truth, but rather presupposes it and adds a deeper and hidden meaning to it.

Usually the things that we write have just one meaning, which is what we wish to signify by our words. In theology, this is called the literal sense of Scripture: the meaning that the author intended to signify directly by the words, intelligently interpreted.

Literary works, however, also make frequent use of the techniques of foreshadowing and symbolism. Thus a given text will often have more than one level of meaning, by operating on both the literal and symbolic level. The writer can arrange the events of his narrative to

---

[3] See also *Dei Verbum* 19, which affirms the historicity of the Gospels.

foreshadow future events or to symbolize other things and truths. However, this never occurs in works of history, for the historian is not the author of the events and thus he cannot manipulate them to symbolize future events.

Historical narratives in the Bible, however, are a special case, for the primary Author of these narratives is God, who is also the Lord and Author of history, who governs it in such a way that certain key events of sacred history prophetically represent future events in God's work of salvation. Now since God, the infinite wisdom, is the primary Author of Scripture, it should not surprise us that Scripture can have more than one meaning in any given text, even in the historical parts of the Bible. Thus there are two major senses in which Scripture can be understood: the literal sense, and the *typological* sense, which is also called the *figurative* or *spiritual sense*.[4]

The Literal and Spiritual Senses of Scripture

The *Catechism of the Catholic Church* 115 summarizes the traditional teaching of the Church on the literal and spiritual senses of Scripture:

> According to an ancient tradition, one can distinguish between two *senses* of Scripture: the literal and the spiritual, the latter being subdivided into the allegorical, moral, and anagogical senses. The profound concordance of the four senses guarantees all its richness to the living reading of Scripture in the Church.

The literal sense is defined by the *CCC* 116 as "the meaning conveyed by the words of Scripture and discovered by exegesis, following the rules of sound interpretation: 'All other senses of Sacred Scripture are based on the literal.'"

The spiritual sense or typological sense is what is signified by the events or realities that are narrated in the literal sense of Scripture. As the *CCC* 117 says: "Thanks to the unity of God's plan, not only the text of Scripture but also the realities and events about which it speaks can be signs." The spiritual or typological sense is divided into three categories: allegorical, moral, and eschatological.

1. The *allegorical* sense is said to be present when a narrative in the Old Testament or an aspect of the Law of Moses represents a reality in the New Testament, such as Christ, the Church, or the sacraments. The *CCC* 117 states: "We can acquire a more profound understanding of

---

[4] The fact that it is sometimes called the *spiritual* sense should not lead us to think that the literal sense is not also "spiritual," in the ordinary sense of the word, especially when it teaches us directly about God, about spiritual realities, and our moral obligations.

example events by recognizing their significance in Christ; thus the crossing of the Red Sea is a sign or type of Christ's victory and also of Christian Baptism."

The *moral* sense is present when a historical event in Scripture symbolizes a truth of the moral or spiritual life. The *CCC* 117 states: "The events reported in Scripture ought to lead us to act justly. As St. Paul says, they were written 'for our instruction.'"

The spiritual sense is said to be *anagogical* or *eschatological* when a reality of the Old Testament represents heaven (the Church *example* Triumphant) or the Last Judgment. The crossing of the Red Sea and the entering into the Promised Land represents not only the entrance into the Church through Baptism, but also the entrance into the kingdom of heaven. The *CCC* 117 states: "We can view realities and events in terms of their eternal significance, leading us toward our true homeland: thus the Church on earth is a sign of the heavenly Jerusalem."

Thus the Fathers and Doctors of the Church arrived at the common doctrine that recognizes four Biblical senses: literal, allegorical, moral, and anagogical.[5] Of these three senses, the allegorical sense is the most important, and we shall be principally concerned with it here.

The four senses of Scripture can be illustrated by the Exodus of Israel from Egypt. The literal sense is simply the historical narration of the event as we find it in the book of Exodus. This sense is the basis of any further spiritual significance.

The literal or historical sense, according to this terminology, is what the author intended to convey by his words. If the words are metaphorical or symbolic, then the literal sense means precisely what the words were intended to convey through the metaphor or symbol, intelligently understood. For example, when Scripture speaks about the "outstretched arm of God" by which He brought the Chosen People out of the house of bondage, we are not to understand the literal sense of these texts as implying that God—in the divine nature—has arms or hands. The literal sense is what the figure intends to represent: the power of God to accomplish His will. Similarly, Christ is said to be

---

[5] This doctrine is taught by St. Thomas Aquinas in *ST* I, q. 1, a. 10: "Therefore that first signification whereby words signify things belongs to the first sense, the historical or literal. That signification whereby things signified by words have themselves also a signification is called the spiritual sense, which is based on the literal, and presupposes it. Now this spiritual sense has a threefold division. Therefore, so far as the things of the Old Law signify the things of the New Law, there is the allegorical sense; so far as the things done in Christ, or so far as the things which signify Christ, are types of what we ought to do, there is the moral sense. But so far as they signify what relates to eternal glory, there is the anagogical sense."

seated at the right hand of God in the sense that His sacred humanity in heaven is associated with all the power of God, so that He is King of heaven and earth.

The Exodus also has an allegorical sense in that the entire event symbolizes the Redemption from sin worked by Christ in His Passion and communicated to us through the sacraments, especially Baptism. For example, on the night before they left Egypt, the Israelites were commanded to sacrifice a spotless lamb and paint the blood on the doorposts of their houses so that the angel of death would pass over them and not kill their firstborn, as he did those of Egypt. This mysterious detail of the painting of blood on the doorposts clearly prefigured the salvation of all mankind through the Blood of Christ, the spotless Lamb of God, spilled out for us on Calvary, and applied to us through the sacrament of Baptism.

Likewise, the passage to freedom from Pharaoh through the waters of the Red Sea also represents the sacrament of Baptism, which washes us from the dominion of Satan incurred through sin. Just as the charioteers of Pharaoh were washed away in the waters after the people had crossed, so the sins of those to be baptized are washed away and obliterated.

The same episode also has a moral sense. The people of Israel murmured as they wandered in the desert because of their attachment to the fleshpots of Egypt, and thus were severely punished by God. This signifies that after conversion, we are not to look back with longing on our worldly way of life, in which we give more importance to the things of this world than to the things of Heaven, but rather we should detach ourselves from those fleshpots and set our minds on heavenly things, represented by the manna. The same truth is taught by the episode from Genesis about the wife of Lot who looked back and was turned into a pillar of salt.

Finally, the Exodus has an eschatological or anagogical sense. After wandering in the desert for forty years and being fed by manna from heaven, the Chosen People finally entered into the Promised Land. Now the Promised Land symbolizes the Church Militant, on the one hand, but also symbolizes heaven, our promised homeland after our march in exile in the desert of this life, during which we are fed by the Bread of heaven. We will return to examine these points in greater detail in the following chapters.

The Existence of the Spiritual or Typological Sense

The existence of the typological or spiritual sense is known to us through the New Testament, the writings of the Fathers, and the Church's liturgy. It is reasonable to think that our Lord revealed the principal examples of the typological or allegorical sense of the Old Testament to the disciples on Easter Sunday, to the two disciples on the way to Emmaus, and to the Apostles in the cenacle, when He "opened up the Scriptures for them," causing their hearts to burn within them.

Let us look at the episode of the journey to Emmaus. The two disciples were walking sadly on Easter Sunday from Jerusalem to the village of Emmaus and discussing the events of the Passion, when they were approached by Jesus Himself, who kept Himself from being recognized by them, appearing as a stranger:

> And he said to them, "What is this conversation which you are holding with each other as you walk?" And they stood still, looking sad. Then one of them, named Cleopas, answered him, "Are you the only visitor to Jerusalem who does not know the things that have happened there in these days?" And he said to them, "What things?" And they said to him, "Concerning Jesus of Nazareth, who was a prophet mighty in deed and word before God and all the people, and how our chief priests and rulers delivered him up to be condemned to death, and crucified him. But we had hoped that he was the one to redeem Israel. . . . And he said to them, "O foolish men, and slow of heart to believe all that the prophets have spoken! Was it not necessary that the Christ should suffer these things and enter into his glory?" And *beginning with Moses and all the prophets, he interpreted to them in all the scriptures the things concerning himself.*[6]

These two disciples had lost their faith in Jesus as the Messiah because He had died a miserable death on the Cross and thus failed to "redeem Israel" in the earthly sense in which they were expecting it. Jesus explains to them that Scripture foretells that the Messiah had to "suffer these things" and die to redeem mankind, and so enter into His glory. The importance of the revelation of the typological meaning of the Scriptures is brought out by the comment of the disciples on their return to Jerusalem: "Did not our hearts burn within us while he talked to us on the road, while he *opened to us the scriptures?*" (Lk 24:32).

The same lesson on the inner hidden meaning of the Old Testament was given some hours later when the disciples had returned from Emmaus to Jerusalem and gathered with the eleven Apostles in the upper room. At that moment Jesus walked through the locked doors and said: "*Shalom aleichem.*" After showing them the wounds in His hands and feet, and eating in front of them, He said to them:

---

[6] Lk 24:17–27.

"These are my words which I spoke to you, while I was still with you, that *everything written about me in the law of Moses* and the prophets and the psalms *must be fulfilled.*" Then he opened their minds to understand the scriptures, and said to them, "Thus it is written, that the Christ should suffer and on the third day rise from the dead, and that repentance and forgiveness of sins should be preached in his name to all nations, beginning from Jerusalem. You are witnesses of these things."[7]

Part of this explanation must have concerned the Messianic prophecies. However, the text tells us that Jesus spoke not only of how the prophets spoke of His Passion, but that He began with the books of Moses, showing how they also spoke of His sufferings, death, and glory. The books of Moses contain very little direct prophecy about Christ's Passion, but they contain a great deal of symbolic prefiguring of it—in the sacrifice of Isaac, in the story of Joseph and his brothers, in the Exodus, and in various events during the wandering in the desert. Jesus must have explained not only the Messianic prophecies, but also the spiritual sense of the Old Testament in general, in all that concerned His Passion, death, and Resurrection.

How we wish we had been there with the disciples on the way to Emmaus or in the upper room to hear Jesus open the Scriptures and show how it all spoke of Him! However, even though these particular discourses have not been recorded, they have certainly passed into the Tradition of the Church, molding the way that the Apostles and their successors—the early Fathers of the Church—read the Old Testament. *The Christian interpretation of the Old Testament has its origin in this teaching of the Risen Christ to His disciples and Apostles.*

Identifying the typological or spiritual sense of a particular text is not a matter of imagination or fantasy. It can be shown to be divinely intended, with reasonable certainty, through its presence in the Tradition of the Church, in the liturgy, and in the New Testament itself.

The Sign of Jonah

Let us look at some more examples of this type of interpretation from the mouth of Jesus. He interpreted the book of Jonah as a type or figure of His death, Resurrection, and the conversion of the Gentiles in His name. Some of the Pharisees were saying that He was casting out demons in the name of Beelzebul and they asked for a sign from Him to prove His divine origin. Of course, He had given very many signs already, as recorded in the Gospel. Thus He reproved them for asking for some sign above what had already been given, but promised that

---

[7] Lk 24:44–48.

they would indeed be given the "sign of Jonah" (Mt 12:40–42), consisting in His death, resurrection, and the conversion of the Gentiles:

> For as Jonah was three days and three nights in the belly of the whale, so shall the Son of man be three days and three nights in the heart of the earth. The men of Nineveh will arise at the judgment with this generation and condemn it; because they repented at the preaching of Jonah, and behold, something greater than Jonah is here. The queen of the South will arise at the judgment with this generation and condemn it; for she came from the ends of the earth to hear the wisdom of Solomon, and behold, something greater than Solomon is here.[8]

The story of Jonah is indeed very rich in the spiritual or typological sense. The prophet Jonah represents both Jesus and Israel as a whole with regard to their role in the salvation of the Gentiles. The prophet is told by God to go to preach repentance to Nineveh (the historic persecutors of the Jews). However, he flees from God, taking a boat to Tarshish, in the extreme opposite direction from Nineveh. A great storm arises and he confesses his guilt and at his request is thrown overboard. He is swallowed by a whale, from the belly of which he prays to the Lord, who hears him and allows him to be spit up on the shore.

The fact that the prophet is three days in the belly of the whale represents the three days the Body of Christ spent in the tomb before rising in glory. Jonah's being spit out of the mouth of the whale on the third day represents the Resurrection of Christ. However, the parallel does not end there. For Jonah goes on to preach repentance to the people of Nineveh, and surprisingly they convert and repent, and the city is not destroyed. This also is part of the figure. After His Resurrection, the Apostles preach Christ to the Gentiles, represented by the people of Nineveh, and, very surprisingly, they are converted to the God of Abraham, Isaac, and Jacob, and to the Jewish Messiah, and do penance. This process continues through two millennia, until our time.

However, there is one final aspect to the figure. Jonah is distressed by the conversion of the Ninevites, who were the enemies of the Jewish people, and who in fact took the ten northern tribes into a captivity from which they never returned. It is not unreasonable to see this negative attitude of Jonah as also a figure of the attitude of a large part of Israel to the work of the Apostles in the conversion of the Gentiles to Christianity.

---

[8] See also the parallel passage in Lk 11:30, in which the aspect of the conversion of the Gentiles is especially emphasized: "For as Jonah became a sign to the men of Nineveh, so will the Son of man be to this generation."

The fact is that Israel has played a great part in the conversion of the Gentiles to Christianity, like Jonah with regard to the Ninevites. Indeed, Christ tells us that "salvation is from the Jews" (Jn 4:22). The Messiah was from the seed of Abraham, Isaac, Jacob, and David, and "born under the Law" (Gal 4:4). The Scriptures of the Old Testament were given to the Jewish people and preserved, passed on, and revered by them. The Apostles, finally, were all faithful Jews commissioned to preach the Jewish Messiah to the ends of the earth. Nevertheless, the majority of Israel as represented by rabbinical Judaism, like Jonah, has not rejoiced over this long process of conversion of the Gentiles to faith in the God of Abraham.

In short, Christ used the story of Jonah to make a prophecy about His own death, entombment, resurrection, and the subsequent conversion of the nations that would occur afterwards. What happened in the story of Jonah would be recapitulated in a higher way in the death and Resurrection of Christ and the formation of His Church from all peoples. The story of Jonah is fascinating even without seeing this spiritual sense, but it becomes far more marvelous when we read it in the light of Christ's explanation.

King Solomon

This same text (Mt 12:39–42) also alludes to Solomon as a figure of Christ, and the Queen of Sheba as a figure of the conversion of the Gentiles. Solomon is a figure of Christ through his wisdom, the building of the Temple, the territorial extent of his reign, which was the largest in the history of Israel, and the peace that it enjoyed. The fact that the Queen of Sheba came from "the ends of the earth" to hear the wisdom of Solomon prefigures how the Gentile nations will gradually flock to the true Temple—Christ and His Church—to hear the divine wisdom of salvation.

The Serpent of Bronze

Another example of an Old Testament narrative referred to by Jesus as a figure of Himself is Numbers 21:4–9. This text recounts an episode during the forty years of the wandering of the Chosen People in the desert in which they began to murmur against God and Moses, complaining about the lack of the fleshpots of Egypt and expressing their loathing for the manna sent them by God. As a result, God sent fiery serpents in punishment. As usual the people cried out to Moses in repentance:

> From Mount Hor they set out by the way to the Red Sea, to go around the land of Edom; and the people became impatient on the

way. And the people spoke against God and against Moses, "Why have you brought us up out of Egypt to die in the wilderness? For there is no food and no water, and we loathe this worthless food." Then the Lord sent fiery serpents among the people, and they bit the people, so that many people of Israel died. And the people came to Moses, and said, "We have sinned, for we have spoken against the Lord and against you; pray to the Lord, that he take away the serpents from us." So Moses prayed for the people. And the Lord said to Moses, "Make a fiery serpent, and set it on a pole; and every one who is bitten, when he sees it, shall live." So Moses made a bronze serpent, and set it on a pole; and if a serpent bit any man, he would look at the bronze serpent and live.

It is a mysterious text. All those guilty of this ingratitude and afflicted by serpent bites could be healed by looking at a bronze serpent set on a pole and erected as a kind of standard. What was the significance of the bronze serpent set up on a pole? Read simply in the context of the five books of Moses, the detail of the bronze serpent makes little sense.

Jesus explained this detail in his nocturnal discussion with Nicodemus, a wealthy member of the Sanhedrin, as recorded in John 3:14–15. He said: "And as Moses lifted up the serpent in the wilderness, so must the Son of man be lifted up, that whoever believes in him may have eternal life."

The bronze serpent raised up as a sign to the penitent, and capable of giving life to him, was a sublime figure of Christ who would be raised up on the Cross. Like the serpent, Christ on the Cross appears as a sign of suffering due to sin, but when seen through the eyes of faith, becomes the means of salvation. The difference is that the bronze serpent was a lifeless statue of bronze, working a physical cure in one instance and one place alone, whereas Christ on the Cross works the spiritual salvation of all men of all times and places, if we cooperate with His grace through faith, hope, and charity.

In addition, the serpent is a symbol of sin, and of the Tempter, who drew Adam and Eve to perform the first sin. Thus the serpent on a pole is also a symbol of victory over sin through Christ, who Himself bore all human sin and hung on a Cross in order to redeem men from its slavery. As St. Paul says in 2 Corinthians 5:21, God "made him to be sin who knew no sin, so that in him we might become the righteousness of God."

The Spiritual Sense of the Old Testament According to St. Paul

St. Paul refers to the spiritual sense of the Old Testament in an interesting text from 1 Corinthians 10:1–11, in which he speaks about the moral sense of the wandering of the Chosen People in the desert for forty years:

> For I would not have you ignorant, brethren, that our fathers were all under the cloud, and all passed through the sea. And all in Moses were baptized, in the cloud, and in the sea. And all ate the same spiritual food, and drank the same spiritual drink (for they drank from the spiritual rock which followed them, and the rock was Christ). Yet with most of them God was not well pleased, for "they were laid low in the desert." Now these things came to pass as examples to us, that we should not lust after evil things even as they lusted. And do not become idolaters, even as some of them were. . . . Neither let us tempt Christ, as some of them tempted, and perished by the serpents. Neither murmur, as some of them murmured, and perished at the hands of the destroyer. Now *all these things happened to them as a type, and they are written for our correction,* upon whom the final age of the world has come.[9]

St. Paul, speaking of the repeated rebellions of the Chosen People during their forty-year sojourn in the desert before entering the Promised Land, discovers a typological significance, in the category of the moral sense. As a result of their infidelity and poor disposition, God punished the Israelites by prolonging their stay in the desert for two generations, so that all but two of the original Israelites who left Egypt died in the desert without entering the Promised Land. St. Paul says this happened to them to serve as a lesson to Christians of the necessity of vigilance and of resistance to temptation. The Israelites were allowed to fall into a series of archetypical sins of rebellion in the desert, followed by exemplary punishments, to provide a graphic example of spiritual temptations. Just as the first generation of Israelites perished in the desert for lack of docility to God, so it may happen that Christians fail to reach the spiritual Promised Land through the same cause.

Typology: A Divine Bridge between the Old and New Testaments

Biblical typology provides a divine bridge between the Old and New Testaments. I say "divine" because this bridge was prepared by God Himself, guiding the events and religious ceremonies of the Old Testament so as to make them figures, signs, or symbols of the New. We may ask why God wished to make this bridge between the Testaments, creating a subtle symbolism that most readers would never

---

[9] Confraternity of Christian Doctrine translation (New York: Benziger Bros., 1958).

understand unless they were expressly taught. Why did God create these figures?

First of all, God uses a *progressive pedagogy*, preparing for what is perfect by means of imperfect representations, which, although imperfect, are nevertheless easier to understand. Secondly, it is fitting for human nature in general to have abstract spiritual realities presented with the aid of sensible and material examples, analogies, and stories. All our abstract and spiritual ideas find their beginning in sense knowledge. Thus it is out of respect for our nature that God reveals spiritual truths through sensible images and historical narratives.

In reality, our question here is deeper. Why did God wish to create two covenants and frame two divine laws, the Law of Moses and the law of the New Testament? Why did the New Testament and the New Covenant sealed with the Blood of Christ need to be preceded by an Old Testament and an Old Covenant, sealed with the blood of animals at Mt. Sinai?

As mentioned above, the covenant with Abraham, the election of the Chosen People, and the Law of Moses were all given as a *preparation* for the coming of the Messiah, who was promised as a blessing to all peoples. He would crush the head of the infernal serpent and free man from slavery to the devil and sin, offering to God the Father a satisfaction for all human transgression. The Chosen People was elected to receive the prophecies concerning the Messiah and His Church, and to prepare for His coming *also through the symbolism of their ceremonies and their history.* The Fathers of the Church, following the teaching of Jesus and of St. Paul, see the entire framework of the Old Testament—its history and ceremonial laws—as essentially a sensible figure of future spiritual realities that would be brought by Christ. The sensible figures prepared mankind to receive and understand the spiritual blessings that were represented under the sensible figures.

The Old Testament Offers Material Rewards

The fact that the Old Testament represents spiritual realities through sensible figures can be seen very clearly if we compare the rewards for fidelity and the punishments for sin in the Old and New Testaments. The Old Testament focuses on temporal rewards and punishments whereas the New Testament focuses on eternal and spiritual ones.

This can be seen most clearly in the promises that are expressly given as the reward for fidelity. In the Old Covenant, the reward is expressed in a *material* way: the Promised Land flowing with milk and honey—the land of Canaan promised to Abraham for his descendants. This reward is a sensible reality that can be understood by all.

For example, in Exodus 3:8, God promises: "I have come down to deliver them out of the hand of the Egyptians, and to bring them up out of that land to a good and broad land, a land flowing with milk and honey, to the place of the Canaanites, the Hittites, the Amorites, the Perizzites, the Hivites, and the Jebusites." This promise is repeated with great frequency in the books of Moses,[10] as in Deuteronomy 6:1–12:

> Now this is the commandment, the statutes and the ordinances which the Lord your God commanded me to teach you, that you may do them in the land to which you are going over, to possess it; that you may fear the Lord your God, you and your son and your son's son, by keeping all his statutes and his commandments, which I command you, all the days of your life; and that your days may be prolonged. Hear therefore, O Israel, and be careful to do them; that it may go well with you, and that you may multiply greatly, as the Lord, the God of your fathers, has promised you, in a land flowing with milk and honey. . . . And when the Lord your God brings you into the land which he swore to your fathers, to Abraham, to Isaac, and to Jacob, to give you, with great and goodly cities, which you did not build, and houses full of all good things, which you did not fill, and cisterns hewn out, which you did not hew, and vineyards and olive trees, which you did not plant, and when you eat and are full, then take heed lest you forget the Lord, who brought you out of the land of Egypt, out of the house of bondage.

The Promised Land flowing with milk and honey, in the literal sense, means the geographical land of Israel. However, it also has an allegorical and eschatological sense revealed by Christ in the New Testament. The Promised Land represents a spiritual kingdom in which the citizens become the children of God, and thus it represents the Church, first on earth, and then in heaven.

The New Testament Promises Heavenly Realities

Christ begins the Sermon on the Mount, which is the synthesis of the New Law, with the beatitudes (Mt 5:5–12), which promise heavenly realities as the reward for fidelity: "Blessed are the poor in spirit, for theirs is the kingdom of heaven. Blessed are the meek, for they shall possess the land." Obviously we are to understand this to refer to a spiritual rather than a temporal "land," which is a synonym for the kingdom of heaven. The third beatitude promises consolation for those

---

[10] See, for example, Lev 20:24: "You shall inherit their land, and I will give it to you to possess, a land flowing with milk and honey. I am the Lord your God, who have separated you from the peoples."

who mourn, referring to a heavenly and eternal reward. The fourth and fifth beatitudes promise the plenitude of justice and mercy that we shall obtain in the Kingdom of God. The sixth beatitude is more explicit, promising the vision of God to the pure in heart. This is the essence of our heavenly beatitude: to see God face to face. The peacemakers are promised the beatitude of being children of God. The eighth and last beatitude for those who suffer persecution for the sake of the Kingdom promises the same reward as is promised to the poor in spirit: "for theirs is the Kingdom of God."

This promise of a heavenly reward is found again in the sublime teaching of our Lord to His Apostles at the Last Supper. He solemnly tells them: "In my Father's house there are many mansions. If not, I would have told you: because I go to prepare a place for you. And if I shall go, and prepare a place for you, I will come again, and will take you to myself; that where I am, you also may be" (Jn 14:2–3).[11]

The beatific vision promised to the pure in heart by Jesus is explained also by St. Paul and St. John. In 1 Corinthians 13:9–12, St. Paul writes:

> For our knowledge is imperfect and our prophecy is imperfect; but when the perfect comes, the imperfect will pass away. . . . For now we see in a mirror dimly, but then *face to face*. Now I know in part; *then I shall understand fully*, even as I have been fully understood.

And St. John says in 1 John 3:2: "We know that when he appears we shall be like him, for we shall see him as he is."

Why did God only promise material rewards for fidelity to the Old Covenant?[12] Could not the Jews also win heaven by fidelity to their covenant? Surely they could and did, through the grace of God which was not lacking to them. Why then did God not more explicitly promise them a heavenly reward, which of course is the only one worth desiring with all our hearts? The reason is that the Promised Land flowing with milk and honey is a sensible and material *figure* of our true spiritual reward—a heavenly homeland. Just as the Jews gained or lost the Promised Land through fidelity to the covenant, so Christians—and all men—shall gain or lose heaven through fidelity or infidelity to the moral law revealed to Moses, and perfected by Christ. God wished spiritual

---

[11] Douay-Rheims version.

[12] Although the beatific vision is not directly promised in the Old Testament, many texts express the longing for the vision of God. For example, in Ps 16:15, the Psalmist says: "As for me, I shall behold thy face in righteousness; when I awake, I shall be satisfied with beholding thy form."

and supernatural realities to be represented first by sensible and material likenesses.

The Old Testament Threatens the Chosen People with Temporal Punishments

In the same way, infidelity to the Old Covenant was punished with *temporal punishments* that were *material and sensible,* involving the loss of the Promised Land. Warning of these temporal punishments is found in a terrifying passage from Deuteronomy 28:15–65:

> But if you will not obey the voice of the Lord your God or be careful to do all his commandments and his statutes which I command you this day, then all these curses shall come upon you and overtake you. Cursed shall you be in the city, and cursed shall you be in the field. . . . They shall besiege you in all your towns, until your high and fortified walls, in which you trusted, come down throughout all your land; and they shall besiege you in all your towns throughout all your land, which the Lord your God has given you. And you shall eat the offspring of your own body, the flesh of your sons and daughters, whom the Lord your God has given you, in the siege and in the distress with which your enemies shall distress you. . . . Whereas you were as the stars of heaven for multitude, you shall be left few in number; because you did not obey the voice of the Lord your God . . . and you shall be plucked off the land which you are entering to take possession of it. And *the Lord will scatter you among all peoples,* from one end of the earth to the other; and there you shall serve other gods, of wood and stone, which neither you nor your fathers have known. And among these nations you shall find no ease, and there shall be no rest for the sole of your foot; but the Lord will give you there a trembling heart, and failing eyes, and a languishing soul.

These temporal punishments were no idle threats, but history tells us that they were realized on two terrible occasions: the destruction of Jerusalem and the captivity in Babylon in 597 BC; and the second destruction of Jerusalem and the Temple in 70 AD, followed by the second Diaspora and exile from the Promised Land, lasting nearly two millennia. Josephus, in his account of the siege of Jerusalem in 70 AD, narrates the notorious action of a mother who killed her own child to eat his flesh.[13]

The New Testament, on the contrary, also threatens punishment for infidelity to the New Covenant, but one which is no longer temporal,

---

[13] Josephus, *The Wars of the Jews,* in *Josephus, Complete Works,* trans. William Whiston (Grand Rapids, MI: Kregel, 1978), 6.3.4–5, pp. 578–79.

material, and earthly, but spiritual and eternal. In fact, it is much more terrible. Our Lord speaks of the fires of hell on numerous occasions. He speaks of the unprofitable servants that are to be cast into the "outer darkness, where there shall be weeping and gnashing of teeth" (Mt 25:31).[14] In the solemn representation of the Last Judgment in Matthew 25:32–46, Jesus explains that the criterion for the Judgment is whether we have been charitable or hard-hearted to all who have needed our charity:

> And all nations shall be gathered together before him, and he shall separate them one from another, as the shepherd separates the sheep from the goats. And he shall set the sheep on his right hand, but the goats on his left. . . . Then he shall say to them also that shall be on his left hand: Depart from me, you cursed into everlasting fire which was prepared for the devil and his angels. For I was hungry, and you gave me not to eat. . . . And these shall go into everlasting punishment, but the just, into life everlasting.

Nevertheless, it would be wrong to think that the Old Testament does not teach eternal rewards and punishments for fidelity or infidelity. The everlasting punishment of hell and the beatitude of heaven are revealed in the Old Testament in Daniel 12:2–3:

> And many of those who sleep in the dust of the earth shall awake, some to everlasting life, and some to shame and everlasting contempt. And those who are wise shall shine like the brightness of the firmament; and those who turn many to righteousness, like the stars for ever and ever.

Thus the great rabbis like Maimonides taught that the Judgment, the Resurrection of the dead, and the final reward or punishment for our works occur in the world to come, after the Messianic age.

However, although the spiritual and eternal aspect of punishment and reward is present in the Old Testament (and in rabbinical Judaism), it does not generally receive the principal focus. Why is this? Why was ancient Israel given mainly the threat of a temporal punishment in this world or the incentive of temporal rewards?

The reason is to be found in God's progressive pedagogy. In the education of children, punishments and rewards must at first be sensible and not long delayed. These punishments and rewards are applied to those who cannot yet understand spiritual realities so that later—in their maturity—they will come to love virtue and fidelity for the honor and glory of God.

---

[14] See also Mt 24:51.

Likewise, the sensible rewards and punishments of the Old Testament were not an end in themselves, but were applied by God as *figures of spiritual rewards and punishments that are infinitely more important*, in that they are eternal and concern eternal blessedness in our final end, or eternal shipwreck in the permanent failure to achieve that end.

Only those who were properly disposed for understanding heavenly things were given the grace to pierce the veil. St. Thomas Aquinas and the Fathers maintain that the great Patriarchs, saints, and prophets of the Old Testament understood the spiritual realities behind the sensible figures, although most of the people perhaps did not. In the Letter to the Hebrews, chapter 11 beautifully describes the faith of the Patriarchs of the Old Testament, by which we see that they indeed had understood the figures and had placed their hope not in an earthly and temporal reward, but in a spiritual and eternal one:

> By faith Abraham obeyed when he was called to go out to a place which he was to receive as an inheritance; and he went out, not knowing where he was to go. By faith he sojourned in the land of promise, as in a foreign land, living in tents with Isaac and Jacob, heirs with him of the same promise. For he looked forward to the *city which has foundations, whose builder and maker is God.* . . . These all [the faithful descendants of Abraham] died in faith, not having received what was promised, but having seen it and greeted it from afar, and having acknowledged that they were strangers and exiles on the earth. For people who speak thus make it clear that they are seeking a homeland. . . . They desire a better country, that is, a *heavenly one.* Therefore God is not ashamed to be called their God, for he has prepared for them a city. . . . And all these, though well attested by their faith, did not receive what was promised, since God had foreseen something better for us, that apart from us they should not be made perfect.[15]

The Promised Land that God prepared for the Patriarchs and all their faithful descendants is realized in the Church in a higher way: in the Church Militant on earth in which we have the seven sacraments of grace (and God Incarnate present in the Blessed Sacrament), and above all in the Church Triumphant in heaven, in which Abraham and his faithful descendants now see God face to face.

---

[15] Heb 11:8–16, 39.

CHAPTER 6

Biblical Typology in Genesis

Typology of the Days of Creation

The book of Genesis provides a very rich supply of Biblical typology which prefigures the mystery of Christ and the Church. A marvelous example of typology can be found in the first chapters of Genesis, which, by the way, are not to be regarded simply as myth and legend, but rather as true history, although told in archaic language and style.[1]

In the beginning of Genesis, we read of the seven "days" of creation. Should this be understood in the literal or historical sense as referring to a "day" of twenty-four hours? The Church (through a document of the Pontifical Biblical Commission of 1909) tells us that this is not necessarily the case.[2] The term "day" (*yom* in Hebrew) may be taken metaphorically as meaning an undetermined period of time. Indeed, how can we speak of a 24-hour day when the sun was not created until the fourth day? The six "days" of creation thus intend to speak of six "stages" of creation, portrayed as an unfolding temporal process. This is still the *literal* or historical sense, rightly understood.

The seventh day in which God took His rest is more mysterious. It signifies that the goal of material creation was the creation of man, at which point the process reached its fulfillment. As we rest after fulfilling our projects and purposes and rejoice in contemplating them, so God is said to have "rested."[3] It also has a spiritual (eschatological) sense, interpreted by the Letter to the Hebrews 4:9–11, according to which

---

[1] See Pius XII, encyclical *Humani generis* 38–39 (1950).

[2] See the Response of the Pontifical Biblical Commission of June 30, 1909, DS 3519 (D 2128).

[3] See John Paul II, apostolic letter *Dies Domini* 11 (1998): "The divine rest of the seventh day does not allude to an inactive God, but emphasizes the fullness of what has been accomplished. It speaks, as it were, of God's lingering before the 'very good' work (Gen 1:31) which his hand has wrought, in order to cast upon it *a gaze full of joyous delight*. This is a 'contemplative' gaze which does not look to new accomplishments but enjoys the beauty of what has already been achieved. It is a gaze that God casts upon all things, but in a special way upon man, the crown of creation. It is a gaze which already discloses something of the nuptial shape of the relationship which God wants to establish with the creature made in his own image, by calling that creature to enter a pact of love."

God's rest signifies the end of creation, which is heaven, in which we shall fully enter into God's rest, rejoicing in the contemplation of all of God's works: "So then, there remains a sabbath rest for the people of God; for whoever enters God's rest also ceases from his labors as God did from his. Let us therefore strive to enter that rest."

The days of Creation also have a mystical parallel with the Passion and Resurrection of Christ. Genesis tells us that on the sixth day, God crowned His work with the creation of Adam, culminating the work of the preceding days. The seventh day was then designated as the mystical "day of rest" of the Lord.

The Fathers see in these days a mystical significance. It is surely no accident that the Passion of Our Lord occurred on a Friday, the sixth day, the day on which man had been created. In the Passion of Our Lord, man was "recreated," in that the price was paid to redeem all sin. The creation of man on the sixth day was the masterpiece of the material creation and its crowning glory. However, the re-creation of man on Good Friday, the sixth day of the week, was much more marvelous still. The creation of man cost God nothing; He had but to say the word, "Let it be." However, the re-creation of man cost God something: all the Blood of the Incarnate Word.

On the seventh day, Jesus' Body rested in the tomb and did no work, fulfilling the Sabbath precept by resting in the sleep of death after all the labors of His life, especially those of His Passion. Holy Saturday was the Sabbath of all Sabbaths. Nevertheless, His soul was not idle. Christ's human soul, separated from His body, went to the "limbo of the just" to bring full salvation to those who had long awaited it in the bosom of Abraham.[4] All the patriarchs were there, beginning with Adam, Eve, and Abel, and all the just of the Old Covenant, from Abraham, Isaac, Jacob, and David, to John the Baptist and St. Joseph. Their faith was finally rewarded on this *great Sabbath*, as they were introduced to God's rest: the vision of God. The veil covering the Holy of Holies—the face of God—was finally rent for them in virtue of Christ's Passion. The Old Covenant was thus brought to its consummation through the power of the Blood of the New.

Finally, the Resurrection of our Lord took place on Sunday, the first day of the week. The fact that the Resurrection took place on the first day of the week is fitting in that it shows us that this central event of history constitutes a *"new creation" and a new beginning*, as it were.[5] On the

---

[4] See *CCC* 632–37.

[5] See John Paul II, *Dies Domini* 1–2: "It is *Easter* which returns week by week, celebrating Christ's victory over sin and death, the fulfilment in him of the first creation and the dawn of 'the new creation' (see 2 Cor 5:17). It is the day which recalls in grateful adoration the world's first day and looks forward in active hope to

first day, God began creation with the command: "Let there be light." In the Resurrection of Christ, a spiritual light was ignited that will never be extinguished. *The light of glory entered into our world on that Sunday* of Easter. The entering of that light into the world is celebrated liturgically every year in the Easter Vigil Mass, the most solemn Mass of the year, which begins with the lighting of the Easter candle and the proclamation of the light of the Messiah: *lumen Christi.*

This is the meaning of the Christian celebration of Sunday, the first day of the week,[6] the day of the new creation. John Paul II speaks of this magnificently in his Apostolic Letter *Dies Domini* 18:

> What God accomplished in Creation and wrought for his People in the Exodus has found its fullest expression in Christ's Death and Resurrection, though its definitive fulfillment will not come until the *Parousia,* when Christ returns in glory. In him, the "spiritual" meaning of the Sabbath is fully realized, as Saint Gregory the Great declares: "For us, the true Sabbath is the person of our Redeemer, our Lord Jesus Christ." This is why the joy with which God, on humanity's first Sabbath, contemplates all that was created from nothing, is now expressed in the joy with which Christ, on Easter Sunday, appeared to his disciples, bringing the gift of peace and the gift of the Spirit (see Jn 20:19–23). It was in the Paschal Mystery that humanity, and with it the whole creation, "groaning in birth-pangs until now" (Rom 8:22), came to know its new "exodus" into the freedom of God's children who can cry out with Christ, "Abba, Father!" (Rom 8:15; Gal 4:6). In the light of this mystery, the meaning of the Old Testament precept concerning the Lord's Day is recovered, perfected and fully revealed in the glory which shines on the face of the Risen Christ.

If God had wished, He could have had Christ resurrected on the Sabbath, so that the Christian day of rest and celebration would have

---

'the last day,' when Christ will come in glory (see Acts 1:11; 1 Thes 4:13–17) and all things will be made new (see Rev 21:5). . . . Therefore, in commemorating the day of Christ's Resurrection not just once a year but every Sunday, the Church seeks to indicate to every generation the true fulcrum of history, to which the mystery of the world's origin and its final destiny leads." See also no. 24: "Christian thought spontaneously linked the Resurrection, which took place on 'the first day of the week,' with the first day of that cosmic week (see Gen 1:1–2:4), which shapes the creation story in the Book of Genesis: the day of the creation of light (see 1:3–5). This link invited an understanding of the Resurrection as the beginning of a new creation, the first fruits of which is the glorious Christ, 'the firstborn of all creation' (Col 1:15) and 'the firstborn from the dead' (Col 1:18)."

[6] See *Dies Domini* 26.

coincided with that of the Old Testament. This is what perhaps we would have expected. However, the divine wisdom did not judge this to be fitting. The fact that our Holy Day of rest falls on the day after that of the Old Law is also a figure of the fact that the Christian dispensation completes and fulfills the ceremonial or liturgical aspect of the Mosaic Covenant,[7] as the figures give way to the light of glory.

The fact that the holy day has been transferred from the seventh to the first day points to a change in Covenant, which is symbolized by a change in ceremonial or liturgical law, and a change in priesthood from that of Aaron to that of Christ, as explained in Hebrews 7–8.

The Church Is Born from the Side of Christ as the New Eve

Christ Is the New Adam

The second and third chapters of Genesis on Adam and Eve are even richer in Biblical typology. Adam and Eve themselves are figures of the Second Adam, who is Christ, and the New Eve, who is the Virgin Mary (as well as the Church). That Christ is the new Adam is explained by St. Paul in Romans 5:14–15:

> *Adam . . . was a type of the one who was to come.* But the free gift is not like the trespass. For if many died through one man's trespass, much more have the grace of God and the free gift in the grace of that one man Jesus Christ abounded for many.

As Adam was the first head of the human race and we have inherited the effects of his sin, so Christ is the new head of a redeemed human race in which the fruits of His merits are communicated to us through the Church.

---

[7] See *Dies Domini* 59–60: "Far from being abolished, the celebration of creation becomes more profound within a Christocentric perspective, being seen in the light of God's plan 'to unite all things in [Christ], things in heaven and things on earth' (Eph 1:10). The remembrance of the liberation of the Exodus also assumes its full meaning as it becomes a remembrance of the universal redemption accomplished by Christ in his Death and Resurrection. More than a 'replacement' for the Sabbath, therefore, Sunday is its fulfilment, and in a certain sense its extension and full expression in the ordered unfolding of the history of salvation, which reaches its culmination in Christ. In this perspective, the Biblical theology of the 'Sabbath' can be recovered in full, without compromising the Christian character of Sunday." See also 62: "It is the duty of Christians therefore to remember that, although the practices of the Jewish Sabbath are gone, surpassed as they are by the 'fulfilment' which Sunday brings, the underlying reasons for keeping 'the Lord's Day' holy— inscribed solemnly in the Ten Commandments—remain valid, though they need to be reinterpreted in the light of the theology and spirituality of Sunday."

Mary Is the New Eve

The early Fathers of the Church develop this parallelism also with regard to Mary, the new Eve. We see it first particularly in St. Justin, St. Irenaeus, and Tertullian, three early Fathers, as mentioned above,[8] and it then becomes a standard theme of Patristic and medieval exegesis. The Fathers see the work of our redemption in Christ as an undoing of the work of original sin. As in the original sin there was a collaboration of guilt between Eve and Adam, so likewise in our Redemption there was cooperation in merit between Christ and the Virgin Mary, especially in the Annunciation and at the foot of the Cross.

St. Justin says:

> From a Virgin the Son of God was made man, so that by the same road from which the disobedience was begun, it could have its reparation. Eve was an incorrupt virgin, who, having conceived by the word of the serpent, gave birth to disobedience and death. Mary, also a Virgin, having conceived faith in the Annunciation of the angel Gabriel . . . responded: 'Be it done unto to me according to thy Word.' From her was born the one whom the Scriptures predicted would destroy the head of the serpent.[9]

Tertullian says that the sin of the first Eve "was abolished by the faith of the second."[10] St. Irenaeus says: "As the first Eve, . . . a disobedient virgin, was the cause of the death of the whole human race, so the second Eve . . . , an obedient virgin, was the cause of salvation for the whole human race."[11]

The Church Is the New Eve

The creation of Eve from the side of the sleeping Adam to be his bride is also a mysterious figure of Christ and the Church. This is indicated in the New Testament itself, as well as in the Fathers and in the liturgy.

St. Paul speaks of this typology of Adam and Eve with regard to Christian matrimony. In Ephesians 5:22–32, he says:

> Wives, be subject to your husbands, as to the Lord. For the husband is the head of the wife as Christ is the head of the church, his body, and is himself its Savior. . . . Husbands, love your wives, as Christ loved the church and gave himself up for her, that he might sanctify her, having cleansed her by the washing of water with the word, that he might present the church to himself in

---

[8] Chapter 2, pp. 18–19.
[9] St. Justin, *Dialogue with the Jew Trypho*, ch. 100, *ANF* 1:249.
[10] Tertullian, *On the Flesh of Christ* 17, *PL* 2:782.
[11] St. Irenaeus, *Against Heresies* 3.22.4, *ANF* 1:455; see also 5.19.1, *ANF* 1:547.

splendor, without spot or wrinkle or any such thing, that she might be holy and without blemish. . . . "For this reason a man shall leave his father and mother and be joined to his wife, and the two shall become one flesh." This mystery is a profound one, and I am saying that it refers to Christ and the Church.

In other words, the union of the first husband and wife—Adam and Eve—and the institution of matrimony itself, are figures of the union between Christ and the Church. The Church is the spouse of Christ; she is the new Eve created from the pierced side of the New Adam. We read in Genesis that Eve was created from the side of Adam during his sleep. The image is very strange. Why did God choose to create Eve in this way, and to have it revealed to us in Genesis? The mysterious significance of this detail can only be grasped through the Passion of Christ.

When Christ died on the Cross, the centurion pierced His sacred side, and there flowed blood and water (see Jn 19:33–35). The Church sees in this flow of blood and water a representation of the sacraments: water signifying Baptism and blood signifying the Eucharist. The Church can in fact be said to receive its life from these two sacraments, for the members of the Church are born in the waters of Baptism and nourished on the heavenly food of the Eucharist.

Thus the Fathers commonly teach that just as Eve, the spouse of Adam, was created from his side during sleep, so the Church, the Bride of Christ, is born from the side of the New Adam, asleep in death upon the Cross, through the flow of water and blood. This mysterious spiritual meaning of the creation of Eve was veiled through all preceding centuries, and revealed only on Good Friday.

The Deluge

Another marvelous Old Testament story, very rich in typological meaning, is the great Flood, recounted in Genesis 6–9. The waters of the Deluge, which represent Baptism, separate the just from the unjust, and those who are saved through the waters are called to be the founders of a new humanity. Here again, as in all typology, physical and material elements mystically represent spiritual realities, which become intelligible to us only after their revelation through Christ.

The key element in this typology is the ark itself, which is a figure of the Catholic Church, the universal ark of salvation through her sacraments. "Catholic" means universal. Her universality is prefigured in the fact that the ark of Noah was to contain every species of animal. The animal species figuratively represent the various peoples of the earth, with their various cultures and tongues.

The fact that the Church alone is the necessary means for salvation is indicated in the fact that the ark was the only means of safety. All men outside the ark were drowned. This is expressed in a Patristic axiom: just as there was no physical salvation outside the ark, so there is no spiritual salvation outside the Church.[12] Boniface VIII, in his dogmatic bull *Unam sanctam* of 1302, on the necessity of communion with the Church for salvation, writes: "Indeed, in the time of the Deluge, *the ark of Noah prefigured the one Church*. It had one pilot and governor, Noah, and we read that outside of it was drowned all that existed on the face of the earth."[13] Just as later in Egypt, all the firstborn were exterminated except those who were protected by the blood of the paschal lamb, so here all of sinful humanity is drowned, except those protected by the wood of the one ark.

We know that it is possible to be saved without being members of the visible Church, but not without being united to the soul of the Church, which is the Holy Spirit. In other words, it is impossible to be saved without receiving sanctifying grace through the merits of Christ's death on Calvary, through at least an implicit faith in Him and in His Church, and through sincere repentance for sins. The Creed of the People of God, promulgated by Paul VI in 1968, states:

> We believe that the Church is necessary for salvation, because Christ, who is the sole mediator and way of salvation, renders Himself present for us in His body which is the Church. But the divine design of salvation embraces all men, and those who without fault on their part do not know the Gospel of Christ and His Church, but seek God sincerely, and under the influence of grace endeavor to do His will as recognized through the promptings of their conscience, they, in a number known only to God, can obtain salvation.

The waters of the Deluge themselves represent both the Last Judgment, in which the good are saved and the wicked damned, and Baptism, by which we are saved from condemnation. This figure is spoken of in the First Letter of St. Peter, 3:20–21:

> God's patience waited in the days of Noah, during the building of the ark, in which a few, that is, eight persons, were saved by water.

---

[12] See St. Cyprian, *On the Unity of the Church* 6, trans. Maurice Bévenot, in *De Lapsis and De Ecclesiae Catholicae Unitate* (Oxford: At the Clarendon Press, 1971), 67: "You cannot have God for your Father if you no longer have the Church for your mother. If there was any escape for one who was outside the ark of Noah, there will be as much for one who is found to be outside the Church."

[13] DS 870 (D 468).

Baptism, which corresponds to this,[14] now saves you, not as a removal of dirt from the body but as an appeal to God for a clear conscience, through the resurrection of Jesus Christ.

There are other typological elements as well. The dove sent out by Noah, which returns with an olive branch, represents the gifts of the Holy Spirit given to the neophytes in Baptism, bringing peace to the soul, a peace which the world cannot know or appreciate. Finally, Noah himself, who is a kind of second Adam, the father of all generations succeeding him, is a figure of Christ, the new Adam.

St. John Chrysostom summarizes as follows:

> The story of the deluge is a mystery, and its details are figures of things that were to come. The ark is the Church, Noah is Christ, the dove is the Holy Spirit, the olive branch is the divine charity. Thus as the ark in the midst of the sea protected those who found shelter inside it, so the Church saves all those who had gone astray. However, the ark only protected; the Church does more. For example, the ark received irrational animals and they remained just that, whereas the Church receives unreasonable men, and not only protects them, but transforms them.[15]

Let it be observed that this symbolic meaning in no way should be taken to deny or diminish the historical truth of the story of the Deluge. The typological or spiritual meaning builds on the literal historical meaning and presupposes it. Evidence of many kinds supports the historical reality of a spectacular devastating flood that occurred in prehistoric times.[16]

There is also a moral sense to the story of the Deluge, which is not hard to understand. Jesus refers to this in Luke 17:26–30. Just as the Flood came upon the world unawares, so the Second Coming will come upon the world when it least expects it (like our own individual particular judgment). Therefore, we must be always prepared.

The Tower of Babel

The building of the tower of Babel, which we should understand as a historical event at the beginning of human civilization, also has a clear moral and allegorical sense. It represents the attempt of man to make a name for himself on earth, to create a technological civilization that

---

[14] The Greek word used here is "antitype," which refers to the reality signified by an Old Testament figure or "type."

[15] *Homily on Lazarus* 6, *PG* 48:1037–38.

[16] See Patrick O'Connell, *Science of Today and the Problems of Genesis* (Rockford, IL: TAN Books, 1993).

rivals God, reaching up to heaven. Such a society has no use for God or heaven. St. Augustine sees it as a perfect symbol of the "earthly city": a civilization opposed to the City of God (the Kingdom of God), focused on the love of self to the point of contempt for God.[17] The City of God, on the contrary, is that civilization built on the love of God up to the point of contempt for self, building a pathway to heaven not through pride in man's works, but through the divine condescension of the Incarnation and Passion of Christ.

It is deeply fitting that the divine punishment for Babel and its cult of pride was the proliferation of tongues and the dispersal of peoples. In this sense, it is the opposite of the Church, which, beginning with Pentecost, speaks in all tongues. The task of the Church is to reunite into the Kingdom of God what man has dispersed through pride.

The Sacrifice of Isaac

A glorious figure of the Passion of Christ is Abraham's sacrifice of Isaac. Although God had promised that all nations would be blessed in his seed, Abraham's wife Sarah had given him no children, until finally in their old age, God worked a miracle in bringing forth Isaac from an aged and barren womb. This child of the miracle, Isaac, was said by God to be the child of the promise, rather than Ishmael, the firstborn of Abraham from his wife's handmaid. Thus all nations were to be blessed in the line of Isaac.

Now it is precisely Isaac, the child of the promise, whom God commands to be sacrificed on Mount Moriah, which Tradition identifies with Mount Zion in Jerusalem. God asked for the sacrifice not only of Abraham's only son from his legitimate wife, but much more!

Obviously there is a great mystery here. Why did God command Abraham to sacrifice the son of the promise? The principal reason, according to the Bible, was to test Abraham's faith, and give him to us as a paradigm of faith, the father of the faithful.

However, there is more to the story than this. Isaac is clearly a figure of Christ, the beloved Only-begotten Son of God the Father, in whom all the promises to the human race are contained. The promises were contained in Isaac as forefather of the Messiah. As Abraham was ordered to sacrifice Isaac, so God the Father, in His eternal Providence, had determined the sacrifice of His Only-begotten Son for the redemption of the human race. As Isaac is a figure of Christ, the sacrificed Son, so Abraham, in this episode, corresponds to God the Father, a Father who sacrifices the object of His greatest love. And as Abraham's readiness to perform the sacrifice showed his faith in the

---

[17] St. Augustine, *City of God* 14.28.

future resurrection of his son, that the promises might be fulfilled,[18] so God the Father had His Son sacrificed in virtue of the divine decree for the Resurrection of Christ that would fulfill the promises of blessing to the human race.

Abraham is also a figure of all Christians who believe in the Resurrection of the Messiah. Through this belief, Christians share the faith of Abraham, and are his descendants through faith. Thus both Jews and Gentile Christian believers are true descendants of Abraham, the former by blood, and both in the spirit through faith.

Other elements of the story of the sacrifice of Isaac are significant as well. Abraham has Isaac carry the wood for his own sacrifice. The Fathers[19] and the liturgy[20] see in this a figure of Christ carrying the Cross up to Calvary.

At the last moment the angel stayed the hand of Abraham and a ram appeared with his horns caught in a thicket of thorns. This ram, offered as a holocaust as a substitute for Isaac, was also—like Isaac—a figure of Christ. Christ also was crowned with thorns, offered as a holocaust in substitution not for one individual, but for all sinners. Christ is a vicarious victim for the sins of every man. Thus it is fitting that He be represented by a vicarious sacrifice in the Old Testament figure.

Abraham's readiness to sacrifice Isaac merited a renewal of the promise of blessing to all nations, confirmed by the oath of God. God said (Gen 22:16–18):

---

[18] The Letter to the Hebrews (11:19) confirms this, saying: "Reasoning that God has power to raise up even from the dead; whence also he received him back as a type."

[19] See, for example, the early third-century work of Tertullian, *Adversus Marcion* 3.18, *ANF* 3:336: "And no doubt it was proper that this mystery [the Passion] should be prophetically set forth by types, and indeed chiefly by that method: for in proportion to its incredibility would it be a stumbling-block, if it were set forth in bare prophecy; and in proportion too, to its grandeur, was the need of obscuring it in shadow, that the difficulty of understanding it might lead to prayer for the grace of God. First, then, Isaac, when he was given up by his father as an offering, himself carried the wood for his own death. By this act he even then was setting forth the death of Christ, who was destined by His Father as a sacrifice, and carried the cross whereon He suffered."

[20] See the great liturgical hymn *Lauda Sion* by St. Thomas Aquinas: "It [the Eucharist] was *prefigured in type when Isaac was brought as an offering*, when a lamb was appointed for the Passover, and when manna was given to the Jews of old."

This figure is also mentioned in the Roman canon in the Mass (first Eucharistic prayer): "Look with favor on these offerings and accept them as once you accepted the gifts of your servant Abel, *the sacrifice of Abraham, our father in faith*, and the bread and wine offered by your priest Melchisedech."

By my own self have I sworn . . . because thou hast done this thing, and hast not spared thy only begotten son for my sake, I will bless thee, and I will multiply thy seed as the stars of the heaven, and as the sand that is by the sea shore. . . . And in thy seed shall all the nations of the earth be blessed, because thou hast obeyed my voice.

The figure, of course, magnificent as it is, falls far short of the reality of the Passion which it prefigured. Isaac was spared, whereas Christ was not. Isaac was not the promise itself, but only the forefather of the Promise that was Christ, in whom all nations are truly blessed.

Typology of Isaac and Ishmael, according to Galatians

According to St. Paul in the Letter to the Galatians, the Law of Moses is essentially a kind of pedagogy leading towards faith in Christ. The newly evangelized Gentile Christians of Galatia had been persuaded by certain Jewish Christians that they needed to observe the ceremonial rites of the Law of Moses in addition to the precepts of Christ in order to be saved. St. Paul wrote his letter to them, explaining that these ceremonial rites were not obligatory for them, since it was but a figure of the realities they had received through faith in Christ, in which the Old Testament was completely fulfilled. To follow the ceremonial law of the Old Testament after the coming of the Messiah would be to continue to use the figures when the reality represented by the figures—Christ and His Redemption of mankind—had already been revealed and accomplished, giving rise to a new and everlasting covenant.

He says in Galatians 3:23–25: "Now before faith came, we were confined under the law, kept under restraint until faith should be revealed. So that the law was our tutor until Christ came, that we might be justified by faith. But now that faith has come, we are no longer under a tutor." Later, in Galatians 4:21–31, he applies Biblical typology in service of his argument that they were not to observe the Law of Moses:

Tell me, you who desire to be under law, do you not hear the law? For it is written that Abraham had two sons, one by a slave and one by a free woman. But the son of the slave was born according to the flesh, the son of the free woman through promise. Now this is an allegory: these women are two covenants. One is from Mount Sinai, bearing children for slavery; she is Hagar. Now Hagar is Mount Sinai in Arabia; she corresponds to the present Jerusalem, for she is in slavery with her children. But the Jerusalem above is free, and she is our mother. For it is written, "Rejoice, O barren one who does not bear; break forth and shout, you who are not in travail; for the children of the desolate one are many more than the children of her that is married." Now we, brethren, like Isaac, are children of promise. But as at that time he who was born according to the flesh persecuted him who was born according to the Spirit, so it is now. But what does the scripture say? "Cast out the slave and her son; for the son of the slave shall not inherit with the son of the free woman." So, brethren, we are not children of the slave but of the free woman.

St. Paul teaches that Isaac, physically the forefather of the Jewish people, nevertheless allegorically represents the Church, the heavenly Jerusalem, whereas Ishmael, physically the forefather of Arab nations, allegorically represents the synagogue, the physical Jerusalem that is here below. The Church is here said to be free in that she possesses the spiritual realities—the channels of grace to attain to heaven—that were only prefigured in the Old Covenant.

This is not to denigrate the dignity of the Chosen People. Their dignity consists in being specially prepared to receive the Messiah and Redeemer, and for this reason they were under the tutorship of the Law, an *immense privilege*. Nevertheless, the Old Covenant was never meant to be an end in itself, but was always conceived by God as a preparation for the Church that was to issue from it.

St. Paul speaks of the Old Covenant as a servant, the child of a bondwoman, in the sense that, although it prepared for the Church and symbolically represented it, it did not yet attain to "the glorious freedom of the sons of God." It did not have the seven glorious sacraments of the New Law, which not only represent grace, but actually confer grace to all those who pose no obstacle to its action. The Old Covenant is allegorically a "bondwoman" because it only attained to the figure, and not to the spiritual reality signified by the figure, which is the treasure of the Church: sanctifying grace.

Jacob and Esau

There is a recurring pattern in the Old Testament that the younger son receives the blessing from the father that should, by right, have gone to the firstborn son, who at times receives a curse. What mystery is concealed here?

The most famous of these occurrences is the blessing of Jacob in the place of his older twin brother, Esau, who emerged first from the womb, although not without a struggle from Jacob, who was clasping his heel. Esau, however, sold his birthright to Jacob for a bowl of lentils (Gen 25:30–34). Isaac did not know this as he blessed his sons on his deathbed, for Isaac favored Esau, a hunter who brought fresh venison to his father. Through the aid of Rebecca, his mother, Jacob disguised himself as Esau, and received the blessing that his father had destined for his older brother (Gen 27:27–29):

> See, the smell of my son is as the smell of a field which the Lord has blessed! May God give you of the dew of heaven, and of the fatness of the earth, and plenty of grain and wine. Let peoples serve you, and nations bow down to you. Be lord over your brothers, and may your mother's sons bow down to you. Cursed be every one who curses you, and blessed be every one who blesses you!

St. Augustine comments:

> Thus the blessing of Jacob is the proclamation of Christ among all nations. This is happening; this is actively going on. Isaac is the Law and the Prophets; and Christ is blessed by the Law and the Prophets . . . as by someone who does not know what he is doing, because the Law and the Prophets are themselves not understood. The world is filled like a field with the fragrance of the name of Christ; and his is the blessing of the dew of heaven, that is, of the showers of divine words. . . . It is Christ whom the nations serve, and to whom the princes do reverence. . . . He it is to whom the sons of his father do reverence, that is, the sons of Abraham according to faith. . . . Our Christ, I repeat, is blessed, that is, he is truly spoken of, even by the lips of Jews who, although in error, still chant the Law and the Prophets: and they suppose that another is being blessed, the Messiah who is still awaited by them, in their error.
>
> Look at Isaac! He is horror-stricken when his elder son asks for the promised blessing, and he realizes that he has blessed another in his place . . . and yet he does not complain that he has been deceived. . . . The great mystery is straightway revealed to him, in the depths of his heart, and he eschews indignation and confirms his blessing. . . . One would surely expect at this point the curse of an angry man, if all this happened in the ordinary course of events, instead of by inspiration from above. *Historical events, these, but events with prophetic meaning! Events on earth, but directed from heaven!* The actions of men, but the operation of God![21]

St. Augustine gives a perfect description of Biblical typology in these words: "*Historical events...but events with prophetic meaning.*" Just as Jacob, the younger son, received the blessing reserved for the firstborn,

---

[21] St. Augustine, *The City of God*, trans. Henry Bettenson (New York: Penguin Books, 1972), 16.37, p. 700 (my italics).

so the Church, the younger descendant of Abraham according to faith, received the blessing of Isaac, after the synagogue, elder brother of the Church, had fulfilled its sublime mission to prepare for the Messiah.

According to a moral sense, Esau represents carnal man, who puts no value on things of the spirit, represented in his birthright, and who afterwards through jealousy opposes the recipient of the promises of God.

St. Augustine tells us that Isaac represents the Law and the Prophets, whereas Jacob—the son of the promise according to the secret intention of God—represents Christ. Isaac blesses Jacob without knowing the object of his blessing. St. Augustine tells us that this represents the blessing given by the Law and the Prophets to Christ. These books truly prophesy His coming, even though so many who reverence the Law and the Prophets have not yet received the gift of faith to see this. We pray that there may be an ever fuller outpouring of grace to enable more and more to see.

There is yet another dimension of Biblical typology in this marvelous story. It is extremely interesting how Rebecca plays a key role in helping Jacob to attain the blessing, which he never would have received without her expert counsel, even though he had acquired the birthright of Esau.

The saints see in this event a figure of the intercession of the Blessed Virgin in favor of all the members of the Mystical Body of Christ. This is an example of typology in its moral dimension, in service of the spiritual life. St. Louis de Montfort develops this typology very beautifully in his great classic, *True Devotion to the Blessed Virgin* (chapter 5). The saint writes:

> Before explaining this beautiful story, let me remind you that, according to the early fathers and the interpreters of Holy Scripture, Jacob is the type of our Lord and of souls who are saved, and Esau is the type of souls who are condemned. We have only to examine the actions and conduct of both in order to judge each one.
>
> 1. Esau, the elder brother, was strong and robust, clever, and skilful with the bow and very successful at hunting.
>
> 2. He seldom stayed at home and, relying only on his own strength and skill, worked out of doors.
>
> 3. He never went out of his way to please his mother Rebecca, and did little or nothing for her.
>
> 4. He was such a glutton and so fond of eating that he sold his birthright for a dish of lentils.
>
> 5. Like Cain, he was extremely jealous of his brother and persecuted him relentlessly.

This is the usual conduct of sinners:

1. They rely upon their own strength and skill in temporal affairs. They are very energetic, clever and well-informed about things of this world but very dull and ignorant about things of heaven.

2. And so they are never or very seldom at home, in their own house, that is, in their own interior, the inner, essential abode that God has given to every man to dwell in, after his own example, for God always abides within himself. Sinners have no liking for solitude or the spiritual life or interior devotion. They consider those who live an interior life, secluded from the world, and who work more interiorly than exteriorly, as narrow-minded, bigoted and uncivilized.

3. Sinners care little or nothing about devotion to Mary the Mother of the elect. It is true that they do not really hate her... Nevertheless they cannot bear to see anyone love her tenderly, for they do not have for her any of the affection of Jacob; they find fault with the honour which her good children and servants faithfully pay her to win her affection. . . .

4. Sinners sell their birthright, that is, the joys of paradise, for a dish of lentils, that is, the pleasures of this world. They laugh, they drink, they eat, they have a good time, they gamble, they dance and so forth, without taking any more trouble than Esau to make themselves worthy of their heavenly Father's blessing. . . .

5. Finally, sinners continually hate and persecute the elect, openly or secretly. The elect are a burden to them. They despise them.

St. Louis de Montfort characterizes Jacob in opposition to these characteristics of Esau. He particularly stresses the fact that Jacob preferred to stay home with his mother, to whom he was submissive in all things, as can be seen in the obedience with which he followed her counsel so as to win the blessing of his father. Jacob can thus be seen as a figure of all God's elect:

They stay at home with their mother—that is, they have an esteem for quietness, love the interior life and are assiduous in prayer. They always remain in the company of the Blessed Virgin, their Mother and Model, whose glory is wholly interior... It is true, at times they do venture out into the world, but only to fulfill the duties of their state of life, in obedience to the will of God and the will of their Mother.

Finally, the Saint shows that Rebecca is a figure of the Blessed Virgin Mary:

She loves them not only affectively but effectively, that is, her love is active and productive of good like Rebecca's love for Jacob— and even more so, for Rebecca was, after all, only a symbolic figure of Mary. . . .

1. Like Rebecca she looks out for favorable opportunities to promote their interests, to ennoble and enrich them. . . .

2. She gives them excellent advice, as Rebecca did to Jacob. "My son, follow my counsels.". . .

3. . . . As she alone knows perfectly what the divine taste is and where the greatest glory to God is to be found, she alone without any fear of mistake can prepare and garnish our body and soul to satisfy that infinitely refined taste and promote that infinitely hidden glory.

4. Once this good Mother has received our complete offering ... and has stripped us of our own garments, she cleanses us and makes us worthy to appear without shame before our heavenly Father. She clothes us in the clean garments of Esau, the firstborn, namely her Son Jesus Christ. . . .

5. Finally, Mary obtains for them the heavenly Father's blessing. As they are the youngest born and adopted, they are not really entitled to it. Clad in new, precious, and sweet-smelling garments, with body and soul well-prepared and dressed, they confidently approach their heavenly Father.[22]

How rich are these Biblical stories! St. Augustine and St. Louis de Montfort see two completely different spiritual or typological lessons contained here, and yet there is no conflict between them. The text has a literal or historical meaning, as do all other histories, and yet at the same time it is prophetic of Christ and the Church, and speaks to us of the maternal intercession of the Virgin Mary and of the spiritual life of Christians who are devoted to her.

The Story of Joseph, Sold by His Brothers

The story of Joseph is extremely rich in typology. Joseph the dreamer is hated by his brothers on account of envy. He has prophetic dreams which foretell that all his brothers, and indeed even his father and mother, would worship him; and he is the favorite son of his father, begotten by Rachel in his old age. "Now Israel loved Joseph more than any other of his children, because he was the son of his old age; and he made him a long robe with sleeves. But when his brothers saw that their

---

[22] St. Louis de Montfort, *True Devotion to the Blessed Virgin* (Bay Shore, NY: Montfort Publications, 1980), pp. 94–104 (ch. 5).

father loved him more than all his brothers, they hated him, and could not speak peaceably to him" (Gen 37:3–4).

Jacob sent Joseph to visit his brothers in the field to see how they were doing. The envy of his brothers was such that they planned to kill him, but seeing the opportunity for a profitable transaction, they preferred to sell him into slavery for twenty pieces of silver. They presented the cloak of many colors, stained with the blood of a goat, to their father.

Thus far, it is easy to see in these events a typological, allegorical sense. Joseph represents Christ, the promise of Israel and of the nations, sent by His father to assist his brethren. "He came into his own, but his own received him not" (Jn 1:11). Both the plan to kill him and to sell him for a few pieces of silver were realized in His Passion. His cloak of many colors represents His sacred humanity, which, stained with blood, was presented by his brethren to God the Father.

However, as we know, the allegory does not end here. The treachery and malice worked on Joseph redounds to the salvation of the very same brothers who betrayed him, of their whole house, and indeed of the nations, represented by Egypt, and all those who came to Egypt to buy grain in the time of famine.

Joseph is sold into slavery in Egypt. There, because of his purity in refusing the advances of Potiphar's wife, he is put in prison. In prison he correctly interprets the dreams of the cupbearer and the baker. Much later, when Pharaoh has the dream of the seven fat cows, followed by seven lean ones, the cupbearer tells Pharaoh of Joseph's ability, and Pharaoh summons him to interpret his dream. He is then set over all of Egypt, second only to Pharaoh, who orders that all are to go to Joseph in their need. In this capacity his brothers are sent to him to buy grain during the great famine. Although knowing their treachery, he tries their repentance and forgives them with deep emotion.

How marvelous and mysterious are the plans of God! An abominable crime of betrayal and ingratitude is worked, which results in the salvation of the treacherous brothers, their house, and of the greatest of nations. If Christ is prefigured in the prophetic dreams of Joseph, in his predilection by his father, and in his betrayal for twenty pieces of silver, He is no less prefigured in the wonderful consequences of that betrayal. God permits evil so as to enable an incomparably greater good to be accomplished. He permits Joseph to be sold by his brethren into slavery so as to save all—both his family and the gentile Egyptians—thereby prefiguring how the betrayal of Christ would work the salvation of the children of Israel and of all the Gentiles. Here we can apply the profound phrase that the liturgy of the Church says of the sin of Adam: "O happy fault (*felix culpa*), which merited us so great a Redeemer."

Pascal summarizes beautifully:

Christ prefigured by Joseph. Innocent, beloved of his father, sent by his father to see his brothers, is sold for twenty pieces of silver by his brothers. Through this he becomes their lord, their savior, savior of strangers and savior of the world. None of this would have happened but for their plot to destroy him, the sale, and their rejection of him.

In prison Joseph, innocent between two criminals. Jesus on the cross between two thieves. He prophesies the salvation of the one and the death of the other when to all appearances they are alike. Christ saves the elect and damns the reprobate for the same crime. Joseph only prophesies, Jesus acts. Joseph asks the man who will be saved to remember him when he comes in glory. And the man Jesus saves asks to be remembered when He comes into His Kingdom.[23]

In fact, it is easy to see in this story a figure not only of Christ, but of the centuries of Christendom. In Egypt, Joseph was first put into prison, which could signify the 300 years of brutal Roman persecution of the Church. He was then raised up to the right hand of Pharaoh, to whom all pay deference, which can be seen as a figure of the social kingship of Christ during the centuries of Christendom. Joseph ruled for fourteen years (and more), as a parallel to the same number of centuries in which the nations publicly recognized Christ. In the end, the once perfidious brethren themselves come to be reconciled, in the final triumph of providence worked through Joseph. This final element of the story is, it would seem, a figure of an event foretold, but not yet fully realized: the final conversion of Israel to faith in Christ in the last times before Christ our Lord comes a second time in majesty to judge the living and the dead.[24]

---

[23] Pascal, *Pensées*, section 2, series 23, n. 570 (New York: Penguin Classics, 1966), 223.

[24] St. Paul foretells this event in enigmatic language in Rom 11:23–26. The idea is that God has permitted the unbelief of the Jews in their promised Messiah, which in itself is a heart-breaking tragedy, so as to permit the accomplishment of a greater good: the conversion of the multitude of the Gentiles and their insertion into the Covenant. And after the time of the conversion of the Gentiles has been completed with the preaching of the Gospel in the whole world, Israel shall be aided by God to come to faith in Christ. See chapters 10 and 11 below.

CHAPTER 7

Typology of the Feasts of Israel

Let us turn now to discuss the spiritual or typological meaning of the principal religious festivals in the Law of Moses: Passover (*Pesach*),[1] Pentecost (*Shavuot*), the Feast of Booths (*Sukkot*), and the Day of Atonement (*Yom Kippur*). Day

All the great Jewish feasts commanded in the books of Moses commemorate the events of the Exodus. At the same time, however, they also celebrate the gifts of God in nature. For example, the celebration of Pentecost/*Shavuot* is tied to the spring harvest, and *Sukkot* to the harvest of the fall. Each feast also has an element of sacrifice offered solemnly to God. Finally, since the event of Exodus is itself a figure of Messianic deliverance, the great Jewish festivals have a forward-looking aspect in which they prefigure the Redemption worked by the Messiah. Thus there are four levels in the great Jewish feasts: (1) celebration of the historic deliverance of Israel from Egypt, (2) celebration of creation, (3) sacrifice offered to God in the Temple, and (4) prefiguring the Messianic deliverance which is the object of hope.

Today the element of sacrifice has disappeared from Jewish worship because of the destruction of the Temple, the only place in which all sacrifice could be offered. However, in Biblical times it was absolutely central. The Law of Moses commands the Israelites to make a pilgrimage to appear before God (in the Temple) to offer sacrifice three times a year: on Passover, Pentecost (*Shavuot*), and the Feast of Booths (*Sukkot*).[2] All the sacrifices of the Old Testament prefigure that of Christ, which alone has the intrinsic value to atone for sin.

---

[1] This is the root of the word "Paschal."

[2] Deut 16:16: "Three times a year all your males shall appear before the Lord your God at the place which he will choose: at the feast of unleavened bread, at the feast of weeks, and at the feast of booths. They shall not appear before the Lord empty-handed." See also Ex 23:14–17 and Ex 34:23: "Three times in the year shall all your males appear before the Lord God, the God of Israel. For I will cast out nations before you, and enlarge your borders; neither shall any man desire your land, when you go up to appear before the Lord your God three times in the year."

Typology of Passover

The feast of Passover commemorates the opening and foundational event of the Exodus from Egypt. It begins by celebrating the protection given to Israel from the last of the ten plagues. The angel of death killed the firstborn of Egypt, but the Israelites were protected by the blood of the Paschal lamb. This is celebrated on the first night of the feast, the fourteenth of Nisan. The remaining days of Passover celebrate the liberation from Egypt.

The people of Israel were in a state of slavery and oppression under Pharaoh. This is a material figure for mankind's spiritual state of slavery to sin before our Redemption by Christ. Pharaoh represents the devil, the enemy of our souls.

Before the Israelites were permitted to leave Egypt, the Lord sent the last plague, the death of the firstborn of all the Egyptians, from Pharaoh down to the poorest of the nation, and even to the firstborn of all the animals. However, the Jews were spared through the performance of a mysterious rite. They were told to sacrifice the Passover lamb, which was to be pure and immaculate, with none of its bones broken, and to put its blood on their doorways, so that the exterminating angel would *pass over* their houses, sparing all those protected by the blood of the lamb. Then they were to eat of the lamb, leaving nothing over. The commandment concerning the Passover is given in Exodus 12:3–14:

> Tell all the congregation of Israel that on the tenth day of this month they shall take every man a lamb according to their fathers' houses, a lamb for a household; and if the household is too small for a lamb, then a man and his neighbor next to his house shall take according to the number of persons; according to what each can eat you shall make your count for the lamb. Your lamb shall be without blemish, a male a year old . . . and you shall keep it until the fourteenth day of this month, when the whole assembly of the congregation of Israel shall kill their lambs in the evening. Then they shall take some of the blood, and put it on the two doorposts and the lintel of the houses in which they eat them. They shall eat the flesh that night, roasted; with unleavened bread and bitter herbs they shall eat it. . . . And you shall let none of it remain until the morning, anything that remains until the morning you shall burn. In this manner you shall eat it: your loins girded, your sandals on your feet, and your staff in your hand; and you shall eat it in haste. It is the Lord's passover. For I will pass through the land of Egypt that night, and I will smite all the first-born in the land of Egypt, both man and beast; and on all the gods of Egypt I will execute judgments: I am the Lord. The blood shall be a sign for you, upon the houses where you are; and when I see the blood, I

will pass over you, and no plague shall fall upon you to destroy you, when I smite the land of Egypt. This day shall be for you a memorial day, and you shall keep it as a feast to the Lord.

When the Temple was later established in Jerusalem, another element was added: the Passover lamb had to be sacrificed in the Temple and consumed in Jerusalem (see Deut 16:6). The number of lambs sacrificed in the Temple each Passover was enormous. Josephus, a Jewish historian from the first century AD, reports that in one year it was ascertained by a census that 256,000 lambs were immolated on the eve of the Passover.[3]

Surely there is a great mystery hidden here, which Israel could not grasp until the Passion of our Lord revealed the reality hidden in the figure. What was the significance of the blood of the sacrificed paschal lambs painted on the doorway of the houses, and poured out on the altar in the Temple every year? All Christians can understand that it symbolically represented or foretold our redemption by the Blood of Christ, and our incorporation into that redemption through the sacrament of Baptism.

The paschal lamb sacrificed on the fourteenth of Nisan obviously was a mysterious figure of the bloody sacrifice of Christ on Calvary, which He suffered on the day of Passover (or of the preparation for the Passover), at 3:00 in the afternoon, the same hour that the priests began to immolate the paschal lambs in the Temple.[4] In the Last Supper the night before, Jesus mystically anticipated the sacrifice that He was to make the following day by offering it in the sacramental form of the Eucharist.

By this sacrifice of Calvary, a perfect expiation of sin was made, once and for all, sufficient for the forgiveness of all the sins of the world, sufficient to open the gates of heaven to all who dispose themselves to enter by cooperating with grace. The sacrifice of Christ, the Lamb of God, the new Paschal Lamb, is sufficient to obtain the release of all men (and not just the Israelites, who were a figure of the whole human race) from the bondage of sin and the devil, and from the threat of the exterminating angel in the judgment.

The Letter to the Hebrews 9:13–14 speaks of how the sacrifice of Christ fulfilled the figures of the Old Testament:

---

[3] Josephus, *Wars of the Jews* 6.9.3. The census was taken by the governor Cestius during the reign of Nero.

[4] See Hayyim Schauss, *The Jewish Festivals: A Guide to Their History and Observance* (New York: Schocken Books, 1996), 53. See also Josephus, *Wars of the Jews* 6.9.3.

For if the sprinkling of defiled persons with the blood of goats and bulls and with the ashes of a heifer sanctifies for the purification of the flesh, how much more shall the blood of Christ, who through the eternal Spirit offered himself without blemish to God, purify your conscience from dead works to serve the living God?

It is clear that the blood of the paschal lamb was but a figure of the Blood of Christ, spilt out on Calvary on the feast of the Passover. The blood of brute animals has no efficacy in itself to satisfy for sin and restore us to God's friendship. It was only a figure that pointed to the true Sacrifice of Calvary, by virtue of which we are washed from the stain of sin.

The Sacrifice of Calvary had this peculiarity: Christ was at one and the same time both *priest and victim,* as well as the God to whom it was offered, so as to reunite man with God. The Sacrifice had infinite value from the dignity of the Person who offered it, from the sheer magnitude of the suffering that was offered, and especially from the inconceivable excess of charity with which it was offered.

However, this redemption must be applied to men individually. It is not enough that the Lamb has been sacrificed. We must be protected by His Blood which must be applied to the doorway of our own life. Obviously this ceremony of the Law of Moses is a metaphor or figure of an interior application of the grace of God. How is it to be applied?

Christian doctrine teaches us that the forgiveness of sins and the sanctifying grace earned by the Blood of the Paschal Lamb is applied to us principally through the seven sacraments of the Church, which are channels of grace. The first step, the gateway of all the sacraments and of grace itself, is the sacrament of Baptism, by which we are given a new spiritual birth. The culmination of the sacraments, however, is the Eucharist, celebrated and instituted by Jesus on the night before His sacrifice on Calvary. The fullness of the grace won for us on Calvary is applied to our souls when we attend Mass devoutly, and especially when we receive Holy Communion with good dispositions.

The Eucharist

Just as the Passover prefigures the sacrifice of Jesus on Calvary, so it likewise prefigures the institution of the Eucharist, which Jesus celebrated during the Passover on the night before He fulfilled the feast in His bloody sacrifice on Good Friday. The Eucharist is so tied to the sacrifice of Calvary that they are essentially identical. The sacramental or mystical re-presentation of the sacrifice of Calvary is accomplished in the Eucharist, in which the Blood of Christ is mystically separated from His Body in the separate consecration of the Body and Blood.

Just as Christ was simultaneously priest and victim in offering the sacrifice of Calvary, so He is in the sacrifice of the Eucharist. Through the ministerial priest, who acts in the person of Christ through the power of the sacrament of Holy Orders, the miracle of transubstantiation is brought about: Christ is made present on the altar under the appearances of bread and wine, and is mystically offered to God the Father. Thus in every Eucharist, the true Paschal Lamb—the Lamb of God—is immolated on our altars in a mystical and unbloody fashion through Christ the High Priest, who acts through His ordained ministers. And that Body and Blood, together with His soul and divinity, is then received by the faithful as spiritual nourishment. Just as the circumcised Israelites were commanded to partake of the meat of the immolated Paschal Lamb, so the new Israelites in the Church—the baptized faithful—partake of the true Lamb of God, which saves us from the wrath of Satan and makes us pleasing to God, ever more conformed to His Son by whom we are spiritually nourished.

Furthermore, just as the Jewish Passover was a sign of the covenant between God and Israel, the Eucharist is both the sign and the reality of the New Covenant. In the words of consecration given in Luke 22:20, Jesus states: "The cup which is poured out for you is the new covenant in my blood." The Eucharist is the New Covenant because it contains Jesus Himself—Body, Blood, soul, and divinity—immolated for us mystically on the altar and containing in Himself all the promises of God.

Baptism

The Passover is also a figure or type of Baptism. In the Exodus, which the Passover commemorates, the Israelites cross in safety and tranquility through the waters, and once secure on the other side they look back exultingly to see their enemies covered by the waves, annihilated, and their corpses and weapons cast up on the shore.

The neophytes, likewise, emerging from the baptismal font, see through the eyes of faith that their sins which have tyrannized them, preventing them from being able to enter into the kingdom of heaven, have been wiped out through the waters of Baptism, whose salvific power comes from the Blood of Christ shed on the Cross on the very day that the Jews celebrated Passover.

Pharaoh pursued the Israelites but lost his dominion over them when they passed through the Red Sea. He was not allowed to pass with his chariots. The Israelites were saved by water, by which the pursuing Egyptians were annihilated. Sin likewise pursues humanity until it is blotted out by forgiveness in the waters of Baptism received with living faith.[5]

For this reason, in the liturgy of the Easter Vigil, traditionally the most solemn and important liturgy of the year, Catholics hear this reading from Exodus on the Crossing of the Red Sea. It is perfectly fitted for the administration of Baptism, which was traditionally administered to adult converts in this night. St. Augustine, for example, received Baptism at the hands of St. Ambrose in the Easter Vigil.

There is a moral typology here as well. It is not enough that the sins of our past life be wiped clean through the sacrament of Baptism. Baptism is only the beginning of the Christian life: many temptations and obstacles remain before we will be able to attain our homeland and final destination. Thus, after triumphantly crossing the Red Sea, the Israelites wandered and were tempted in the desert for forty years. This is a very important figurative event as well. The Christian likewise must continue to do battle with the world, the devil, sin, and vice, during the period of this mortal life.

The Feast of Pentecost (Shavuot)

The journey through the desert was marked by a fundamental event: the giving of the Law on Mt. Sinai, recounted in Exodus 19–20, which occurred exactly seven weeks—that is, fifty days—after the Passover. Hence the Greek-speaking Jews called it "Pentecost," which means fifty,[6] while in Hebrew it was called the feast of "weeks" (*shavuot*), for the seven weeks which separate the Passover from the solemn covenant on Mt. Sinai.

The Israelites were commanded at Sinai to celebrate a feast to commemorate this second foundational event of their existence, and also to give thanks for the harvest by the offering of the first fruits in

---

[5] See St. Augustine, Sermon IV on Jacob and Esau, n. 9, in *The Works of Saint Augustine. Sermons I (1–19) on the Old Testament*, trans. Edmund Hill (Brooklyn, NY: New City Press, 1990), 189: "The people, according to the old testament, are liberated from Egypt; the people, according to the new testament, are liberated from the devil. . . . Just as the Egyptians pursue the Jews as far as the sea, so Christians are pursued by their sins as far as baptism. Observe, brothers, and see; through the sea the Jews are liberated, in the sea the Egyptians are overwhelmed. Through baptism Christians are liberated and quit of their sins, while their sins are destroyed. Those ones come out after the Red Sea and journey through the desert; so too Christians after baptism are not yet in the promised land, but live in hope. This age is the desert, and desert indeed it is for Christians after baptism, if they understand what they have received. . . . They will understand that they are living as wandering exiles, longing for their native land."

[6] See Tob 2:1; 2 Macc 12:32.

the Promised Land.[7] The Jewish feast of Pentecost is in a certain sense the completion of what was begun in the Passover and the Exodus. It marks the end of the season of Passover—just as for Christians it marks the end of the season of Easter—and celebrates the first fruits of the Promised Land. Thus the feast has two principal aspects: thanksgiving for the gift of the Ten Commandments and the Covenant of Sinai, and thanksgiving for the first fruits of the land.

It is important to know this background to the Jewish feast of Pentecost/Shavuot in order to understand the Christian feast of Pentecost, for it was not by chance that on this day the Lord chose to communicate to the Apostles and disciples the fullest gifts of the Holy Spirit, accompanied by the miracle of speaking in tongues.

Just as the written Law of the Ten Commandments and the sealing of the covenant with Israel was given fifty days after Passover, so too the New Law of the Holy Spirit was given fifty days after Easter, which celebrates the Resurrection of the true Passover Lamb.

As we have seen, the giving of a new covenant written on our souls rather than on tablets of stone had been announced by the prophets—especially Jeremiah and Ezekiel (Ez 36:24–27)—some six centuries before its fulfillment. Jeremiah, in 31:31–33, proclaims: "Behold, the days are coming, says the Lord, when I will make a new covenant with the house of Israel. . . . I will put my law within them, and I will write it upon their hearts . . . for I will forgive their iniquity, and I will remember their sin no more." This promise was fulfilled first in a manifest and public way on the day of Pentecost, when three thousand Israelites were baptized, as recounted in Acts 2.

This event was also the first "celebration" of the sacrament of Confirmation. In this case, it was not offered by ministers of the Church, but by God Himself to the Apostles.

What is the relationship between the giving of the Law on Mt. Sinai and the outpouring of the Holy Spirit on the same day of Pentecost? St. Thomas Aquinas and the other great doctors of the Church see the New Law of Christ as principally the grace of the Holy Spirit, which enables us to accomplish God's Law in charity.

In other words, the parallelism between the Pentecost of the Old Testament and that of the New shows us the respective characters of the Old and the New Law. The Ten Commandments are holy indeed, for they show us what we must do and refrain from doing. The New Law of Christ presupposes the Ten Commandments, but crowns and

---

[7] See Ex 34:22: "And you shall observe the feast of weeks, the first fruits of wheat harvest." See also Ex 23:16: "You shall keep the feast of harvest, of the first fruits of your labor"; and Lev 23:15–21.

transcends them, for it consists essentially in supernatural charity, "the bond of perfection" (Col 3:14), giving us love for what we have been commanded, and the interior capacity to put it into practice in a holy way.

Mt. Sinai and Pentecost

The difference between the two covenants is spoken of at length in the Letter to the Hebrews. The letter culminates with the comparison between the revelation of God in the two covenants as manifested in two very different kinds of theophanies—that of Mt. Sinai and that of Pentecost on Mount Zion:

> For you have not come to what may be touched, a blazing fire, and darkness, and gloom, and a tempest, and the sound of a trumpet, and a voice whose words made the hearers entreat that no further messages be spoken to them. For they could not endure the order that was given, "If even a beast touches the mountain, it shall be stoned." Indeed, so terrifying was the sight that Moses said, "I tremble with fear." But you have come to Mount Zion and to the city of the living God, the heavenly Jerusalem, and to innumerable angels in festal gathering, and to the assembly of the first-born who are enrolled in heaven, and to a judge who is God of all, and to the spirits of just men made perfect, and to Jesus, the mediator of a new covenant, and to the sprinkled blood that speaks more graciously than the blood of Abel. See that you do not refuse him who is speaking. For if they did not escape when they refused him who warned them on earth, much less shall we escape if we reject him who warns from heaven.[8]

God appeared to Moses on Mt. Sinai in the darkness of a cloud, preceded by awe-inspiring physical prodigies, which terrified the Israelites. In Exodus 19:18–19 and 20:18–19 we read:

> And Mount Sinai was wrapped in smoke, because the Lord descended upon it in fire; and the smoke of it went up like the smoke of a kiln, and the whole mountain quaked greatly. And as the sound of the trumpet grew louder and louder, Moses spoke, and God answered him in thunder. . . . Now when all the people perceived the thunderings and the lightnings and the sound of the trumpet and the mountain smoking, the people were afraid and trembled; and they stood afar off, and said to Moses, "You speak to us, and we will hear; but let not God speak to us, lest we die."

---

[8] Heb 12:18–25.

It was at this moment that the Lord gave Moses the Ten Commandments on Mt. Sinai (fifty days after the Passover). This most solemn event of the Old Testament, the center of the life of Israel, corresponds to the first Christian Pentecost, fifty days after the Passion and Resurrection of our Lord.

What a contrast between the two feasts! The giving of the Law of Moses was marked by the emotions of extreme fear and trembling, accompanied by great supernatural thunder, lightning, and smoke; whereas the giving of the new law of the Holy Spirit is marked by spiritual exultation and great confidence in God on the part of the Apostles who begin to preach without fear, speaking in tongues so that they are understood by all the Jewish pilgrims in Jerusalem who had come from the Diaspora. In place of the terrible fire and smoke, each disciple has a tongue of fire over his head, indicating that the New Covenant is to be spread by the fire of preaching.

And on that very day, the preaching of St. Peter won for the Church three thousand who were immediately baptized. Thus the Christian Pentecost corresponded mystically to the Jewish feast of the first fruits, offered on that same day. The material first fruits of the harvest correspond to the spiritual first fruits of the Apostolic preaching—three thousand adult converts—as well as to the gifts and fruits of the Holy Spirit in the souls of the disciples. Thus the first fruits were of grace and apostolate.

The fact that the Apostles miraculously spoke in tongues is itself a figure of future events. It was a prophetic indication of the universality of the Church, called to be the ark of salvation of the whole human race and to speak all tongues and be understood by all. The event of Pentecost was thus the antitype of Babel with its confusion and "pluralism" of tongues. Although the plurality of tongues continues, and will doubtless continue until the end of time, in the Church the original harmony is recomposed in the unity of faith. Although materially there continue to be many languages, they are united in proclaiming the same Creed. In the words of St. Paul (Eph 4:3–6), the faithful should be "eager to maintain the unity of the Spirit in the bond of peace. There is one body and one Spirit, just as you were called to the one hope that belongs to your call, one Lord, one faith, one baptism, one God and Father of us all, who is above all and through all and in all." There is no room for "pluralism" in the faith, for the truth is one.

The Veil of Moses

The book of Exodus tells us that after speaking with the Lord on Mt. Sinai, and in the tabernacle of the witness, Moses' face shone with a supernatural light which the Israelites could not bear to look at. Thus when Moses spoke with the people, he put a veil on his face, which he removed when speaking with the Lord.[9] There is a mystery concealed here. The veil worn by Moses when speaking with the people represents the veil of figures by which the mysteries of Christ were both concealed and obscurely represented, revealed only for those who had the key to penetrate beneath the veil. The key, of course, is faith in Christ. St. Paul speaks of this in 2 Corinthians 3:6–16:

> He also it is who has made us fit ministers of the new covenant, not of the letter but of the spirit; for the letter kills, but the spirit gives life. Now if the ministration of death, which was engraved in letters upon stones, was inaugurated in such glory that the children of Israel could not look steadfastly upon the face of Moses on account of the transient glory that shone upon it, shall not the ministration of the spirit be still more glorious? . . . For if that which was transient was glorious, much more is that glorious which abides. Having therefore such hope, we show great boldness. We do not act as Moses did, who used to put a veil over his face that the Israelites might not observe the glory of his countenance, which was to pass away. But their minds were darkened; for to this day, when the Old Testament is read to them, the selfsame veil remains, not being lifted to disclose the Christ in whom it is made void. Yes, down to this very day, when Moses is read, the veil covers their hearts; but when they turn in repentance to God, the veil shall be taken away.[10]

The Old Testament is said to be in the letter and not in the spirit for two reasons. First, because the Old Testament speaks of spiritual realities and promises principally through material and temporal figures (the letter), which do not "give life" until they are spiritually understood. These figures are symbolized by the veil worn by Moses when he spoke to the Israelites. For this reason, St. Paul says that the veil still remains for them when they read the Old Testament, because they cannot penetrate the figurative meaning of the Old Testament until they come to have faith in the New, at which point the veil is lifted.

Secondly, the Old Testament is said to be in the "letter" rather than in the "spirit" because its rites and ceremonies do not give and contain the grace of the Holy Spirit, as do the seven sacraments of the New. It is through sanctifying grace that we are enabled to observe the Law not just in the letter, but in its inner spirit of supernatural charity. Of course,

---

[9] To represent this light emanating from his face, artists frequently put horns on his head, as in the famous statue by Michelangelo. This followed the Vulgate translation of these rays of light as "horns."

[10] Confraternity of Christian Doctrine translation (1958).

to do this we must cooperate with the grace of God in the pursuit of perfection.

When St. Paul says that the letter "kills," this must not be understood to mean that every written code is bad, or that the Old Law of Moses is not from God, or that it is not good. The letter "kills" in the sense that the commandments of the Law—the Ten Commandments in particular—tell us what we must do to please God, and what we must not do; but it does not give us new inner strength to put it in practice. The Ten Commandments are a written law, very holy and true, inscribed in stone, but nevertheless they only tell what is our obligation, and they condemn us when we transgress them. It is in this sense only that they "kill."[11] St. Thomas notes that although the Old Law of Moses is most certainly not evil, it is still *imperfect*, for it does not remove the *cause* of the transgressions which it justly condemns. They were written in stone to symbolize their immutable character as absolute norms for all time, but they were not yet written on our hearts.

The essence of the New Covenant is not a new written law, but sanctifying grace, from which flow the theological virtues (faith, hope, and charity) and the gifts of the Holy Spirit, and which make possible the indwelling of the Spirit. These supernatural gifts give the faithful the inner strength to put the Law into practice and to merit eternal life.

In summary, just as the giving of the Law on Mt. Sinai on the fiftieth day after Passover was the central event in the life of ancient Israel, bringing it to birth in a certain sense, so likewise the event of Pentecost is at the center of the life of the Church, and her true birth.

Feast of Booths (Sukkot)

The third great feast on which all adult Jewish males were to make a pilgrimage to Jerusalem was *Sukkot*, the feast of Booths or Tabernacles. *Sukkot* is a Hebrew word meaning "huts" or "booths." It is celebrated five days after Yom Kippur, in the month of Tishri (Sept.–Oct.). The feast is commanded in Leviticus 23:39–43:

> On the fifteenth day of the seventh month, when you have gathered in the produce of the land, you shall keep the feast of the Lord seven days; on the first day shall be a solemn rest, and on the eighth day shall be a solemn rest. And you shall take on the first day the fruit of goodly trees, branches of palm trees, and boughs of leafy trees, and willows of the brook; and you shall rejoice before the Lord your God seven days. You shall keep it as a feast to the

---

[11] See the interpretation of St. Thomas Aquinas in his commentary on 2 Cor, ch. 3, lecture 2, v. 6, in Aquinas, *Super epistolas S. Pauli lectura*, ed. Raphael Cai (Turin: Marietti, 1953), 1:460 (n. 91).

Lord seven days in the year; it is a statute for ever throughout your generations; you shall keep it in the seventh month. You shall dwell in booths for seven days; all that are native in Israel shall dwell in booths, that your generations may know that I made the people of Israel dwell in booths when I brought them out of the land of Egypt: I am the Lord your God."[12]

Levels of Meaning

The feast of Sukkot, like all the great Jewish feasts, has various levels of meaning. On the one hand, it is a festival commemorating the ingathering of the harvest, and the corresponding joy (Lev 23:39). Secondly and more importantly, it has a historical meaning, which commemorates the wandering of the Israelites in the desert under God's miraculous protection (Lev 23:42) as He led them in a pillar of cloud by day and a pillar of fire by night. Third, it involved the offering of a great number of sacrifices in the Temple (Lev 23:36–38). Finally, the festival also has a spiritual sense in which it prefigures the eternal tabernacles of heaven and the communion of saints. For this reason it must be celebrated with joy and, if possible, with guests.

This festival is marked by the construction of huts or booths (tabernacles), covered by leafy branches which give shade, but through which one can see the stars at night. All meals during the week of the festival are taken in these huts. By tradition the walls are decorated with tablets bearing the names of seven patriarchs who represent the heavenly guests who are invited to dwell within for the seven days of the feast.[13]

The feast of Sukkot thus reminds the Jews that they are pilgrims on earth, sojourners in the desert awaiting a heavenly dwelling place, or eternal tabernacle, as Jesus says in Luke 16:9. They too realize that in this pilgrimage we live by faith and not yet by vision. We yearn for God and for heaven, a yearning expressed by the sight of the stars through the branches that form the roof of the *sukkah*. This yearning, although not yet satisfied, is nevertheless a source of joy through hope for what lies beyond this vale of tears.[14] The joy is produced also by gratitude for God's providing us in this pilgrimage with both physical and spiritual means of sustenance.

This sense of our existence as pilgrims wandering for forty years in the desert of this world is beautifully expressed in Hebrews 11:13–16:

---

[12] The feast is also described in Deut 16:13–15.

[13] This is marvelous affirmation of the communion of saints between heaven and earth.

[14] It is interesting that the book of Kohelet, which speaks of the vanity of all earthly things, is read in the synagogue on the Sabbath during the festival of Sukkot.

These [Abraham and the patriarchs] all died in faith, not having received what was promised, but having seen it and greeted it from afar, and having acknowledged that they were strangers and exiles on the earth. For people who speak thus make it clear that they are seeking a homeland. If they had been thinking of that land from which they had gone out, they would have had opportunity to return. But as it is, they desire a better country, that is, a heavenly one. Therefore God is not ashamed to be called their God, for he has prepared for them a city.

Another aspect of the ritual of Sukkot, no longer practiced, concerns water. On the morning of the first day of the feast, after the daily sacrifice and daily libation of wine, a procession went from the Temple mount to the spring of Shiloah. A priest drew the water and returned to the Temple through the Water Gate which led to the inner court. There he chanted the words of Isaiah: "With joy shall ye draw water out of the wells of salvation" (Is 12:3), and poured out the water on the altar as a libation.[15] A rabbinic commentary stated: "He who has not witnessed the joy of the water drawing has never in his life experienced real joy."[16]

This ritual had an obvious agricultural significance, for it was a prayer for rain (which in Israel occurs in winter). It also had an important historical significance, for it was associated with the miraculous water that Moses drew from the rock in the desert during the seven weeks of wandering before arriving at Mt. Sinai.

The New Testament sees this water coming from the rock as referring spiritually to Christ and His grace. St. Paul tells us in 1 Corinthians 10:4 that the rock was Christ. In John 7:37–39, Jesus speaks of this element of water in the feast of Sukkot:

On the last day of the feast, the great day, Jesus stood up and proclaimed, "If any one thirst, let him come to me and drink. He who believes in me, as the scripture has said, 'Out of his heart shall flow rivers of living water.'" Now this he said about the Spirit, which those who believed in him were to receive; for as yet the Spirit had not been given, because Jesus was not yet glorified.

In this way Jesus reveals that the inner meaning of this aspect of the feast points to man's sanctification through sanctifying grace and the gifts of the Holy Spirit—symbolized by the water drawn from the spring of Shiloah—which enable God's people to carry out and accomplish His

---

[15] See Hayyim Schauss, *The Jewish Festivals. A Guide to Their History and Observance* (New York: Schocken Books, 1996), 181.

[16] Babylonian Talmud, Tractate Sukkah 5:1–3.

Torah. They produce spiritual joy and peace of heart in God—that "joy in the Torah" (*simhat Torah*) which is celebrated on the final day of Sukkot in a feast called *Simhat Torah*.

Carnal man sees the Law of God all too often as something negative that limits our freedom and imposes a burden. However, the spiritual man rejoices in the Law of God and sees it as true freedom: freedom to do good and to walk with God. This transformation in our inner attitude to the Torah can only occur through the great gift of God's grace in our hearts, merited for mankind by the Passion of the Messiah.

The gift of the Holy Spirit is spoken of through the image of water because it is the Spirit who satisfies the thirst of the heart for God. Every man's heart secretly desires complete happiness which is only found in God, in His love and forgiveness. It can be said of every heart that it secretly yearns for the waters of grace. In the words of Psalm 42:1–5:

> As a hart longs for flowing streams,
> so longs my soul for thee, O God.
> My soul thirsts for God, for the living God.
> When shall I come and behold the face of God?
> My tears have been my food day and night,
> while men say to me continually, "Where is your God?"
> These things I remember, as I pour out my soul:
> how I went with the throng,
> and led them in procession to the house of God,
> with glad shouts and songs of thanksgiving,
> a multitude keeping festival.

Jesus spoke of this water of His grace and the gift of the Holy Spirit in His conversation with the Samaritan woman in John 4:10: "If you knew the gift of God, and who it is that is saying to you, 'Give me a drink,' you would have asked him and he would have given you living water." Not surprisingly, the woman fails to understand Jesus' meaning, thinking that He is speaking of physical water. So she asks for that. He responds: "Everyone who drinks of this water will thirst again, but whoever drinks of the water that I shall give him will never thirst; the water that I shall give will become in him a spring of water welling up to eternal life" (Jn 4:13–14). The water springing up to eternal life that Jesus gives is sanctifying grace, by which we are made sons of God in the Son, pleasing to God, and heirs of heaven. It is the water by which the thirst of our hearts for the living God is satisfied.

The water by which the Israelites were nourished in the desert was a symbol or figure of Christ and His grace. The pillar of cloud was likewise a symbol of Christ and the Holy Spirit leading us in the pilgrimage of this life, until we reach the Father and our heavenly mansion.

Sukkot and the Transfiguration of Christ

We have said that Jesus chose the feast of Passover to institute the Eucharist and offer His Body and Blood on Calvary as the Lamb of God. Is there any parallel for the feast of Sukkot in Christ's public ministry?

It is very interesting to connect the feast of Sukkot with the event narrated in the Gospels concerning the Transfiguration of Jesus on Mt. Tabor, in which Jesus appears in glory with two special guests: Moses and Elijah. Pope Benedict XVI has recently written about the relation of these two feasts in *Jesus of Nazareth*.[17] The Transfiguration of Jesus is described by Matthew as follows (Mt 17:1–8):

> And after six days Jesus took with him Peter and James and John his brother, and led them up a high mountain apart. And he was transfigured before them, and his face shone like the sun, and his garments became white as light. And behold, there appeared to them Moses and Elijah, talking with him. And Peter said to Jesus, "Lord, it is well that we are here; if you wish, *I will make three booths here, one for you and one for Moses and one for Elijah.*" He was still speaking, when lo, a bright cloud overshadowed them, and a voice from the cloud said, "This is my beloved Son, with whom I am well pleased; listen to him." When the disciples heard this, they fell on their faces, and were filled with awe. But Jesus came and touched them, saying, "Rise, and have no fear." And when they lifted up their eyes, they saw no one but Jesus only.

Peter's reference to making three booths for Jesus, Moses, and Elijah makes sense if the context of the event is the Feast of Booths. This is especially appropriate for several reasons. First of all, Sukkot has an eschatological aspect. Its commemoration of the wandering of the Israelites in the desert without a permanent abode is a figure of longing for the eternal tabernacles of the just in heaven. The Transfiguration was a glimpse of that glory of Heaven, radiating from the person of Jesus, and giving a foretaste of the glory of all the just in heaven.

Secondly, the leafy branches overhead which let through the light of the stars is a figure of the cloud that represented the special presence of God, referred to in Hebrew as the *Shekinah*. This cloud covered the tent of Meeting with the Ark of the Covenant during the wandering of the

---

[17] Joseph Ratzinger, *Jesus of Nazareth: From the Baptism in the Jordan to the Transfiguration*, trans. Adrian J. Walker (New York: Doubleday, 2007), 306–17.

Chosen People in the desert, and later it descended on the Temple in Jerusalem. As Peter, James, and John were watching, a cloud descended on Jesus as it had a millennium earlier on the Temple of Solomon, but now with a new element. The voice of God the Father is heard: "This is my beloved Son, with whom I am well pleased; listen to him."

In addition, Sukkot is a time in which one seeks to entertain heavenly guests, and here Moses and Elijah appear conversing with Jesus. It is interesting to consider what they are speaking about. According to Luke 9:31, their conversation concerned Jesus' *"exodus* which he was to accomplish in Jerusalem." The Greek word "exodus" means "departure," and clearly refers to His upcoming Passion. The use of the word "exodus" to indicate the Passion underscores the typology. Jesus is the new Moses who will pass out of the Egypt of this world, redeeming all humanity in the waters of His "Baptism"/"Exodus."

Day of Atonement (Yom Kippur)

Five days before the beginning of the feast of Sukkot, Israel celebrates the solemn Day of Atonement (*Yom Kippur*). The essential meaning of Yom Kippur concerns the imploring of God's forgiveness for sin. This was symbolized in the purifying of the sanctuary and the rite of the scapegoat. This feast is commanded in Leviticus 23:27–29:

> On the tenth day of this seventh month is the day of atonement; it shall be for you a time of holy convocation, and you shall afflict yourselves and present an offering by fire to the Lord. And you shall do no work on this same day; for it is a day of atonement, to make atonement for you before the Lord your God. For whoever is not afflicted on this same day shall be cut off from his people.

The feast had two other important elements: the rite of the scapegoat, and the solemn invocation of the sacred name of God by the High Priest in the Holy of Holies behind the veil and before the Ark of the Covenant. The holy name was pronounced only on this day. The rite of the scapegoat is described in Leviticus 16:7–22:

> Then he [Aaron] shall take the two goats, and set them before the Lord at the door of the tent of meeting; and Aaron shall cast lots upon the two goats, one lot for the Lord and the other lot for Azazel. And Aaron shall present the goat on which the lot fell for the Lord, and offer it as a sin offering; but the goat on which the lot fell for Azazel shall be presented alive before the Lord to make atonement over it, that it may be sent away into the wilderness to Azazel. . . . Then he shall kill the goat of the sin offering which is for the people, and bring its blood within the veil, and do with its

blood as he did with the blood of the bull, sprinkling it upon the mercy seat and before the mercy seat; thus he shall make atonement for the holy place, because of the uncleannesses of the people of Israel. . . . And when he has made an end of atoning for the holy place and the tent of meeting and the altar, he shall present the live goat; and Aaron shall lay both his hands upon the head of the live goat, and confess over him all the iniquities of the people of Israel, and all their transgressions, all their sins; and he shall put them upon the head of the goat, and send him away into the wilderness by the hand of a man who is in readiness. The goat shall bear all their iniquities upon him to a solitary land; and he shall let the goat go in the wilderness.

It is obvious that no goat can bear the sins of the people of Israel, and make expiation for them. This graphic image of the scapegoat is clearly a figure for the true sacrifice that expiates sin: the sacrifice of the Suffering Servant, the Passion of Jesus Christ.

Hebrews 9:6–15 explains how the sacrifices offered solemnly on Yom Kippur are but a figure of the sacrifice of Christ, the High Priest of the new and eternal covenant between God and mankind:

The priests go continually into the outer tent, performing their ritual duties; but into the second only the high priest goes, and he but once a year, and not without taking blood which he offers for himself and for the errors of the people. By this the Holy Spirit indicates that the way into the sanctuary is not yet opened as long as the outer tent is still standing (which is symbolic for the present age). According to this arrangement, gifts and sacrifices are offered which cannot perfect the conscience of the worshiper, but deal only with food and drink and various ablutions, regulations for the body imposed until the time of reformation. But when Christ appeared as a high priest of the good things that have come, then through the greater and more perfect tent (not made with hands, that is, not of this creation) he entered once for all into the Holy Place, taking not the blood of goats and calves but his own blood, thus securing an eternal redemption. For if the sprinkling of defiled persons with the blood of goats and bulls and with the ashes of a heifer sanctifies for the purification of the flesh, how much more shall the blood of Christ, who through the eternal Spirit offered himself without blemish to God, purify your conscience from dead works to serve the living God. Therefore he is the mediator of a new covenant, so that those who are called may receive the promised eternal inheritance.

Miracle of the Scarlet Thread on Yom Kippur

The Talmud and the Zohar relate that certain miracles occurred regularly on Yom Kippur in the time of the Second Temple. A scarlet thread over the door of the sanctuary would miraculously turn white, as a sign that God had found the sin-offering acceptable. This was understood in reference to Isaiah 1:18: "Though your sins are like scarlet, they shall be as white as snow." This miracle, accompanied by a miraculous continuation of the burning of the western lamp, and a miracle by which a lot for the scapegoat was always drawn in the right rather than the left hand, occurred every year during the time of a holy high priest, Simeon the Upright,[18] and only sometimes after his time. The Talmud relates:

> Our rabbis have taught on Tannaite authority: Throughout the forty years that Simeon the Righteous served as high priest, the lot would always come up in the right hand. From that time onward, sometimes it would come up in the right hand, sometimes it would come up in the left hand. And during that same span of time the crimson thread would turn white. From that time, sometimes it would turn white, sometimes it would not turn white. So long as Simeon the Righteous was alive, the Western lamp remained permanently lit. When he died, they went and found that it had gone out. From that time forward, sometimes they find it extinguished, and sometimes lit.[19]

The Zohar also relates this account, and explains that the people would rejoice when the crimson thread turned white, for they took this to indicate that their sacrifice had been accepted by God. Similarly, they would grieve when the miracle would fail to occur, taking it as a sign that their sacrifice was not accepted in heaven.[20]

The above Talmudic tractate also reports that these miracles completely ceased to occur forty years before the destruction of the Second Temple in 70 AD:

---

[18] Simeon the Righteous was high priest at the time of Alexander the Great, and the Talmud reports a meeting between the two men (313 BC), after which Alexander decided not to destroy the Temple.

[19] Yoma 39a, in Jacob Neusner, *The Babylonian Talmud: A Translation and Commentary*, vol. 5, *Tractate Yoma. Tractate Sukkah* (Peabody, MA: Hendrickson Publishers, 2005), 140–41.

[20] See the discussion of the miracle of the scarlet thread and its cessation at the time of Christ's crucifixion in Roy Schoeman, *Salvation Is from the Jews* (San Francisco: Ignatius Press, 2003), 131–32.

Our rabbis have taught on Tannaite authority: *Forty years before the destruction of the sanctuary,* the lot did not come up in the right hand, and the *thread of crimson never turned white,* and the westernmost light never shone, and the doors of the courtyard open by themselves, until Rabban Yohanan b. Zakkai rebuked them. He said, "Temple, Temple, why will you yourself give the alarm [that you are going to be destroyed? You don't have to, because] I know that in the end you are destined to be destroyed. For Zechariah . . . has already prophesied concerning you: 'Open your doors, Lebanon, that fire may devour your cedars'" (Zech 11:1).[21]

A similar account of the same miracle of the scarlet thread and its cessation is found in a different Talmudic tractate: *Rosh hashana* 31b. The context is a discussion of the same great rabbi, Yohanan ben Zakkai, who was said to have regulated the use of the crimson thread:

For it is taught on Tannaite authority: At first, [on the Day of Atonement, after the high priest performed his special worship], they would tie a crimson thread to the outside of the door of the [Temple] entrance-way. [If] it turned white, [the people] would rejoice; [if] it did not turn white, [the people] would be grieved. They ordained that they should tie it to the inside of the door of the [Temple] entrance-way, but still [the people] would peek. . . They ordained that they should tie half of it to the rock and half of it to the goat sent [to the wilderness].[22]

This tractate then questions how Rabbi Yohanan could have given this ordinance, if he taught only at the time the miracle had ceased. As it considers this question, the Talmud states: "And it is [additionally] taught on Tannaite authority: *For forty years prior to the destruction of the Temple, the crimson thread did not turn white but, rather remained red.*"[23]

The Talmud does not enter into speculation as to why God completely ceased to work this miracle forty years before the destruction of the Temple. It is presented simply as a sorrowful and humiliating fact and as a foreshadowing of the great tragedy of the destruction of the Temple which occurred in the year 70 AD. However, it is surely not coincidental that forty years before the destruction of the Temple is the date of the Crucifixion of Christ.

---

[21] Yoma 39b, in Jacob Neusner, *The Babylonian Talmud,* 5:142. My italics.

[22] Tractate Rosh Hashanah 31b, in Jacob Neusner, *The Babylonian Talmud: A Translation and Commentary,* vol. 6, *Tractate Besah. Tractate Rosh Hashanah* (Peabody, MA: Hendrickson Publishers, 2005), 195–96.

[23] Ibid., p. 196.

Both the miracle of the scarlet thread turning white and its complete cessation belong to the order of typology: events which themselves have a symbolic meaning with reference to the Paschal Mystery. The cessation of the miracle is fitting, for the sacrificial offerings of the Day of Atonement could no longer be an acceptable sacrifice to God after the Sacrifice of Christ was consummated on Calvary. Indeed, all the sacrificial offerings of humanity—including the solemn sacrifices of Yom Kippur—were but figures of that one true Sacrifice that redeemed mankind from sin by offering to God the oblation of charity of the heart of the Incarnate Son, which is more pleasing to God than all sin is displeasing.

Yom Kippur and the Confession of Peter

There is an interesting connection between the holy day of Yom Kippur and the confession of Peter in Matthew 16:16–20. In *Jesus of Nazareth*, Pope Benedict XVI endorses the suggestion made by some exegetes that the confession of Peter was made on the feast of Yom Kippur,[24] which occurs on the tenth of Tishri, five days before the feast of Sukkot. Matthew tells us that the Transfiguration of Jesus, which we have connected with the feast of Sukkot, occurred six days after the Confession of Peter. Thus, according to the Semitic reckoning of time, the confession would have occurred on the Day of Atonement.

This is deeply fitting, for Yom Kippur was the one time of the year in which the sacred name of God, the Tetragrammaton YHWH (יהוה), was pronounced by the high priest in the Temple. In Matthew 16:13–15, Jesus asks the disciples who people say that He is, and then He asks them who they say that He is. Peter answers: "You are the Christ, the Son of the living God." Peter has solemnly confessed the new name by which God has revealed Himself to mankind. The name of God is holy because it indicates the sacred reality that God is. By referring to Jesus as the Son of the living God, Peter has confessed his faith in the sacred mystery of the Trinity and the Incarnation. God is not a solitary, but is Father and Son and Holy Spirit, and the Son has become man in Jesus of Nazareth. This confession of Peter has the same sacred import as the solemn confession of the sacred name of God in the Holy of Holies on Yom Kippur.

And it is pronounced by Peter, who will be ordained High Priest of the New Covenant during the Last Supper. Interestingly, Christ then proclaims His "faith" in Peter, giving him a new name—Cephas or Rock—on whom He will build His Church. And He gives to Peter the power to forgive the iniquities of the new Israel: "I will give you the

---

[24] Joseph Ratzinger, *Jesus of Nazareth*, 306.

keys of the kingdom of heaven, and whatever you bind on earth shall be bound in heaven, and whatever you loose on earth shall be loosed in heaven." This promise thus fulfills what was prefigured in the sacrifices of Yom Kippur.

Importance of Typology

This examination of the typology of the great feasts of Israel should make it abundantly clear that Biblical typology is of crucial importance in grasping the veiled continuity of God's salvific plan, according to which the liturgy of ancient Israel—continually commemorating the Exodus—mystically foreshadows the Paschal mystery of Christ. The typological sense of Scripture binds the contents of the Old and New Testaments intimately together.[25] It also helps the doctrines to take flesh, to live within us, to appeal to our imagination, to be more memorable, to show us the unity of God's providence in history, to show us graphically that Christ and His Passion are the center and fulcrum of history around which everything revolves, and to which all is oriented in the plan of God. It is admirably suited to show God's power and adapted to our sensible and corporeal nature. The Fathers and Doctors of the Church drew heavily on this way of understanding Scripture.

It is a great shame that present-day Christians have very little familiarity with Biblical typology. Scholars pride themselves on their knowledge of history and languages, but most of them do not concern themselves with the typological sense of the Bible, where the deepest and most important meaning of the texts is found. In this respect, the generally illiterate populace of the Middle Ages was better versed in understanding Biblical typology, which fills the Gothic cathedrals and its stained glass windows, the glorious art of the Renaissance, and above all, completely permeates the liturgy of the Church. The typological sense of Scripture is beautiful and sublime precisely because it demonstrates the reality and power of God's providence over history. It shows us the presence of the finger of God in events of this world. It is a divine work of art written within history itself. However, it can only be grasped by those who have the key to the Scriptures, which is Christ and the Church, since this is the principal content of the typological sense.

---

[25] Lev 23:14 proclaims observance of the Passover to be "a statute forever in all your dwellings throughout your generations"; Lev 23:31 proclaims Yom Kippur to be "a statute forever throughout your generations"; and Lev 23:41 proclaims that Sukkot shall be "a statute forever throughout your generations." This perpetual celebration is realized (in a typological sense) insofar as these feasts are figures that are eternally fulfilled in the Sacrifice of Christ, perpetuated throughout all generations in the Holy Mass.

CHAPTER 8

The Law of Moses and Its Fulfillment in Christ

The New Law Is the Fulfillment of the Old Law

What is the status of the Law of Moses in the Messianic age, which is the time of the Church? Has it been perfected? Or has it been revoked or abrogated? If it has not been revoked, has it been changed at all? If so, in what way? and why? Obviously this is a question of the greatest importance.

Jesus addresses this fundamental question in the Sermon on the Mount, as recorded by St. Matthew. The entire Sermon is in fact an event parallel to the giving of the Law on Mt. Sinai.[1] Jesus begins with the promise of the kingdom of heaven in the Beatitudes, which are the spiritual culmination of the formulation of the law. He then addresses the question of the Law of Moses (Mt 5:17–20):

> Think not that I have come to abolish the law and the prophets; I have come not to abolish them but to fulfill them. For truly, I say to you, till heaven and earth pass away, not an iota, not a dot, will pass from the law until all is accomplished. Whoever then relaxes one of the least of these commandments and teaches men so, shall be called least in the kingdom of heaven; but he who does them and teaches them shall be called great in the kingdom of heaven. For I tell you, unless your righteousness exceeds that of the scribes and Pharisees, you will never enter the kingdom of heaven.

It is hard to imagine a more emphatic denial that Jesus intended to abrogate the Law of Moses—the Torah of Israel—so as to substitute a new Law. Rather, His New Law is ordered to the complete fulfillment of the Old Law, expressed not just in our external actions but also in our interior motivations. It aims at the heroic fulfillment of the double commandment of love, which fulfillment is sanctity.

---

[1] It is interesting to observe that Jesus chose a "mountain" that is of a very different character from that of Sinai. According to tradition, this sermon was given on a gentle and exceedingly beautiful hill overlooking the Lake of Genneseret.

131

Abrogation of the Dietary Law

It is not easy, however, to interpret this solemn affirmation of Jesus that He does not come to abrogate the Law, but to fulfill it. It is clear that the Ten Commandments are not abrogated by Jesus, for He goes on to deepen them by showing their full interior meaning. However, the kosher dietary laws and other laws of ritual purity were clearly abrogated after Christ's Resurrection and Ascension, for they would put a limit on evangelization. Such laws served a very valuable purpose in separating the Jewish people from other peoples until the coming of the Messiah. However, with His advent and the extension of the Gospel promises to all peoples, such a separation would be harmful, and prevent the Gospel from going to the Gentiles. This abrogation of the dietary laws was indicated by Jesus in the Gospel when He spoke about what makes one pure or impure (Mk 7:14–23):

> And he called the people to him again, and said to them, "Hear me, all of you, and understand: there is nothing outside a man which by going into him can defile him; but the things which come out of a man are what defile him." And when he had entered the house, and left the people, his disciples asked him about the parable. And he said to them, "Then are you also without understanding? Do you not see that whatever goes into a man from outside cannot defile him, since it enters, not his heart but his stomach, and so passes on?" (Thus he declared all foods clean.) And he said, "What comes out of a man is what defiles a man. For from within, out of the heart of man, come evil thoughts, fornication, theft, murder, adultery, coveting, wickedness, deceit, licentiousness, envy, slander, pride, foolishness. All these evil things come from within, and they defile a man."

However, the fact that Christ had declared all foods clean was not immediately clear to the Apostles, nor would it become so until several years after Christ's Resurrection. It was finally understood by St. Peter when he was called to the house of the centurion, a Gentile, after seeing a vision in which he was told to eat animals that were unclean according to the Mosaic Law (Acts 10:9–16):

> Peter went up on the housetop to pray, about the sixth hour. And he became hungry and desired something to eat; but while they were preparing it, he fell into a trance and saw the heaven opened, and something descending, like a great sheet, let down by four corners upon the earth. In it were all kinds of animals and reptiles and birds of the air. And there came a voice to him, "Rise, Peter; kill and eat." But Peter said, "No, Lord; for I have never eaten anything that is common or unclean." And the voice came to him

again a second time, "*What God has cleansed, you must not call common.*"
This happened three times, and the thing was taken up at once to
heaven.

After seeing this vision, messengers from Cornelius arrived at the
house where Peter was staying, and he went to them, preached the word
of God, after which they received the Spirit and were baptized. It can be
seen from Peter's reaction to the vision that he had never before broken
the kosher dietary laws and had never stayed in the house of a non-Jew.
This vision was necessary to make clear the full implications of the
missionary commandment to teach and baptize all nations, which Jesus
gave the Apostles before His Ascension.

The pagan centurion was baptized without needing first to be
circumcised and instructed in the Jewish ceremonial law. The same thing
occurred shortly thereafter on a larger scale in the great city of Antioch,
where many pagan converts were made. Barnabas and St. Paul
ministered to them, and later St. Peter as well. The Apostles and other
Jewish Christians shared table fellowship with the non-Jewish disciples.

However, a great turmoil later broke out when a certain branch of
the disciples (many converted from the sect of the Pharisees) began to
teach that the ceremonial law of Moses continued to bind the Jewish
Christians and even the pagan converts. This was the great and burning
issue behind the Council of Jerusalem, recounted in Acts 15.

Different Types of Law

Much light can be shed on this subject by making a distinction between
different types of laws, following St. Thomas Aquinas and the Catholic
tradition. Law is defined as an ordinance of reason, promulgated by the
legitimate authority, for the sake of the common good of society.[2] The
highest kind of law is the eternal law of God, which exists eternally in
the mind of God and orders all of creation according to the divine
wisdom.

Secondly, there is natural law, which is a participation or share in the
eternal law of God that every man discovers written in his conscience in
virtue of the gift of reason. The natural law is based on a few self-
evident principles that all men naturally know: seek good and avoid evil;
love your neighbor as yourself; do unto others as you would have them
do unto you; give to each one his due; God is to be loved above all; God
is to be obeyed; the common good is to be preferred to the private
good; etc.

---

[2] See Thomas Aquinas, *ST* I–II, q. 90, a. 4.

On the basis of these first principles, the mind naturally grasps the basic content of the Ten Commandments. The first three commandments follow from the principle that God is to be loved above all things. 1) Idol worship obviously goes against the supreme love and reverence due to God alone. 2) In order to offer the reverence due to God, His name is to be sanctified, and worship is to be given to Him. 3) In order to do so, it is necessary to set aside a time that is sacred and given to God rather than to our own secular pursuits. This is the essential meaning of the third commandment.

All of the other commandments are based on the golden rule and the principle of justice: give to each his due. The fourth commandment tells us to give to our parents a respect and honor that is due to them for having brought us into the world and educated us. That honor is a certain participation in the honor due to God.

The fifth through tenth commandments protect fundamental goods that all men naturally understand as such: life, matrimony and the family, property, and honor. The fifth commandment is based on the fundamental good of innocent human life that must always be respected in others as we would have it respected in ourselves. The sixth protects the great good of marital fidelity and intimacy, and the sanctity of marriage. The seventh protects private property, and the eighth commandment protects honor and the good name of others against false witness. The ninth and tenth commandments extend the sixth and seventh commandments to include desires of the heart.

The Ten Commandments, therefore, pertain to natural law, and can be discovered "written on the heart" of all men who come to the age of reason, as St. Paul says in Romans 2:15: "They show that what the law requires is written on their hearts, while their conscience also bears witness and their conflicting thoughts accuse or perhaps excuse them."

Below natural law, there is human positive law[3]—or civil law—which binds not because it is written on the heart, but because it has been promulgated by the legitimate authority. It depends on natural law, however, for its binding character. If a civil law is contrary to the natural law, it is not a true law.

For example, the law to drive on the right side of the road is civil law. In England, they drive on the left. Such laws depend on the general principle of natural law that commands travelers to respect the safety of all, which obviously could be put into practice in various ways. Civil law delineates a particular way that this general principle of natural law must be put into effect in a particular society.

---

[3] "Positive" here is related to the word "posit," and comes from the past participle of the Latin verb *ponere*: to lay down.

In addition to the eternal law of God, natural law, and human law, there is also divine positive law: a written law given by God. This law is twofold: the Law of Moses and the law of Jesus Christ. Furthermore, the written law of God is accompanied by an oral tradition that gives the key to interpreting the written Torah. In Judaism, this is called the oral Torah and is regarded by Jews as coming from God through Moses and the succession of sages in Israel. Catholics likewise hold that there is an authoritative oral Tradition that comes from the Messiah, the incarnate Wisdom of God, and was handed down to the Apostles and to their successors. This is called the apostolic Tradition.

A consideration of the Law of Moses brings various questions to mind. If natural law is already written on the human heart, why would God give a publicly promulgated law? Furthermore, does divine positive law reveal only the natural law, or does it add to it? For example, do the Ten Commandments correspond exactly to natural law, or include other kinds of law as well?

The first question is not difficult. Even though the moral law of God can be discovered in the human conscience and is written on the heart, we all know that conscience can be obscured and overruled, to the point where its protests are only dimly heard. Conscience can also err, due to rationalization or ignorance.

Furthermore, since man is a social creature, we need the moral law proclaimed in a social way, so that it may form the fabric of society. Human law serves this function, and it proclaims in words what is already understood by the human heart: thou shalt not steal, etc. However, since God is the supreme Governor of all human society, it is fitting that He too should promulgate the moral Law of which He is the supreme and first Author. In this way, the moral law will be free from error, and proclaimed with an authority that commands the obedience of every man. Thus it was very fitting for God to promulgate the Ten Commandments to Israel on Mt. Sinai, and it was a great gift to mankind.

Does the Torah simply correspond to the natural law written on the hearts of all men? The Ten Commandments contain the essence of the natural law, and set it forth in a perfect manner, in perfect order, in a way worthy of God. In the third commandment, however, a particular day of the week is singled out for giving worship to God. What pertains to natural law is that some time be singled out as sacred to God. The particular day on which it is done does not pertain to natural law as such, and cannot be said to be written on the human heart. A similar example regards the prohibition of eating pork, which cannot be said to be written on the heart of man. The same is true of all the commandments concerning the special feasts of Israel, the particular way they were to conduct divine worship, and the laws regarding ritual purity.

These laws are referred to by St. Thomas Aquinas and the Catholic tradition as ceremonial laws. They have a basis in the natural law, which commands us to worship God with special tokens of honor and to separate what is sacred from what is profane. However, the particular ways in which this is to be realized are not directly dictated by the natural law, and thus they have a certain contingent quality which needs to be determined by positive law.

There are other laws in the books of Moses which neither belong directly to the natural law, nor to the ceremonial law, but which likewise have their basis in the natural law. Such laws contain particular ways of realizing the natural law by setting up particular penalties and judicial procedures. St. Thomas Aquinas refers to such precepts as "judicial";[4] they are like the precepts of human civil law, but mandated by God for Israel.

A good example of judicial precepts is found in Exodus 21:12–21:

> Whoever strikes a man so that he dies shall be put to death. But if he did not lie in wait for him, but God let him fall into his hand, then I will appoint for you a place to which he may flee. . . . Whoever strikes his father or his mother shall be put to death. Whoever steals a man . . . shall be put to death. Whoever curses his father or his mother shall be put to death.

The basis for these laws is obviously the fourth and fifth commandments. However, the particular punishment cannot be said to be written on man's heart. Such punishments and judicial procedures were given by God for a particular type of society in the course of human history.

Can the Law of God Change?

If God gives a law, could it change, or even be entirely abrogated? One might be tempted to think that a law given by God, who is eternal,

---

[4] St. Thomas Aquinas distinguishes the three kinds of precepts in *ST* I–II, q. 99, a. 4: "We must therefore distinguish three kinds of precept in the Old Law; viz. '*moral*' precepts, which are dictated by the natural law; '*ceremonial*' precepts, which are determinations of the Divine worship; and '*judicial*' precepts, which are determinations of the justice to be maintained among men. Wherefore the Apostle (Rom 7:12) after saying that the 'Law is holy,' adds that 'the commandment is just, and holy, and good': 'just,' in respect of the judicial precepts; 'holy,' with regard to the ceremonial precepts (since the word 'sanctus'—'holy'—is applied to that which is consecrated to God); and 'good,' i.e. conducive to virtue, as to the moral precepts."

should likewise be eternal. Does God "change His mind"? Of course not. However, that does not mean that God's laws governing mankind could not be subject to a change eternally decreed in the mind of God. After all, we give different laws and different penalties to children and to adults, for they need to be treated differently. Thus it would not be inappropriate for God to give different laws to mankind in different periods of human history and salvation history.

To better understand this question, let us take a closer look at the different categories of law mentioned above: natural, ceremonial, and judicial. The natural law itself is unchangeable, for it rests on the very nature of man. Reason naturally grasps the first principles of the moral life, such as the golden rule and the principle of justice (to give to each their due). The precepts of the natural law are necessary conclusions based on these first principles, and thus they are not subject to change. This is the case of the Ten Commandments (if we except the particular day of the week commanded in the third commandment). They bound mankind before the giving of the Law on Mt. Sinai, and will continue to do so until the end of time. Jesus did not change these precepts, but perfectly fulfilled them in His own person and perfectly taught them by word and example.

However, the ceremonial and the judicial precepts are intrinsically subject to change, for they depend on particular historical circumstances. It is easy to see that judicial precepts could require modification. Penalties can vary in different contexts so as to best preserve the intent of the Law, which is to promote justice. As a society changes, what was formerly beneficial in particular judicial precepts can become less beneficial and in need of modification.

The Catholic teaching on the death penalty reflects this awareness that social and historical circumstances change the types of penalties that should be imposed for different crimes. For example, the *Catechism of the Catholic Church* 2267 states:

> Assuming that the guilty party's identity and responsibility have been fully determined, the traditional teaching of the Church does not exclude recourse to the death penalty, if this is the only possible way of effectively defending human lives against the unjust aggressor.
>
> If, however, non-lethal means are sufficient to defend and protect people's safety from the aggressor, authority will limit itself to such means, as these are more in keeping with the concrete conditions of the common good and are more in conformity to the dignity of the human person.
>
> Today, in fact, as a consequence of the possibilities which the state has for effectively preventing crime, by rendering one who

has committed an offense incapable of doing harm—without definitely taking away from him the possibility of redeeming himself—the cases in which the execution of the offender is an absolute necessity "are very rare, if not practically non-existent."

Can ceremonial precepts also change? Ceremonial precepts—of which liturgical rites are the principal part—are symbolic, containing sacred signs that commemorate the great events in salvation history. The ceremonial precepts of the Law of Moses in large part commemorate the events of the Exodus and prefigure the sacrifice of the Messiah.

It is fitting that there be a change of ceremonial law to commemorate the events of the new Exodus and the New Covenant established by God with the new Israel in the Blood of the Messiah. Thus the ceremonial law of the new Israel centers on the seven sacraments instituted by Christ to give grace through the merits of the Blood He shed for us on Calvary. Christ instituted a new priesthood to continue His own High Priestly office as the one perfect Mediator between God and man. This new priesthood requires a new ceremonial law, as stated in Hebrews 7:12: "For when there is a change in the priesthood, there is necessarily a change in the law as well."

Does Jesus Place the Law and the Gospel in Opposition?

In traditional Lutheran thought, Law and Gospel are opposed. The Old Covenant gave us the Law with its burden of culpability, and Jesus gives us the Gospel which frees us from the incrimination of the Law through the forgiveness of sins. The purpose of the Law according to Luther is simply to condemn us by showing that we have not been able to keep it and are therefore in need of redemption. Thus the opposition between Jesus and Moses becomes extreme.

This is not the complete Catholic understanding, nor is it compatible with Matthew 5:17–20. The Catholic tradition sees the Law of God as good—incredibly good—but nevertheless above the strength of natural man to accomplish. Therefore, the principal work of the Redeemer is to give us the grace to be able to accomplish the Law of God ever more perfectly. He does this by giving us charity, for it is charity that accomplishes the Law.

How Does Jesus Fulfill the Law?

The Moral Law

It is above all the moral law that Jesus said that He came not to abrogate, but to fulfill. He fulfilled it by perfectly carrying out the double commandment of love.[5] This can be seen in all the acts of His life, but most especially in His Passion, in which He shed all His Blood and suffered utmost humiliation and pain in order to reconcile mankind with God and restore the glory of His Father which is trampled upon by every human sin. In Christ's earthly life, the moral law received an infinitely perfect accomplishment.

Jesus fulfills the Law also in us, His Mystical Body, by giving us the grace to put it in practice, if we correspond to that grace. He fulfills it also by giving His Church an infallible living teaching office that can determine, in His name, all questions regarding the moral law throughout human history. This Magisterium can treat issues that no one dreamed of 2,000 years ago, such as in-vitro fertilization, cloning, embryonic stem cell research, etc.

The Ceremonial Law

Although Jesus established a new ceremonial law consisting principally in the sacraments of the Church and the liturgy, He perfectly fulfilled the ceremonial law of the Old Covenant precisely by realizing in His Person what was symbolized in that Law. He Himself was the true Paschal Lamb, the true holocaust, sin-offering, peace-offering, the true offering of the firstborn, the first fruit of the Resurrection, the Blood of the Covenant, the scapegoat, the living water, the true High Priest, the true Temple of God, etc.

Judicial Precepts

It is interesting and significant that Jesus does not legislate judicial precepts in the New Testament. This is left to particular societies. An example of this can be seen in His forgiveness of the woman caught in adultery. What Jesus comes to offer mankind is not a new judicial code of precepts similar to what is found in the books of Moses, but rather a sacramental office of forgiveness.

One case in which one might think that He does enter into this type of legislation concerns marriage. As we know, Jesus rescinds the right to divorce given in the Law of Moses. Is this a judicial precept? Not really. His intervention consists in restoring the natural law concerning marriage to its original intent and integrity. Divorce had been allowed under the Law of Moses as a kind of dispensation given "for the hardness of men's hearts."

---

[5] Deut 6:5 with Lev 19:18. For a Thomistic explanation on how Christ fulfills the three types of precepts in the Mosaic Law, see Matthew Levering, *Christ's Fulfillment of Torah and Temple: Salvation according to Thomas Aquinas* (Notre Dame, IN: University of Notre Dame Press, 2002), 54–66.

The fact that the New Law of Christ does not contain judicial precepts is a consequence of the fact that the Kingdom inaugurated by Christ is not intended to be a theocracy like that of the Davidic kingship in Israel. The Church is a spiritual society that does not claim to usurp temporal power and offer a new civil code. This can be seen in the saying of Jesus: "Give unto Caesar what is Caesar's, and give unto God what is God's."

Nevertheless, the Church does aid civil societies to institute just judicial precepts, through her Magisterium, which authoritatively teaches also on social issues. The social doctrine of the Church has great light to shed on the principles that should govern the temporal order. This is one way in which the Church is a "light to the Gentiles."[6]

Thus Christ fulfills the Law by accomplishing the moral law perfectly in His own person and by assisting men through His grace to do so as well; He fulfills the ceremonial law because He is the reality to which the old rites referred; and He fulfills the judicial law through the Church, to which He has given the infallible power to judge moral issues and thus to be a light for the governing of nations.

Christians Can Learn from Jewish Reverence for the Torah

One of the most beautiful things about Orthodox Judaism, in my view, is the reverence and gratitude of Jews for the gift of the Law, or Torah. The word "Torah" is understood by Jews to be one of the most beautiful words in Hebrew language and culture. Another such word is "mitzvah," which means commandment. The fulfilling of the commandments is seen to be a *good deed*, as indeed it is.

Can we say the same about our Western Christian culture? Are the words "law" and "commandment" seen to be among the most beautiful in our languages? Is it not rather the opposite? Do not these words bring to the minds of most people the idea of a burden, something imposed upon us that limits and restricts our freedom? We often think of the relationship between God's law and our freedom as a kind of battle between conflicting wills. The reality, of course, should be exactly the opposite. The law of God is a gift enabling our freedom to achieve the goal we naturally desire: perfect happiness and fulfillment, which in

---

[6] See Joseph Ratzinger, *Jesus of Nazareth*, 118: "Concrete juridical and social forms and political arrangements are no longer treated as a sacred law that is fixed *ad litteram* for all times and so for all peoples. The decisive thing is the underlying communion of will with God given by Jesus. It frees men and nations to discover what aspects of political and social order accord with this communion of will and so to work out their own juridical arrangements."

fact can only lie in knowing and loving God and living in conformity with His adorable will.

The proper relationship between freedom and God's law is a key point for human life. Our freedom is made possible by our ability to order means to ends, and is for the sake of our true final end. In order to arrive at our end, we need to be guided by the eternal law of God. Our freedom, therefore, has an intrinsic need of the moral law to guide it to our naturally desired end. Freedom of choice would not be a blessing but the cause of ruin were it not accompanied by light to see the good and the strength to choose it even when it is seen to involve sacrifice. The light to see the good comes from our natural capacity to grasp natural law, and is strengthened both by the Revelation of God's Law in the Old and New Testaments and through the gift of grace.

This relationship between freedom and law or truth has become particularly obscured in contemporary society. The correct presentation of this fundamental relationship is therefore an urgent need of the new evangelization. We tend to see freedom as a "freedom-from," whereas true freedom should always be understood as a "freedom-for." Freedom is given to us so that we can freely choose to live according to God's law and thus achieve the fulfillment of our being and perfect happiness in God.

The relationship between freedom and law can also be stated in terms of the relationship between freedom and truth, for the law of God states the *truth* about the way to live rightly and achieve our sublime end, which is total happiness in God. In the eighth chapter of the Gospel of John, Jesus has a conversation with the crowd, which centers on the true meaning of freedom and bondage, and the relation of freedom and truth: "Jesus then said to the Jews who believed in him, 'If you continue in my word, you are truly my disciples, and you will know the truth, and the truth will make you free'" (Jn 8:31–32).

There is a fundamental link between freedom and truth. Truth alone has the power to liberate man. Falsehood and vice bind man, destroying his liberty. Jesus is speaking here about the full truth about man and God, the truth of Revelation. That truth sets man free first of all because it shows man his most exalted end and the means that lead there. Man is liberated to achieve what he already desires by nature: complete happiness, which can only lie in union with God.

The crowd took exception to Jesus' saying that "the truth will make you free" because it seemed to imply that they were not yet free. So they responded:

> "We are descendants of Abraham, and have never been in bondage to anyone. How is it that you say, 'You will be made free?'" Jesus

answered them, "Truly, truly, I say to you, everyone who commits sin is a slave to sin. The slave does not continue in the house for ever; the son continues for ever. So if the Son makes you free, you will be free indeed."[7]

Just as truth liberates man, so sin and falsehood enslave man. This may seem paradoxical, for sin is a product and an exercise of human freedom. How can the exercise of freedom enslave someone?

Enslavement by sin has several levels of meaning. Sin enslaves in the sense that it engenders vice which results in the constant strengthening of disordered passions. These disordered passions seduce the will with increasing power as the vice develops. Thus it becomes ever harder to resist the disordered passion in order to avoid sin. One has become a slave of that particular passion, in bondage to it. This is particularly evident in the case of addictions. One is enslaved to the object of the addiction, even though one would very much like to be free of it.

Sin enslaves also because it brings man down to the animal level, in that it makes him respond more to his passions than to his reason. However, it is precisely by virtue of reason that man is free. By reducing the efficacy of reason with respect to passion, sin brings man into the bondage of irrational passion.

Finally, sin enslaves in that it makes it impossible for the will to attain its natural desire, which is true happiness. Only communion with God can make a man happy; sin separates him from that end.

It is in this sense that we should read the texts from the Old Testament that thank and praise God for giving us His Law of truth which sets us free. An example of this is Psalm 119, which is a lengthy hymn of thanksgiving for the gift of the Torah, an expression of delight in it, petition for the grace to keep it faithfully, and sorrow over its transgression: "My eyes shed streams of tears because men transgress thy law."[8]

Another beautiful example is Psalm 147:12–20, in which Israel is urged to praise God for the unique privilege of receiving the gift of the Torah, for the Lord "has not dealt thus with any other nation; they do not know his ordinances. Praise the Lord!" (Ps 147:20).

Another eloquent hymn of praise for the Torah is found in Psalm 19:7–10, in which the Psalmist says that the law of the Lord is perfect, certain, true, pure, eternal, more precious than gold, and sweeter than honey.

---

[7] Jn 8:33–36.
[8] Ps 119:136.

Let us ask God for appreciation of the Law of God in the spirit of the Psalmist, and in the spirit of Jesus Christ who shows us the way to keep the double commandment of love "to the end" (Jn 13:1), and gives us the grace to do so through the sacraments of the Church.

CHAPTER 9

The Prayer of Israel and the Prayer of the Church

In this chapter we will look at Jewish and Christian prayer, examining the nature of prayer in general, and then looking at the continuity between Jewish and Christian prayer, and what distinguishes them.

The Nature of Prayer

"Prayer is the raising of one's mind and heart to God or the requesting of good things from God,"[1] conversing with Him intimately. St. Teresa of Avila has given a beautiful definition: "For mental prayer in my opinion is nothing else than an intimate sharing between friends: it means *taking time frequently to be alone with him who we know loves us.*"[2]

Prayer presupposes some level of faith, hope, and charity. We cannot pray unless we believe that God hears our prayer, and we would not pray unless we hoped in God to attain to true happiness in Him. Faith and hope lead to charity by which we come to love God for Himself, for His majesty and love. The greater the faith, hope, and charity, the greater the power of prayer. However, we need to pray for these gifts, for they cannot be acquired by human effort.

Charity is essentially a love of friendship for God, as the Spouse and Beloved of our soul. Friendship is a mutual love of benevolence, which means to will the good for another for their own sake. We can have a love of friendship with God because He has taken the first step and revealed Himself to us as our Father, Redeemer, and divine Spouse.

As we know from our human experience, love of friendship needs to be nourished by frequent contact and conversation. This is no less true of the love of friendship with God, and this is the primary reason for prayer. Without frequent contact and conversation, friendship grows weak and dies. Thus without frequent prayer, charity languishes and dies, and gives way to more profane loves.

---

[1] St. John Damascene, *De fide orthodoxa* 3.24, *PG* 94:1089C, quoted in *CCC* 2590.

[2] St. Teresa of Avila, *The Life of Teresa of Jesus* (Garden City, NY: Image Books, 1960), 8.5.

144

This is the most fundamental meaning of the Sabbath: a time set aside for God, the liturgy, prayer, and the Word of God. Friendship with God cannot be maintained without dedicating time to Him and speaking with Him in the liturgy and in the heart.

The Four Aspects of Prayer: Adoration, Thanksgiving, Petition, and Sacrifice (*penance*)

Jewish tradition and Catholic doctrine identify four essential purposes of prayer: adoration, thanksgiving, petition, and penance (which involves confession and sacrifice). All four of these bind us to God, and this bond is the essence of religion.

Our first duty to God is to adore Him for His divine majesty and holiness. Adoration is our response to who God is in Himself. By adoration we join with the angels in the celestial liturgy as they proclaim: "Holy, holy, holy is the Lord of hosts; the whole earth is full of His glory" (Is 6:6). The psalms, the prophets, and the Jewish and Christian liturgies are full of prayer of adoration.

Our second duty is to thank Him for all the gifts we have received in creation and in the sanctification of our souls. The psalms constantly exhort us to "give thanks to the Lord for He is good, and His mercy endures forever" (Ps 136:1). This psalm goes on to thank God for all His works in favor of Israel. Another beautiful prayer of thanksgiving is Psalm 92, which begins: "It is good to give thanks to the Lord, to sing praises to thy name, O Most High; to declare thy steadfast love in the morning, and thy faithfulness by night." Psalm 119 gives thanks for the gift of the Torah in 176 verses.

The duty of thanksgiving is beautifully expressed in the Passover liturgy in which fifteen favors of God to Israel are commemorated with the refrain, *Dayyenu* ("it would have been enough"), which dramatically emphasizes the complete gratuitousness of every step in God's work of salvation:

> God has bestowed many favors upon us.
> Had He brought us out of Egypt, and not executed judgments
>   against the Egyptians, it would have been enough—Dayyenu....
> Had He satisfied our needs in the desert for forty years, and not
>   fed us the manna, it would have been enough—Dayyenu.
> Had He fed us the manna, and not given us the Sabbath, it would
>   have been enough—Dayyenu.
> Had He given us the Sabbath, and not brought us to Mount Sinai,
>   it would have been enough—Dayyenu.
> Had He brought us to Mount Sinai, and not given us the Torah, it
>   would have been enough—Dayyenu.

Had He given us the Torah, and not brought us into Israel, it
would have been enough—Dayyenu.
Had He brought us into Israel, and not built the Temple for us, it
would have been enough—Dayyenu.

We have seen that the Exodus was fundamentally a figure of the
spiritual exodus and liberation from sin worked by Christ in the Paschal
mystery. If such thanks were given for the temporal liberation that is a
figure, how much greater is our obligation to give thanks for the
Redemption worked by the Passion of Christ. Catholics could continue
the recitation by repeating the refrain for each step of the Paschal
mystery:

If God had given us the Incarnation, but not the example of His
life—Dayyenu.
If God had given us the example of the life of the Messiah, but He
had not died for us—Dayyenu.
If Christ had died for us, but not risen gloriously from the dead—
Dayyenu.
If Christ had risen, but not ascended into heaven—Dayyenu.
If Christ had ascended into heaven but not sent the Holy Spirit on
Pentecost—Dayyenu.
If Christ had sent the Holy Spirit, but had not founded a Church
on the rock of Peter—Dayyenu.
If Christ had founded the Church on the rock of Peter, but not
given us Mary to be our Mother in the order of grace—
Dayyenu.
If Christ had given us Mary to be our Mother, but had not
instituted the blessed sacrament of the Eucharist—Dayyenu.
Since God in His great mercy has done all these things, how great
our need to give thanks.

Prayer of thanksgiving and prayer of adoration are intimately
connected, for all the gifts for which we thank God manifest His glory
and thus incite adoration. In other words, it is natural to move from
thanksgiving for God's gifts to praise for His glory and mercy
manifested by those gifts, and vice versa.

The third purpose of prayer is petition: to ask God for help in all
our needs. This is also a duty which gives glory to God, for it shows
Him to be the Giver of all good gifts, whose aid must be constantly
invoked. Petition shows us the truth about who God is and who we are.
The psalms are full of petitionary prayer: "Be pleased, O God, to deliver
me! O Lord, make haste to help me!"(Ps 70:1). "Out of the depths I cry
to Thee, O Lord! Lord, hear my voice! Let thy ears be attentive to the
voice of my supplications!" (Ps 130:1–2).

Our fourth duty of prayer is to confess our sin and to seek to appease God through the offering of sacrifice. In the Law of Moses, this was done through all the myriad sacrifices prescribed in the Law, and through the confession of sin to God. Psalm 51:17 states this beautifully: "The sacrifice acceptable to God is a broken spirit; a broken and contrite heart, O God, thou wilt not despise."[3]

All four of these purposes of prayer are constantly evident in the prayer of Israel as we see it in the Old Testament. Today the element of ritual sacrifice is no longer present in Jewish prayer, not through any heresy or deviation, but simply because the Temple in Jerusalem has been destroyed, and the Law ordains that all sacrifice be offered in the Temple.

These four purposes of prayer are united in the most admirable way in the Eucharist, and in the Our Father, as we shall see below.

Jewish Prayer and Pagan Prayer

How does Jewish prayer as we see it in the Old Testament and as it continues today, relate to the prayer of the Church, and to the prayer of those outside both the Church and the synagogue? This is a difficult question.

Prayer is a universal human phenomenon, found wherever we find man. The pagan peoples surrounding Israel also prayed, and we find prayer—consisting in adoration, thanksgiving, sacrifice, and petition—in every human culture. These four aspects of prayer are something due from man to God, and thus prayer pertains to natural law, and its necessity is written on the human heart, as are the commandments to honor our parents, not to kill or steal, etc. The *Catechism of the Catholic Church* 2566 states this beautifully: "Even after losing through his sin his likeness to God, man remains an image of his Creator, and retains the desire for the one who calls him into existence. All religions bear witness to man's essential search for God."

Insofar as the human mind can grasp that the world has a Creator and Governor, we can know that a supreme reverence must be shown to Him, special thanks are to be given, petitions addressed to Him, and sacrifice offered for the forgiveness of sins.

However, for the peoples to whom God has not revealed Himself, all this is done as by an orphan who does not know the face of his father or mother, and thus pagan prayer generally involves great ignorance, error, and distance from God. Let us look at three great deformations of prayer in the pagan world: idolatry, pantheism, and the distortion of the face of God.

---

[3] See also Ps 32:5.

Within polytheistic religions, cult is given to the various gods to obtain temporal benefits for man. To each kind of particular temporal benefit there corresponds a particular deity to whom sacrifice is offered and to whom petition is addressed. In such a context, man's relation to God is not marked by love and total gift of self, but by self-interest, division of attention, and multiplicity. Man's relation to God would be like that of a king to his harem. The multiplicity of idols worshipped in the temple tends to correspond to the multiplicity of idols of temporal interest in the heart. Without recognition of the oneness of God, there can be no complete oblation of love given to God for His own sake.

The second deformation of pagan prayer is typical of Eastern religions—pantheism—according to which God is everything, and no ultimate distinction is made between God and the world. In such a context, prayer is not directed to a Person, to God our Father and Creator, but to the All of which we are simply a part. Pantheism aspires to a false and impossible mysticism, seeking a total oneness without maintaining the distinction between man and God, between the lover and the Beloved. Prayer is no longer a dialogue between two lovers, but a monologue between the self and the self. It aspires to an inner silence in which all duality is extinguished. This is not the goal of Jewish or Christian prayer, which is essentially a loving *dialogue*, even when it takes place in the deepest silence.

A third deformation of pagan prayer occurs when God is represented as bloodthirsty or tyrannical, like the gods of the Aztecs, rather than the God of infinite Love and Mercy.

Israel was preserved from these deformations of prayer by God's Revelation to them. His Chosen People were taught to pray not as orphans to an unknown father, but as children adopted by God Himself, who revealed Himself as Love, and as seeking love from His people, which He required from them as their most fundamental duty. Instead of the multiplicity of idols, Israel received the great revelation of the oneness of God. Instead of pantheism, Israel was instructed to pray as children to their Father, and as brides to the heavenly Bridegroom.

This awesome privilege of Israel is summarized above all in the great text of the *Shema Yisrael*, recited morning and evening by the devout Jew: "Hear, O Israel: The Lord our God is one Lord; and you shall love the Lord your God with all your heart, and with all your soul, and with all your might" (Deut 6:4–5).

It is not insignificant that the revelation of the oneness of God is the foundation of the great commandment to love God with all our heart, mind, and soul. Only in the recognition of His oneness do we clearly see Him as the absolute and total source of all goodness and being, and the one and only final end, the supreme good, infinite Love, who merits all our love in return. Only in the recognition of the oneness of God does our life gain a unity in direction to love and serve Him.

Polytheism represents the gods as powers that can satisfy the needs of men. The cult of the gods is ultimately directed to the advantage of men, and not to the love of the gods above all things! I cannot imagine that Zeus and his kin could have been loved with all the heart, mind, and soul of their devotees. They did not claim to be *the source* of all goodness and being, infinite love, and thus infinitely loveable. Quite the contrary. It follows that polytheism logically makes true charity with regard to God (love of God above all things for His own sake) incomprehensible and impossible. The same thing is true today of New Age religiosity. The worship of powers and forces is always directed to self, and can never provide the basis for true charity.

We can never overemphasize the privilege received by the Chosen People to be able to address God in prayer on the basis of His Revelation as the one God who created the world out of love for man, who intervenes in history for the sake of man's salvation, and who seeks the oblation of our hearts, minds, and souls.

The prayer of Israel was thus a prayer rooted in the three theological virtues of faith, hope, and charity. It was rooted in faith, for it was based on belief in God's Revelation to His people, in His fidelity to His covenant of love, and in His intervention in the history of Israel.

It is a prayer based on hope in a final redemption, in which God's kingdom shall be definitively established through the work of the Messiah, a new Moses. We can see this hope, for example, in the beautiful prayer of the priest Zechariah, father of John the Baptist (Lk 1:68–79).

The prayer of Israel is also a prophetic prayer in which the voice of the Messiah is heard. We hear the prayer of the Messiah above all in the canticles of the Suffering Servant, and in many psalms, such as Psalm 22, which begins "My God, my God, why have you abandoned me?" and Psalm 40:6–8: "Sacrifice and offering thou dost not desire, but thou hast given me an open ear. Burnt offering and sin offering thou hast not required. Then I said, 'Lo, I come; in the roll of the book it is written of me; I delight to do thy will, O my God; thy law is within my heart.'" In the Letter to the Hebrews 10:5–10, this psalm is applied to Christ in the moment of the Incarnation, and is interpreted as Christ giving consent to His Passion, for that is the will of God that He comes into the world to accomplish.

It is, finally, a prayer of charity, for its ultimate aim is the glorification of God, for the sake of His holy name. A great example of this is the Song of Songs, recited by devout Jews to bring in the Sabbath.

The Song of Songs is essentially a love song in which the bride is Israel (collectively and individually) and the bridegroom is God.

Jewish Prayer and the Prayer of the Church: Continuity

Let us look now at the differences between the prayer of Israel under the Old Covenant, and prayer under the New. Are these differences, we may wonder, as marked as those between pagan peoples and Israel? Certainly not. There is a fundamental continuity, but also a very important novelty.

The fundamental continuity is that the prayer of Israel continues to be the prayer of the Church, in the sense that the Church assumes the prayer of the Old Testament unchanged. She continues to speak to God using the Psalms and other texts of the Old Testament, which form the bulk of the Divine Office of the Church.

There are countless testimonies to this fundamental continuity throughout history. The first Christians continued to pray in the Temple and take part in the Jewish liturgy, as we see from the Acts of the Apostles. In his letter to the Corinthians, Pope Clement I, who was the third successor of Peter in Rome, constantly quotes the Old Testament and concludes with a beautiful liturgical prayer deeply rooted in the liturgy of Israel.

In modern times, an interesting testimony is given by St. Edith Stein. After her conversion she visited her mother and would go with her to the synagogue, during which she followed the Hebrew psalms in her Latin Breviary. Her mother was amazed to find so many Jewish prayers in a Catholic prayer book![4]

The *Catechism of the Catholic Church* speaks of the perennial value of the Psalms in strong terms:

> The Psalter is the book in which the Word of God becomes man's prayer. . . . The words of the Psalmist, sung for God, both express and acclaim the Lord's saving works; the same Spirit inspires both God's work and man's response. Christ will unite the two. In him, the psalms continue to teach us how to pray.[5] . . . The Psalms constitute the masterwork of prayer in the Old Testament.[6] . . . Prayed and fulfilled in Christ, the Psalms are an essential and

---

4 See Waltraud Herbstrith, *Edith Stein: A Biography*, trans. B. Bonowitz (San Francisco: Ignatius Press, 1992), 74.

5 *CCC* 2587.

6 *CCC* 2596.

permanent element of the prayer of the Church. They are suitable for men of every condition and time.[7]

The "Our Father" as a Summary of What We Should Seek in Prayer

The Lord's Prayer is a beautiful example of the continuity between the prayer of Israel and the Church, for there is nothing in the Lord's Prayer that essentially differs from the prayer of Israel under the Old Covenant. On the contrary, it stands as a perfect summary of it.

The invocation to God as our Father is common to many Jewish prayers, for the fatherhood of God marks Israel's most fundamental privilege.[8] As we have seen, Israel was adopted as God's people, in preparation for the Incarnation of Christ. Their adoption as sons was intimately linked to the future Incarnation of God's natural Son. In fact, the Son of God was made man so that men could become sons and daughters of God. We can invoke God as our Father because He has adopted us through sanctifying grace, giving us a mysterious share in the divine nature.

A Jewish prayer which petitions God as "Our Father, our King," was written by Rabbi Akiba in the early second century: "Our Father, our King, we have no king but you; our Father, our King, have mercy upon us for Your own sake!" Today a lengthier version is sung as a prayer of petition in services from Rosh Hashana to Yom Kippur.

Seven petitions in perfect order form the rest of the Our Father. The first petition, like the first commandment, concerns the sanctification or glorification of the name of God. We are taught to pray first and foremost that the glory due to God be given to Him, for His name's sake.

God has created all things to manifest His goodness and glory, and so it is fitting that all things serve to give glory to God. We pray here that the very goal of the universe be accomplished. And it is above all in the human heart that this goal of the sanctification of God's name is to be realized. We pray that our heart and every human heart unite to give glory to God above all.

The glorification of the name of God is the central theme of one of the classic Jewish prayers, the Kaddish, recited in the daily liturgy: "Exalted and sanctified is God's great name, in the world which He has created according to His will."

---

[7] *CCC* 2597.

[8] See, for example, Ex 4:22: "Say to Pharaoh, 'Thus says the Lord, Israel is my first-born son. . . . Let my son go that he may serve me.'" See also Deut 32:6, Is 63:16, Is 64:8, Jer 3:4, Jer 3:19, and Mal 2:10.

But how are we to glorify God's name? We know the weakness of our own prayer and of our own human efforts. The sanctification of God's name must be accomplished through the work of God. Thus the second petition is for the kingdom of God, a kingdom in which God's name will be perfectly sanctified.

Jewish prayer is full of invocations for the establishment of God's kingdom. The Kaddish continues: "May He establish His kingdom during your life and during your days, and during the life of all of Israel." As in the Our Father, this refers to the Messianic kingdom.

It is true that the prayer for God's kingdom was not infrequently misunderstood as a kingdom in an overly temporal sense: the reestablishment of Israel as a sovereign state as in the time of King David. This is a perennial temptation of the human spirit. Similarly in our times, Marxism, socialism, and liberation theology have inspired a desire for the kingdom of God conceived as a reform of certain social structures rather than a reform of the human heart by grace.

We pray here for God to reign in us—as individuals and as societies—so that God's name will be sanctified in us. This reign of God has to be principally a reign of interior grace, by which our hearts are moved to conform to God's law and will, for this is what sanctifies God's name. The kingdom of God must be primarily interior and invisible, as Jesus says in Luke 17:21.[9]

This leads us to the next petition: Thy will be done on earth as it in heaven. The kingdom of God in us, by which we can glorify God's name, consists in the conformity of our wills with the will of God, as expressed in His eternal Law. Conformity with God's will is the very soul of the Torah, God's great gift to Israel. The Jew prays for his soul to be opened to God's Law. Conformity of our wills with God's holy will is likewise the essence of sanctity.

God's will is made known to us in four principal ways: (1) through God's commandments, (2) through the evangelical counsels, the Beatitudes, and the example of Christ; (3) through the inspirations of the Holy Spirit in our hearts in prayer, (4) through the events of our lives in which God's providence is made manifest. Nevertheless, the commandments have a primacy, and the other three means of knowing God's will always lead us to a more perfect realization of the commandments, especially the double commandment of love.

And how are we to gain the strength to conform our will to God's will? This leads us to the next petition: "Give us this day our daily

---

[9] Being asked by the Pharisees when the kingdom of God was coming, he answered them, "The kingdom of God is not coming with signs to be observed; nor will they say, 'Lo, here it is!' or 'There!' for behold, the kingdom of God is in the midst of you [or: within you]."

bread." This petition can be interpreted in two senses: (a) as referring to our temporal needs, symbolized in the gift of bread, and (b) as referring to our spiritual needs, which are filled through the gift of the Eucharist, the bread from heaven. I would say that the principal meaning is the second, although without excluding the first. Above all, we need spiritual food, and God has supplied us in a superabundant way by giving us the Body of Christ as our spiritual nourishment in the Eucharist. It is only through the grace given to us in the Eucharist that we are made able to glorify God's name, that His Kingdom may be realized in us, and that His will be accomplished in our lives.

What else do we need from God beside temporal and spiritual nourishment? Above all, we need the forgiveness of sins, which is made contingent on our forgiveness of the sins of our neighbors against us. This is the great theme of Yom Kippur: prayer for the forgiveness of sins.

The sixth petition—lead us not into temptation—asks that God not permit us to be ensnared by the devil, as were Adam and Eve in the Fall. We do not pray that we be spared trials, for this is impossible, but that we not be allowed to fall into the trap and be taken.

Finally, the petition that we be delivered from evil is common to the Jewish liturgy. Here we pray for freedom from all evils that have afflicted mankind since the Fall, and ultimately we pray for the fullness of God's kingdom in heaven where all evil shall be banished forever.

The entire prayer of the Our Father is profoundly Jewish—a perfect summary of Jewish prayer, and a model for all Christian prayer.

Jewish Prayer and the Prayer of the Church: Distinction

Let us look now at the distinction of Christian prayer from that of the synagogue. I would say that there are fundamentally three differences. One is that the Gentiles have been introduced into the prayer of Israel in the Church. The sanctification of God's name, the adoption as sons, the incorporation into God's kingdom, the quest for conformity with God's will, the forgiveness of sins, the power not to be ensnared by the deceits of the devil—all of these privileges have now been given to all nations through the Church.

In this sense, the Gentiles have been incorporated into the prayer of Israel, according to the analogy of the olive tree used by St. Paul in Romans 11. The prayer of Israel is the domesticated olive tree, into which the Gentiles, as wild olive branches, have been engrafted. The prayer of the Church is thus "Catholic," which means universal. It is the prayer of mankind grafted into Christ and thus into Israel in its fullness.

The second novelty is yet more substantial. The prayer of the synagogue was the prayer of *hope* in the coming of the Redeemer, the

Messiah who is to be the Bridegroom of Israel. The prayer of the Church, on the other hand, is principally the prayer of Christ already come. The Church prays with and through her divine Bridegroom, to whom she is already united. She is given the inconceivable privilege of being enabled to pray with the very prayer of the Messiah, her Spouse. As the Mystical Body of Christ, *she can address God the Father through the prayer of God the Son*. The prayer of the Church centers on the prayer of the Messiah. The Church prays to the Father with Christ, through Christ, and in Christ. We see this constantly in the liturgy of the Church, in which almost all prayers are addressed to the Father through Christ.

Third, the prayer of the Church is Trinitarian. The *Compendium of the Catechism of the Catholic Church* 534 describes Christian prayer as "the personal and living relationship of the children of God with their Father who is infinitely good, with his Son Jesus Christ, and with the Holy Spirit who dwells in their hearts."

Finally, Christian prayer is marked by the Passion of Christ. Our relationship with God cannot bypass the fact that we have been redeemed by the Cross, and that all human suffering has been redeemed by that Cross and rendered capable of being redemptive, of participating in the redemption worked by Christ's Passion.

In other words, Christian prayer is distinguished by being (at least implicitly) Christological and Trinitarian. This is especially true in the prayer of the liturgy.

The Christian Liturgy

The word "liturgy," as the *Catechism of the Catholic Church* 1069 explains,

> originally meant a "public work" or a "service in the name of/on behalf of the people." In Christian tradition it means the participation of the People of God in "the work of God" [*opus Dei*]. Through the liturgy Christ, our redeemer and high priest, continues the work of our redemption in, with, and through his Church.

The liturgy of the Church should be understood, first and foremost, as the prayer of Christ to the Father, in the Holy Spirit. Christ does not pray alone, but enables His spouse, His Mystical Body, the Church, to pray with Him to the Father. Thus the liturgy should be understood as the prayer of the "whole Christ," Head and members. The members are joined to Christ by the ties of sanctifying grace and the character imparted at Baptism, which allows them to participate in the offices of Christ as Priest, Prophet, and King.

The prayer of the Church is also a participation in and foretaste of the celestial liturgy, in which the angels and saints praise the blessed

Trinity eternally in heaven.[10] This principle has tremendous pastoral implications. One of the key ways that faith, hope, and charity are nourished is through the foretaste of heaven given by the beauty and transcendence of liturgical prayer, which has led to many conversions. Indeed, one could say that the "normal" way of conversion occurs through reverent and awe-inspiring liturgy.

This foretaste of the heavenly liturgy is one of the key points of the Second Vatican Council's Constitution on the Sacred Liturgy, *Sacrosanctum concilium*, that have not been implemented in the "typical" celebration of the post-conciliar liturgy in the Latin rite. Very often the result has been the complete contrary, producing a liturgy that is banal and lacking expression of devotion and reverence.

The heavenly liturgy is the worship of God that takes place in heaven in the communion of the saints and angels, where "celebration is wholly communion and feast" (*CCC* 1136), without the need for the mediation of signs and symbols. Glimpses of this celestial liturgy were seen by Isaiah[11] and Ezekiel.[12] However, it is especially in the book of Revelation that the heavenly liturgy is mentioned most prominently.[13] The visions of Isaiah and Ezekiel are recalled, for example, in Revelation 4:

> And round the throne, on each side of the throne, are four living creatures, full of eyes in front and behind: . . . and day and night they never cease to sing, "Holy, holy, holy, is the Lord God Almighty, who was and is and is to come!" And whenever the living creatures give glory and honor and thanks to him who is seated on the throne, who lives for ever and ever, the twenty-four elders fall down before him who is seated on the throne and worship him who lives for ever and ever; they cast their crowns before the throne, singing, "Worthy art thou, our Lord and God,

---

[10] See Vatican II, *Sacrosanctum concilium* (*Constitution on the Sacred Liturgy*) 8: "In the earthly liturgy we take part in a foretaste of that heavenly liturgy which is celebrated in the holy city of Jerusalem toward which we journey as pilgrims, where Christ is sitting at the right hand of God, a minister of the holies and of the true tabernacle; we sing a hymn to the Lord's glory with all the warriors of the heavenly army; venerating the memory of the saints, we hope for some part and fellowship with them; we eagerly await the Saviour, Our Lord Jesus Christ, until He, our life, shall appear and we too will appear with Him in glory."

[11] Isaiah 6:1–3: "In the year that King Uzziah died I saw the Lord sitting upon a throne, high and lifted up; and his train filled the temple. Above him stood the seraphim; each had six wings: with two he covered his face, and with two he covered his feet, and with two he flew. And one called to another and said: 'Holy, holy, holy is the Lord of hosts; the whole earth is full of his glory.'"

[12] See Ez 1:26–28.

[13] See *CCC* 1137–39.

to receive glory and honor and power, for thou didst create all things, and by thy will they existed and were created."[14]

This idea that the liturgy is a foretaste of the heavenly liturgy came to Christianity from Judaism. The Jewish liturgy is also a participation in the heavenly liturgy. However, it is clear that Christian liturgy, objectively speaking, realizes this participation in a fuller way precisely because it is the prayer of the Messiah and the Church together, whereas the prayer of the synagogue is the prayer of the Messiah only prophetically and through yearning and faith.

A beautiful expression of our participation in the heavenly liturgy is found in the Hasidic tradition:

> When a Jew speaks a word of prayer in love and awe, the power of his word gives birth to God's glory. The angels call out to God: "Who is like Your Israel, a unique people in the world!" How great is even a single word of such prayer: it causes all the angels to sing to God! All the worlds join with man as he serves his Lord. This is the meaning of the Song of Songs—one who sings a song below can arouse many songs on high![15]

The Eucharist

The prayer of the Church reaches its summit in the Eucharistic liturgy, the "source and summit" of Christian life and sanctification. It is above all in the Eucharistic prayer that the Church prays with the voice of Christ, for He becomes present throughout the life of the Church on our altars as the Victim of our Redemption. At Mass the faithful are present at the very sacrifice of Calvary by which the Word Incarnate redeemed our souls by offering the price of His Blood for all the sins of the world.

The faithful are called to participate actively in this prayer of Christ in the Eucharist.[16] Their participation is most fully and actively realized in the liturgy when through a lively faith working in charity they unite their own self-immolation and reparation with that of Christ, especially

---

[14] Rev 4:6–11.

[15] *Your Word Is Fire: The Hasidic Masters on Contemplative Prayer*, ed. and trans. Arthur Green and Barry W. Holtz (New York: Paulist Press, 1977), 26.

[16] Vatican II, *Sacrosanctum concilium* 14 states: "Mother Church earnestly desires that all the faithful should be led to that fully conscious, and active participation in liturgical celebrations which is demanded by the very nature of the liturgy. Such participation by the Christian people as 'a chosen race, a royal priesthood, a holy nation, a redeemed people' (1 Pet. 2:9; cf. 2:4–5), is their right and duty by reason of their baptism."

in the sacrifice of the Mass.[17] We are to put our sacrifices, crosses, hopes, fears, loves, and prayers on the altar and on the paten, so that they may be offered spiritually to the Father together with the sacrifice of Christ that is truly offered in every Mass.

All Christian prayer is deeply tied to the Eucharist, in which Christ exercises His office of Mediator most intimately.

Is Jewish Prayer Still Pleasing to God?

At this point, I think a certain question inevitably comes to mind: Is Jewish prayer, as prayed today and for the past two thousand years, still pleasing to God, as it was before the coming of the Messiah? This question is closely related to that concerning the present status of the Chosen People in salvation history.[18] The Chosen People has not been accursed by God, nor has it lost its condition of being especially chosen. It still has a crucial mission to accomplish in salvation history, which will be revealed in the last times when Jews recognize Jesus as the Messiah.

However, what about the prayer today of Jews who do not recognize Christ? Is their prayer pleasing to God? As long as their unbelief is through no grave fault of their own, the answer is yes. Jewish prayer, insofar as it is based on the writings of the Old Testament, is a form of worship that comes from God Himself. It enabled the Chosen People to pray as adopted children of God, to have an intimacy with God Himself, to pray with true faith, hope, and charity. In the prayer of the synagogue, the Jew prays with texts of Scripture and with other writings steeped in the tradition that comes from God's Revelation. Furthermore, Jewish prayer stands at the basis of the Christian liturgy. How could it not be pleasing to God if it is prayed with a sincere heart?

This brings us to the question of the objective and subjective aspects of prayer. A prayer is pleasing to God if it unites two criteria. The prayer must be in accordance with the truth about God's will and express our true relationship with Him, and secondly, prayer must come from the heart with sincerity, love, and fear of the Lord, which means a recognition of His loving dominion over us. Only God knows the extent to which this second criterion is fulfilled.

---

[17] See Pius XI, encyclical *Miserentissimus Redemptor*, on Reparation to the Sacred Heart, n. 10 (1928): "But the more perfectly that our oblation and sacrifice corresponds to the sacrifice of Our Lord, that is to say, the more perfectly we have immolated our love and our desires and have crucified our flesh by that mystic crucifixion of which the Apostle speaks, the more abundant fruits of that propitiation and expiation shall we receive for ourselves and for others."

[18] See chapter 10 below, and Vatican II, *Nostra aetate* 4.

The Jewish liturgy, as we find it in the *Siddur*,[19] fulfills the first criterion, except insofar as it holds, or is understood to hold, that the Messiah has not yet come. Insofar as Jews are inculpably ignorant that Jesus is the Messiah, the prayer of the synagogue can give glory to God and sanctify man, according to the degree of faith, hope, and charity with which it is prayed.

Does the fact that Jewish prayer comes from God and is pleasing to God mean that there is no need to tell Jews about Christ? Certainly not. For since Jewish prayer is fundamentally marked by hope in the coming of the redemption and the Messiah, *how could it remain indifferent to the truth about the fulfillment of that hope?* Christ is the fulfillment of every aspiration of Jewish prayer. How can it be indifferent to a soul burning for the redemption of Israel to learn that that redemption has already been realized in a higher and more superabundant way than any human heart can conceive?

The Messiah and His Kingdom were promised to the sons and daughters of Israel, in fidelity to the promises made to the Patriarchs. It would be grave disrespect to God's own fidelity and love to intentionally withhold the Gospel from those to whom it was first promised, and who have yearned for it for millennia.

What Can Christians Learn from Jewish Prayer?

The prayer of Israel is a continual means of sanctification through remembrance of God and His Law. The devout Jew repeatedly thanks God for having sanctified the Jewish people with the revelation and gift of His precepts. One of the beautiful aspects of the prayer of the Orthodox Jew is the praise (blessing) given to God on the occasion of ordinary acts of everyday life, such as eating, drinking, washing of hands, dressing, wearing new clothes, even going to the bathroom, in sickness and upon recovery, traveling, at a birth, in mourning, at a family thanksgiving (birthdays, anniversaries), etc. This is a constant reminder of the presence of God and His holy will in all the events of life. It is said that a devout Jew should pray one hundred of these blessings every day.[20]

---

[19] The classical text of Jewish prayer is the traditional Prayer Book, or *Siddur*. In addition, a beautiful collection of Jewish prayers can be found in *Language of Faith: A Selection of the Most Expressive Jewish Prayers*, ed. Nahum N. Glatzer (New York: Schocken Books, 1967).

[20] See Mary Ruth Bede, "The Blessings of the Jewish Prayer Book," in *The Bridge: A Yearbook of Judaeo-Christian Studies*, ed. J. Oesterreicher, 2:224–38.

Personal Prayer in Judaism: the Hasidic Movement

It is appropriate in the context of a discussion of Jewish prayer to look briefly at the Hasidic movement in Judaism, which sought to give greater prominence to contemplative and mystical prayer in Jewish life. It arose in the eighteenth century in Eastern Europe, the period of the Enlightenment. However, Hasidism is not a product of the Enlightenment, but a reaction against it. The word "Hasid" means "devout" or "pious." It comes from the Hebrew root "hesed," which means piety or "loving-kindness."

The founder of Hasidism is a rabbi known as the "Baal Shem Tov," Master of the Good Name, who lived from around 1700 to 1760.[21] His great-grandson, Rabbi Nachman of Breslau (1772–1810), became another great Hasidic master, and was known for his tales, including Messianic tales. A well-known saying of his is that "it is a great *mitzvah* [good deed, or commandment] to be happy."

The key elements of the original Hasidic movement were prayer from the heart as the center of sanctity, ecstatic prayer, seeing the divine presence in all things, devotion (*devekut*) or communion with God in everyday life, and joy in worship. It was opposed to excessive formalism and casuistry in Jewish life, and sought to extend piety also to the unlearned and the common people.

A beautiful statement of the importance of prayer in Hasidism is given by Rabbi Shneor Zalman of Liady (1747–1813), founder of the Chabad group of Hasidism, who wrote:

> The concept of prayer and its essential idea belong to the very foundation of the Torah, namely, to know the Lord, to recognize His greatness and His glory with a serene mind, and, through contemplation, to have these fixed firmly in the mind. A man must reflect on this theme until the contemplative soul is awakened to love the Lord's name, to cleave to Him and to His Torah and greatly to desire His commandments. . . . Anyone who has drawn near to God and has once tasted the fragrance of prayer, knows and appreciates that without prayer no man can lift hand or foot to serve God in truth, rather than as the commands of men who learn by rote.[22]

An important teaching of the Baal Shem Tov was his idea that prayer should involve complete self-abnegation and self-forgetfulness, focusing entirely on God, His glory and presence. Of course, this is an

---

[21] His actual name is Rabbi Israel ben Eliezer.
[22] Louis Jacobs, *Hasidic Prayer* (New York: Schocken Books, 1973), 18.

ideal that can never be fully realized except perhaps in the highest mystical states.

An obvious objection against this ideal concerns the prayer of petition. How can we forget about self when praying for our needs? The Baal Shem Tov and his disciples taught that one should pray for one's needs ultimately for the sake of God's glory.[23] We see this in the rules of prayer written by one of his disciples:

> One should recite the words [of prayer] with great enthusiasm, with great joy, and with great attachment [*devekut*]. It is another great rule that in whatever he does a man should intend only to give satisfaction to the *Shekinah* [presence of God—Holy Spirit]. He should have no thought of self . . . for he is vanity and emptiness so why should he do it for his own pleasure? . . . The main thing is that all his worship should be for the sake of the Shekinah and there should be nothing of self in it, not even to the slightest degree. At times a man is like unto a drunkard in the joy he has of the Torah because a great love burns in his heart.[24]

This is very similar to the Catholic idea that we should do all things, including prayer itself, for the sake of the greater glory of God. Let us pray that the prayer of Israel and the Church may burn with this enthusiasm for the glory of God and joy in the fullness of His Torah, which is Christ.

---

[23] In Hasidic terminology, one should pray for our needs for the sake of the *Shekinah*, which refers to the mysterious presence of God in the world and in the soul.

[24] Rabbi Hayim Haikel, disciple of the Maggid of Meseritch, the successor of the Baal Shem Tov. Quoted in Jacobs, *Hasidic Prayer*, 98.

CHAPTER 10

Role of the Jewish People after the Coming of the Messiah

Here we shall take up a difficult and controversial topic: the continuing role of the Chosen People after the coming of the Messiah. Let me preface this by pointing out that we are dealing with a mystery, in the strict sense of the word.

Israel, the Catholic Church, and the relation between the two, are mysteries hidden in God from all eternity. A mystery in theology is a truth revealed by God which exceeds the full grasp of the human mind. Human reason can never fully understand mysteries through its own power. We know them because they are revealed by God. Furthermore, even after they have been revealed, we still cannot fully grasp them, for it would require the divine wisdom to understand them properly. The Trinity, the Incarnation, the Redemption, the sacraments, and grace, are mysteries in this sense. The Church herself is a mystery. She is not simply a sociological body of believers who gather together in church on Sundays, profess a certain creed, and are united under certain pastors. That is all true, but she is much more than that, for she is the Body of Christ and the Bride of Christ, whose members are given the grace of the adoption of sons and daughters of God.

If this is true of the Church, it is also true of Israel (taking the word in the Biblical rather than political sense). Israel is not simply a sociological reality, a particular people on the face of the earth, with its own particular history, sacred traditions, and books. Israel is a mystery as the Church is a mystery: the mystery of God's intervention in human history to form a people for Himself, a people in which God would become man, a people in which the drama of the salvation of mankind would be played out, a people whose members receive the adoption as sons and daughters of God, a people uniquely elected for God's own plan.

Every mystery jars the human mind. The Trinity, the Incarnation, and the Passion of Christ are the greatest examples. The mysteries of

Israel and the Church also jar the human mind. The election of Israel as a special people chosen from all the nations of the earth raises many questions. Why was Israel picked out? There is no human answer, but only a divine one.

The mystery of Israel contains many dimensions: her election, Law, and peculiar history. Certainly one of the greatest mysteries about Israel is the fact that God allowed a certain spiritual blindness to come upon a part of Israel so that it would not recognize the Messiah who came from her bosom. As we shall see, St. Paul speaks of this very profoundly. Nevertheless, he too finds it tremendously mysterious, as mysterious as it is tragic. God in His inscrutable plans allowed a great part of Israel to remain blinded in that regard for two thousand years. Does this mean that they are no longer chosen or have been repudiated?

The human mind naturally seeks to avoid mysteries. The easy way out of this dilemma would be to say that the Chosen People who have become blinded are no longer chosen. The human mind would eliminate this aspect of the mystery of Israel simply by rejecting the continuing election.

So what is the "status" of the Jewish people today in salvation history? Are they still the Chosen People, or has their election been revoked by God because of lack of belief in Jesus as the Messiah? Is the Old Covenant still in force for the Jewish people? Do they continue to play a role in salvation history after the coming of the Messiah?

As with most theological questions, the truth lies between two extremes. It is like the summit of a mountain between two opposite slopes. One error would be to say that the Jewish people has been completely rejected by God because of its failure to recognize the Messiah and thus no longer has any special role in salvation history.

An opposing error would be to hold a theory of parallel covenants, thinking that after the coming of Jesus there are two parallel and equal covenants for approaching and pleasing God: Christianity for the Gentiles, and Judaism for Jews. Thus there would be no reason for Jews to embrace Christ and enter the Church.

On the basis of what we have seen in previous chapters, we can make the following preliminary conclusions. God's plan for the salvation of the human race, from all eternity, centered on the Incarnation and Passion of God the Son, the Word of God, the Second Person of the Trinity. The Jewish people was chosen precisely for the inestimable privilege of being the people in whom the Messiah—the Word Incarnate—would come into the world, into human history and society; He would be born of a Jewish mother and raised under the Law of Moses. As St. Paul says in Galatians 4:4: "When the fullness of time came, God sent His Son, born of a woman, born under the Law, to redeem those who were under the Law, so that we might receive adoption as sons."

The coming of the Messiah was the blessing promised to Abraham in his descendants: "In your seed shall all the nations of the earth be blessed" (Gen 22:18). The Jewish people was called in Abraham and progressively formed through numerous wondrous interventions of God to be the people in whom God would become man, so as to redeem mankind.

The role of the Jewish people was manifold. First, as we have said, they were to prepare for the coming of the Messiah, so that His coming would be long awaited, ardently desired, and constantly prayed for. They were called also to be a witness to God's entire plan of salvation, announcing the coming of the Messiah, and giving solemn witness to the signs of His coming. They were called to live out in their own history the glorious figures of Christ's work of salvation, as we saw with regard to Biblical typology. Finally, they were called to receive the Law of Moses. As we have seen, the Law of Moses has three aspects: the moral law, the ceremonial law, and judicial precepts which assign penalties and give a particular application of the general precepts of the Law contained in the Ten Commandments.

The moral law of the Old Testament was never abrogated, and could never be so. On the contrary, Christ came to fulfill it perfectly in His Person, and to give us the grace and teaching we need to fulfill it in imitation of Him.

The ceremonial law was abrogated, however, for it was a figure that pointed to Christ's sacrifice on Calvary: the sacrifices of animals and other offerings point to the perfect sacrifice of the Messiah, which is their fulfillment. Thus the ceremonial law, according to God's eternal plan, was to pass into a new ceremonial law centering on the seven sacraments of the Church—divine channels of grace flowing from the perfect sacrifice of the Messiah.

The judicial precepts of the Old Testament remain as a model, but are adapted to the needs of different historical circumstances. Christ does not promulgate new judicial precepts. This is left to the Church in her canon law, and to the nations in their civil codes.

On the basis of these points, how can we understand the current role of the Jewish people in salvation history? First of all, God's choice or election of a particular people in which He would become man *can never be revoked*. Still today, the Jewish people have the inestimable honor and privilege of being the people in which God chose to become man. He was born of a quintessentially Jewish mother, circumcised on the eighth day, raised in pious Jewish fashion, and brought to the Temple three times a year when He came of age. He participated weekly in the synagogue, taught and worked miracles in the streets and marketplaces of Israel. This honor is still theirs, even if they do not yet recognize Him, as Joseph's brothers did not at first recognize Joseph in Egypt.

Secondly, the Jewish people were chosen to be a witness to Jesus' coming through their sacred books, their Law, their traditions, their liturgy, and their history. This is no less true today than it was before His coming.

Third, all the Apostles and first disciples of Jesus, together with Mary, the most perfect disciple of all times, were chosen from the Jewish people. The Church of Pentecost was entirely from Judaism.

Fourth, God is faithful to His promises, even if men are unfaithful to Him. The Jewish people are still singularly beloved on account of the Patriarchs and on account of the covenant of love that He entered into with them. Jesus was born into a people that prayed for His coming for generation after generation.

Thus we can say that the special role of the Jewish people did not come to an end with the coming of the Messiah, as some theologians maintain, because of two crucial facts mentioned above: *God's fidelity, and the fact that the Jewish people continue to be a privileged witness to Christ's coming.* This is true even in their unbelief in Jesus, and it will be even more true if they come to believe that Jesus is the Messiah, as we believe shall happen before His Second Coming, whenever that shall come to pass.

These questions are dealt with authoritatively in two crucial sources: a brief text of Vatican II, *Nostra aetate* 4, and St. Paul's Letter to the Romans, chapters 9–11.

Vatican II, *Nostra aetate*

The declaration of Vatican II on the Relation of the Church to Non-Christian Religions, called *Nostra aetate*, has a beautiful and luminous section on the relation of the Catholic Church to the Jewish people. This brief text has had tremendous importance in diminishing anti-Semitism and in contributing to a proper understanding of the enduring mystery of Israel:

> As the sacred synod searches into the mystery of the Church, it remembers the bond that spiritually ties the people of the New Covenant to Abraham's stock.
>
> Thus the Church of Christ acknowledges that, according to God's saving design, the beginnings of her faith and her election are found already among the Patriarchs, Moses and the prophets. She professes that *all who believe in Christ*—Abraham's sons according to faith (see Gal 3:7)—*are included in the same Patriarch's call*, and likewise that the salvation of the Church is mysteriously

foreshadowed by the chosen people's exodus from the land of bondage. The *Church, therefore, cannot forget that she received the revelation of the Old Testament through the people with whom God in His inexpressible mercy concluded the Ancient Covenant. Nor can she forget that she draws sustenance from the root of that well-cultivated olive tree onto which have been grafted the wild shoots, the Gentiles* (see Rom 11:17–24). Indeed, the Church believes that by His cross Christ, Our Peace, reconciled Jews and Gentiles, making both one in Himself (see Eph 2:14–16).

The Church keeps ever in mind the words of the Apostle about his kinsmen: "Theirs is the sonship and the glory and the covenants and the law and the worship and the promises; theirs are the fathers and from them is the Christ according to the flesh" (Rom 9:4–5), the Son of the Virgin Mary. She also recalls that the Apostles, the Church's mainstay and pillars, as well as most of the early disciples who proclaimed Christ's Gospel to the world, sprang from the Jewish people. . . . *God holds the Jews most dear for the sake of their Fathers; He does not repent of the gifts He makes or of the calls He issues*—such is the witness of the Apostle (see Rom 11:28–29). In company with the Prophets and the same Apostle, the Church awaits that day, known to God alone, on which all peoples will address the Lord in a single voice and "serve him with one accord" (Zeph 3:9).[1]

Since the *spiritual patrimony common to Christians and Jews is thus so great*, this sacred synod wants to foster and recommend that mutual understanding and respect which is the fruit, above all, of Biblical and theological studies as well as of fraternal dialogues.

True, the Jewish authorities and those who followed their lead pressed for the death of Christ (see Jn 19:6); still, what happened in His passion cannot be charged against all the Jews, without distinction, then alive, nor against the Jews of today. Although the Church is the new people of God, the Jews should not be presented as rejected or accursed by God, as if this followed from the Holy Scriptures. All should see to it, then, that in catechetical work or in the preaching of the word of God they do not teach anything that does not conform to the truth of the Gospel and the spirit of Christ.

Furthermore, in her rejection of every persecution against any man, the Church, mindful of the patrimony she shares with the Jews and moved not by political reasons but by the Gospel's spiritual love, decries hatred, persecutions, displays of anti-Semitism, directed against Jews at any time and by anyone.

Besides, as the Church has always held and holds now, *Christ underwent His passion and death freely, because of the sins of men and out of*

---

[1] See Is 66:23; Ps 65:4; Rom 11:11–32.

infinite love, in order that all may reach salvation. It is, therefore, the burden of the Church's preaching to proclaim the *cross of Christ as the sign of God's all-embracing love and as the fountain from which every grace flows.*[2]

The Council stresses that Christ died of His own free will (for He could have avoided it through His omnipotence) for the sins of all men of all times and places. Every man born in sin and who has committed personal sins has in a sense caused the Son of God to die for him, as if he were the only person in the world.

To present the Jews in particular as Christ-killers is absolutely repudiated by the most elementary Christian doctrine: Christ died for all men, on account of all the sins of the world, that all may reach salvation. The Council makes it perfectly clear that Christ's Passion cannot be charged against all Jews, then or now. Rather, every man must reckon himself to be responsible for the Blood of Christ poured out for love of all.

In Matthew 27:25, the crowd of Jews present at the Praetorium before Pontius Pilate cried out: "His blood be on us and on our children." This initially seems to mean that they are assuming the guilt for His death, but it can also be taken as an unwitting plea to come under the redeeming power of the Blood of Christ.

Vatican II emphatically states that God did not reject, nor still less accurse, the Chosen People because of the death of Christ. They remain "most dear for the sake of their Fathers; He does not repent of the gifts He makes or of the calls He issues."

So the answer to our first question is clear: God has not rejected the Chosen People, who remain beloved in a special way and by a special title: God's own calling of them. Their election has not been revoked. We cannot regard them through the eyes of Christian faith as just another people in the world, and still less as a people somehow cursed by God.

Now if God has not rejected the Chosen People, and their election remains forever, then what is their role today in salvation history? The Council does not directly address this issue.

Romans 9

Let us now look at the witness of the New Testament with regard to Israel's continuing role in salvation history. This question is addressed most prominently by St. Paul in his letter to the Romans, chapters 9–11. The text is very profound and deals with great mysteries. He begins by

---

[2] Vatican II, *Nostra aetate* 4 (my italics).

saying that the mystery of blindness on the part of much of Israel causes him unceasing anguish. He goes so far as to say:

> For I could wish that I myself were accursed and cut off from Christ for the sake of my brethren, my kinsmen by race. They are Israelites, and to them belong the sonship, the glory, the covenants, the giving of the law, the worship, and the promises; to them belong the patriarchs, and of their race, according to the flesh, is the Christ, who is God over all, blessed for ever. Amen.[3]

Here St. Paul has recounted the great privileges of the Chosen People. As we have seen, Vatican II's *Nostra aetate* cited this text. Does the blindness that has come over a part of the Chosen People mean that God's promise to Abraham, Isaac, and Jacob has failed? St. Paul answers in Romans 9:6–13 that Israel is not simply a sociological reality comprising a particular ethnic group. Since Israel is a mystery, her full meaning will not be fathomed in this life. In a spiritual sense, Israel refers not to the children of Abraham simply according to the flesh, but rather according to the promise (Rom 9:8). Thus all those who believe in Christ and become members of the Church are the "new Israel," and fulfill God's promise to Abraham. In order to convey this idea, St. Paul observes that not all of Abraham's children, nor all of Isaac's, received the promise concerning the blessing that God would give to Abraham's seed. Ishmael was Abraham's elder son, but he did not receive the promise, and Esau was Isaac's elder son, but he did not receive the promise, either. Thus not all Israel according to the flesh needs to receive the promise to which God remains faithful, but only a remnant.

However, it might seem that God is being unjust in not giving equal grace to all. For example, why is Jacob preferred to Esau? Is God unjust in calling some and allowing blindness to fall on others? Why was St. Paul called to believe with the Apostles, and not Caiaphas and all the sages of the Law, such as Gamaliel? St. Paul points out in Romans 9:14–18 that we are dealing with the great mystery of how God distributes His graces and why He does not give equally to all. God's grace is absolutely gratuitous and unmerited, and He gives it to those whom He chooses.

But here we ask, does this mean that everything is determined by God? St. Paul poses this question (Rom 9:19): "You will say to me then, 'Why does he still find fault? For who can resist his will?'" He answers by underlining the divine sovereignty. God has a plan that includes our free will, our correspondence to God's grace when we correspond, and our resistance when we freely resist, making ourselves vessels fit or apt

---

[3] Rom 9:3–5.

for destruction. However, even man's free, obstinate, and culpable resistance to God's plans, as in the case of Pharaoh[4] and Caiaphas, is made to work to further those very plans.

We know from other Pauline texts that God wills the salvation of all men. In 1 Timothy 2:4 he says that God "desires all men to be saved and to come to the knowledge of the truth," and in 1 Thessalonians 4:3 he says that "this is the will of God, your sanctification." The Catholic Tradition infers from this that God gives *sufficient* grace to all men so that they can be saved, if they freely choose to cooperate perseveringly with that grace. Otherwise, God could not truly be said to will the salvation of all men.

Nevertheless, God has mysteriously elected some to receive a *superabundance* of mercy, by adopting them as His People, revealing Himself intimately to them, and making available to them special channels of grace. And this He has done both with Jews and with Gentiles:

> As indeed he says in Hosea, "Those who were not my people I will call 'my people,' and her who was not beloved I will call 'my beloved.'" And in the very place where it was said to them, "You are not my people," they will be called "sons of the living God."[5]

St. Paul interprets these texts of the prophet Hosea as referring to the conversion of the Gentiles, who had previously not been adopted by God as His people, but who in Christ receive the adoption to become "sons of the living God," and adoption into the privileges of Israel. St. Paul then goes on to quote Isaiah who speaks of a faithful remnant:

> And Isaiah cries out concerning Israel: "Though the number of the sons of Israel be as the sand of the sea, only a remnant of them will be saved; for the Lord will execute his sentence upon the earth with rigor and dispatch." And as Isaiah predicted, "If the Lord of hosts had not left us children, we would have fared like Sodom and been made like Gomorrah."[6]

And why has only a remnant been saved? This also is a mystery. St. Paul says it is because the rest of Israel did not believe in the Messiah, but allowed themselves to be scandalized by Him, as a "stumbling stone" (which is the etymological meaning of scandal). The key error, which is a universal tendency of man, is to seek salvation through one's

---

[4] See Rom 9:17.

[5] Rom 9:25–26.

[6] Rom 9:27–29.

own effort, rather than allowing God to transform the heart through faith in Christ.[7]

Romans 11

Romans 11 brings us to the heart of our question about the continuing role of the Jewish people after the coming of the Messiah. St. Paul poses the question directly in Romans 11:1–8:

> I ask, then, has God rejected his people? By no means! I myself am an Israelite, a descendant of Abraham, a member of the tribe of Benjamin. God has not rejected his people whom he foreknew. Do you not know what the scripture says of Elijah, how he pleads with God against Israel? "Lord, they have killed thy prophets, they have demolished thy altars, and I alone am left, and they seek my life." But what is God's reply to him? "I have kept for myself seven thousand men who have not bowed the knee to Baal." So too at the present time there is a remnant, chosen by grace. But if it is by grace, it is no longer on the basis of works; otherwise grace would no longer be grace. What then? Israel failed to obtain what it sought. The elect obtained it, but the rest were hardened, as it is written, "God gave them a spirit of stupor, eyes that should not see and ears that should not hear, down to this very day."

A first answer to the question of whether God has rejected His people is that part of Israel has been a faithful remnant through the gratuitous mercy of God. This remnant includes Mary, St. Joseph, the Apostles, St. Paul, the disciples gathered into the Church at Pentecost, and the innumerable Jews evangelized by St. Paul and the other disciples throughout the Diaspora, such as Priscilla and Aquila (Jews from Rome with whom St. Paul stayed in Corinth), Timothy, Apollos, and many others. The Acts of the Apostles (6:7; 15:5) tells us that many of the priests and Pharisees came to believe. In Acts 21:20, James tells Paul: "You see, brother, how many thousands there are among the Jews of those who have believed; they are all zealous for the law." However, what about those who failed to recognize Christ? St. Paul asks:

> So I ask, have they stumbled so as to fall? By no means! But through their trespass salvation has come to the Gentiles, so as to make Israel jealous. Now if their trespass means riches for the world, and if their failure means riches for the Gentiles, how much more will their full inclusion mean![8]

---

[7] See Rom 9:30–10:4.
[8] Rom 11:11–12.

Why has God allowed a great part of Israel to fall? Is it simply that they were stiff-necked and obstinate? No, for St. Paul tells us that this has occurred as part of God's plan of salvation and mercy for all. The obstinacy of Israel that we not infrequently see in the Old Testament is a figure of the stiff-necked tendency of all mankind.[9] None of us can think that we would have done any better than Caiaphas, if left to ourselves.[10] And St. Paul knew this from personal experience. He would still have been persecuting the Church if God had not intervened with a superabundant, absolutely unmerited grace.

Somehow, the unbelief of a part of Israel, therefore, is a part of God's plan. Though God certainly did not directly will their disobedience, and gave each person sufficient grace to be saved, He permitted it by not giving to everyone the extraordinary graces that He gave to St. Paul and the Apostles. Why? We have to leave this as a mystery.

St. Paul alludes to the fact that the ingathering of the Gentiles into the early Church was not completely unrelated to the blindness of part of Israel, permitted by God only until the full number of Gentiles are brought in and the "time of the Gentiles" is fulfilled. Then God will have mercy also on the part of Israel that has been permitted to remain blind to the identity of Christ:

> Now I am speaking to you Gentiles. Inasmuch then as I am an apostle to the Gentiles, I magnify my ministry in order to make my fellow Jews jealous, and thus save some of them. For if their rejection means the reconciliation of the world, what will their acceptance mean but life from the dead?[11]

Here St. Paul is alluding to the conversion of the Jewish people before the Second Coming of Jesus, which will precede the Resurrection of the dead.[12] Thus he says that their acceptance will mean "life from the dead" literally as well as figuratively, in that it will mark the approach of the general Resurrection. In the spiritual sense it seems that there is also

---

[9] See Mirjam Prager, "Israel in the Parables," in *The Bridge: A Yearbook of Judaeo-Christian Studies*, ed. John Oesterreicher, vol. 4 (New York: Pantheon Books, 1961), 44: "I look upon Israel as the paradigm of mankind, upon her misstep as the pattern of human failing, upon Scribes and Pharisees as types of those hostile to Jesus in every age and place. Only a perspective so wide can give the parables their full import; only a perspective so universal can free His authentic message to Israel from interpretations that have darkened or overdrawn it."

[10] God always gives to every man *sufficient* grace to be saved. Nevertheless, superabundant and extraordinary graces are not given equally to all.

[11] Rom 11:13–15.

[12] See *CCC* 674.

a double meaning. On the one hand, "life from the dead" indicates the spiritual resurrection of Israel through faith in Christ. On the other hand, it seems to refer to the spiritual resurrection of many Gentile Christians who will fall away from the faith in the time of the great apostasy spoken of by St. Paul in 2 Thessalonians 2:3, and who will be brought back by the witness of the faith in Christ of the people of Israel.

St. Thomas Aquinas holds that the phrase "life from the dead" in Rom 11:15 has all three of these meanings. The conversion of the Jewish people in the latter days means "life from the dead" as indicating (a) the approach of the general Resurrection, but also (b) a spiritual regeneration of the Jewish people, and (c) the spiritual regeneration of Gentile Christians who will have "grown cold" in faith and charity. In his commentary on Romans 11:15, St. Thomas writes:

> If the loss of the Jews provided the occasion for the reconciliation of the world, in that through the death of Christ we are reconciled with God, what will their acceptance be but life from the dead? That is, that the Jews are received again by God. . . . *What will that reception accomplish, if not that the Gentiles be made to rise unto life?* For the Gentile faithful will grow cold, according to Mt 24:12: "And because wickedness is multiplied, most men's love will grow cold." Or also those who completely fall—deceived by the Antichrist— will be *restored to their pristine fervor by the converted Jews.* And thus as through the fall of the Jews the Gentiles were reconciled after being enemies, so after the conversion of the Jews, the end of the world being imminent, there will be the general resurrection, through which men will go from death to immortal life.[13]

This interpretation implies that when Jews come in significant numbers to faith in Christ, they will have an historic ecclesial mission to accomplish: confirming their Gentile brethren—fallen-away Catholics— in the faith.

Charles Cardinal Journet, a great twentieth century theologian, shares the thesis of St. Thomas and develops it. He asks whether "Israel's reintegration will mark the end of history, giving the signal for the Last Judgment and for the final restoration of the universe? Or may one assume that Israel's return will take place within the very web of historic time?" He responds that "both opinions are found within the Church," but nevertheless he prefers the second interpretation as being more in harmony with St. Paul's texts in Romans 11:12 and 15. These

---

[13] St. Thomas Aquinas, Commentary on Romans 11:15, in *Super epistolas S. Pauli lectura*, ed. Raphael Cai (Turin: Marietti, 1953), 1:166, n. 890 (my translation and italics). See also Steven C. Boguslawski, *Thomas Aquinas on the Jews: Insights into His Commentary on Romans 9–11* (New York: Paulist Press, 2008), 98.

texts show that it is "impossible . . . that Israel's restoration should not be of inestimable benefit to the other peoples, since even its stumbling marvelously profited them. . . . According to this second view, Israel's entry will provoke within the Church such a resurgence of love as could be compared to a return of the dead to life."[14]

After speaking in Romans 11:12–15 of Israel's acceptance of Christ in the latter times and the beneficial effects of this conversion for the entire Church, St. Paul goes on to infer from this that the Chosen People retains its holy calling and mission of giving witness to the Messiah and to God's fidelity. In Romans 11:16 he says: "If the dough offered as first fruits is holy, so is the whole lump; and if the root is holy, so are the branches." In this analogy, St. Paul is comparing the Chosen People with the dough from the grain harvest. His point is that if the bread made from the first fruits of the harvest is holy and consecrated to God,[15] this symbolizes that the whole lump—and by extension, the entire harvest—retains a connection with that holiness. The first fruits symbolize the Patriarchs with whom God made a covenant of love (although it can also be taken to refer to Christ and the Apostles). Thus the conclusion is that the whole lump of dough—which would include the Jewish people today—is still holy and will be the recipient of future blessings. They still have a task to accomplish in salvation history. He says the same with the analogy of a tree. If the root is holy, so are the branches. The root here refers to the Patriarchs, and the branches to their descendants called to faith in the Messiah throughout the centuries.

At this point St. Paul uses the figure of an olive tree to describe the relation between Israel and the Church. Israel is God's cultivated olive tree. Some of the natural branches were broken off through unbelief in Christ, which caused Paul "unceasing anguish" (Rom 9:2). However, this tragedy gave an occasion for the engrafting of wild shoots into the cultivated olive tree. The wild shoots are the Gentiles incorporated into the Church. However, St. Paul warns the Christians of Gentile origin that they too can be separated from the olive tree by unbelief, just as had happened to some of the natural branches: "But if some of the branches were broken off, and you, a wild olive shoot, were grafted in their place to share the richness of the olive tree, do not boast over the branches" (Rom 11:17–18).

Furthermore, he stresses that it is the holy root that supports the engrafted branches:

---

[14] Charles Cardinal Journet, "The Mysterious Destinies of Israel," *The Bridge: A Yearbook of Judaeo-Christian Studies*, ed. John Oesterreicher, vol. 2 (New York: Pantheon Books, 1956), 84–85.

[15] See Num 15:19–21.

If you do boast, remember it is not you that support the root, but the root that supports you. You will say, "Branches were broken off so that I might be grafted in." That is true. They were broken off because of their unbelief, but you stand fast only through faith. So do not become proud, but stand in awe. For if God did not spare the natural branches, neither will he spare you.[16]

St. Paul then states that God has the power to graft the separated branches back in: "For if you have been cut from what is by nature a wild olive tree, and grafted, contrary to nature, into a cultivated olive tree, how much more will these natural branches be grafted back into their own olive tree" (Rom 11:24).

Not only does God have the power to graft the natural branches back again, but He will do so in the opportune time, after the fullness of the Gentiles have come into the Church:

Lest you be wise in your own conceits, I want you to understand this mystery, brethren: a hardening has come upon part of Israel, until the full number of the Gentiles come in, and so all Israel will be saved; as it is written, "The Deliverer will come from Zion, he will banish ungodliness from Jacob"; "and this will be my covenant with them when I take away their sins." As regards the gospel they are enemies of God, for your sake; but as regards election they are beloved for the sake of their forefathers. For the gifts and the call of God are irrevocable. Just as you were once disobedient to God but now have received mercy because of their disobedience, so they have now been disobedient in order that by the mercy shown to you they also may receive mercy.[17]

St. Paul thus firmly defends the continuing nature of God's plan for His Chosen People. The election continues because "God's gifts and call are *irrevocable.*" God is faithful, and will show His fidelity by removing the blindness of Israel with regard to the Messiah in the time that He has reserved in His eternal plan. St. Paul tells us that that time will be after "the full number of the Gentiles" has come into the Church. What is meant by the "full number of the Gentiles"? The Gospel must be preached, we know, to all nations and cultures,[18] so that all may receive mercy and the Church may be truly *catholic,* which means

---

[16] Rom 11:18–21.

[17] Rom 11:25–31.

[18] See Mt 24:14: "And this gospel of the kingdom will be preached throughout the whole world, as a testimony to all nations; and then the end will come."

universal. Then it will be time for mercy to be shown superabundantly to all Israel, so that "all Israel will be saved."[19]

One of the most beautiful themes that St. Paul develops in Romans 11 consists in showing that the relationship between Jews and Gentiles in the Church involves a *mutual indebtedness*. The Gentiles are obviously debtors to the Jews, from whom they have received the Messiah and a share in His mercy and salvation, being engrafted into the cultivated olive tree of Israel.[20] As we have seen, the Second Vatican Council has emphasized this in *Nostra aetate* 4:

> The Church, therefore, cannot forget that she received the revelation of the Old Testament through the people with whom God in His inexpressible mercy concluded the Ancient Covenant. Nor can she forget that she draws sustenance from the root of that well-cultivated olive tree onto which have been grafted the wild shoots, the Gentiles (see Rom 11:17–24). . . . She also recalls that the Apostles, the Church's mainstay and pillars, as well as most of the early disciples who proclaimed Christ's Gospel to the world, sprang from the Jewish people.

But Israel that comes to faith in Christ in the latter days will also be indebted to the Gentiles in the Church, from whom they in turn will receive the Gospel. Hebrew Catholics today receive the Gospel from a Church whose members have long been predominantly of Gentile origin.

And then, if we follow the interpretation of St. Thomas Aquinas, finally the Gentiles who will have fallen away in the apostasy will be indebted to the witness of the Jewish believers who will come into the Church, waking them up and thus raising them "from the dead" (Rom 11:15). In this way, God will have mercy on all (Rom 11:32) through the mutual contribution of Jew and Gentile in God's plan of salvation.

---

[19] For a fuller interpretation of Romans 11, see Boguslawski, *Thomas Aquinas on the Jews*, 87–130. For the theme of the conversion of the Jews in the last times, see *CCC* 674, and the discussion in chapter 11 below, pp. 188ff.

[20] See Charles Journet, "The Mysterious Destinies of Israel," in *The Bridge: A Yearbook of Judaeo-Christian Studies*, 2:59: "Christians of Gentile stock, latecomers to the Church, owe to the Jewish people from whom God chose the Christ, His blessed mother, and His first and fervent followers, an admiration tinged with envy; we owe them admiration, which is radically incompatible with contempt, aversion, hatred, in short, with anti-Semitism. Then, to this admiration we must join an everlasting gratitude toward those first Jews who by grace entered the new faith and were given the mission of carrying with them to the Church the sacred patrimony of the Jewish people, notably its most cherished treasure, the Law and the Prophets."

Conversion of Israel and the Two Comings of the Messiah

As we have seen, Biblical prophecy tells us that the last times will be marked by a conversion of Israel to faith in the Messiah. To understand that prophecy, it will be helpful to look at the Jewish presence in the early Church and in salvation history after Christ. As we have seen, the Second Vatican Council teaches that the Chosen People have not been rejected by Christ: they still have a role to play, which will be fully revealed in the last times, when "all Israel will be saved."[1] To understand their role at the Second Coming of Christ, we should first understand their place at the time of His first coming.

First we will look briefly at the notion of conversion with regard to the Catholic Church. Second, we will look at Hebrew Christians in the first centuries. Third, we will look at Hebrew Christians of the present day. Fourth, we will look at the prophecies of the conversion of the Jews in the last times, as revealed by Jesus Himself and by St. Paul.

Conversion

Let us begin with a question of terminology. Should Hebrew Catholics (of the first generation) be considered converts? First we must clarify what we mean by "conversion."

Conversion to Christianity—and in Christianity—always involves a spiritual turning to God. Conversion etymologically means "turning around," indicating a spiritual about-face, moving away from sin and towards God. It means a radical and progressive shift from a consideration of self (and other creatures) as one's final end, to placing one's heart in God as one's final end, and thus it is a glorious thing. John the Baptist and Jesus Himself began their preaching by calling the people to convert. We are called in fact to continual conversion, for spiritual growth means an ever more complete rejection of sin and a more perfect union with God.

---

[1] Rom 11:26. See Vatican II, Declaration on the Relation of the Church to Non-Christian Religions, *Nostra aetate* 4.

Spiritual writers speak of three main conversions in the spiritual life, and illustrate this with the example of the life of the Apostles, especially of St. Peter.[2] First the Apostles left the world—all their possessions—to follow Christ. But they were still worldly: they hoped for a temporal triumph of Israel and they did not understand the redemptive value of suffering. They ran from the scene after Jesus was arrested, and Peter denied Him three times. Peter's bitter sorrow after his denial of Christ was his second conversion, which was predicted by Christ when He said, "When you have turned again, strengthen your brethren" (Lk 22:32). Their third conversion occurred at Pentecost, which introduced them to an intimate knowledge and love of God.

It is true that conversion among ancient societies did mean leaving one's people or tribe to join another, and converting to Judaism still means becoming a member of that people on the natural level. Catholicism, however, has never required a person to leave his people, because the Church is not a natural, but a supernatural society, which therefore does not annul the ties to natural societies which an individual had before conversion. It does not replace natural society, but is *above ethnic and tribal boundaries*, and so a Catholic is always a member of two societies: one natural and the other supernatural. The early Christians knew this, and thus remained patriotic members of their country. A testimony to this consciousness on the part of the early Church can be found in a beautiful anonymous letter from the third century to Diognetus:

> For Christians are not distinguished from the rest of humanity by country, language, or custom. For nowhere do they live in cities of their own, nor do they speak some unusual dialect, nor do they practice an eccentric way of life. This teaching of theirs has not been discovered by the thought and reflection of ingenious people, nor do they promote any human doctrine, as some do. But while they live in both Greek and barbarian cities, as each one's lot was cast, and follow the local customs in dress and food and other aspects of life, at the same time they demonstrate the remarkable and admittedly unusual character of their own citizenship. They live in their own countries, but only as nonresidents; they participate in everything as citizens, and endure everything as foreigners. Every foreign country is their fatherland, and every fatherland is foreign. They marry like everyone else, and have children, but they do not expose their offspring. They share their food but not their wives. They are in the flesh, but they do not live

---

[2] See Reginald Garrigou-Lagrange, *The Three Conversions in the Spiritual Life* (Rockford, IL: TAN Books, 2002).

according to the flesh. They live on earth, but their citizenship is in heaven.[3]

We can speak of converts to Christianity as those who enter this supernatural society of the Church through Baptism and who seek to put on the new man in Christ so as to live in a way worthy of this supernatural society of the Body of Christ. They do not leave their natural society. Jewish converts did not leave their customs and history.

The term "conversion" is also used to describe the loss of belief in one religion and the genesis of belief in another. Thus Roman pagans, Buddhists, Hindus, Muslims, atheists, etc., are considered converts when they reject their former beliefs and enter the Church. When Jewish people enter the Catholic Church, however, they are not rejecting the faith of Israel! On the contrary, they have come to understand that faith as fulfilled in the coming of Christ. One can argue that they have become true and "completed" Jews, following the will of God now expressed in His New Covenant with them and with all people.

The Apostolic Church

The Apostolic Church that we read about in the first eleven chapters of Acts was composed entirely of Jewish people who believed that Christ was the divine Messiah.

Did the members of the Apostolic Church consider themselves as "converts"? Although they did not use that terminology, they were aware that they had entered a new supernatural religious society governed not by the High Priests but by the Apostles, with religious rites centering on the "breaking of the bread."[4] Furthermore, they were aware that they had a grave obligation to live in a new way according to the spirit and not according to the flesh, and that this involved a progressive *turning around*—conversion—to the Lord.

Did they continue to follow the ceremonial law? Here we must make some distinctions. For the first decade, the answer must be yes, as far as we know. Peter followed the kosher laws until he was commanded by God in a vision to kill and eat unkosher animals, and shortly thereafter visited the family of a Roman centurion and ate with them (Acts 10:1–11:18). The Apostles continued to be present at the sacrifices in the Temple and did not separate themselves from the worship practiced by Israel, but used it to proclaim Christ. It would have also

---

[3] Letter to Diognetus 5, in *The Apostolic Fathers: Greek Texts and English Translations*, trans. Michael W. Holmes, 3rd ed. (Grand Rapids, MI: Baker Academic, 2007), 701–703.

[4] See Acts 2:42; 4:32–33.

been natural for them to continue to follow the ceremonial law as a venerable custom of their people and history, especially since at this point there was no sociological division in the Church between Jews and non-Jews, for the Gentiles had not yet entered.

Things began to change, however, when a significant group of Gentiles began to believe in the Gospel in Antioch (where the disciples first came to be known as "Christians"). We gather from St. Paul's Epistle to the Galatians that the Apostles, including Peter and Paul, shared table fellowship also with Gentile converts, which meant that they were not observing all the kosher laws. Obviously this was done to strengthen the fellowship or communion of the Church, and not allow it to be divided into two groups that could not eat with each other.

St. Peter, however, stopped sharing table fellowship with the Gentiles at Antioch when Jewish Christians from Judea from the party of James arrived there, who would be scandalized by the breaking of the kosher laws. St. Peter thought it was better to avoid conflict with them, which apparently had the effect of leading some of the Gentile Christians also to follow the Mosaic ceremonial law. This lasted until St. Paul came and openly confronted Peter on the issue. St. Paul recounts this episode in Galatians 2:11–16:

> But when Cephas came to Antioch I opposed him to his face, because he stood condemned. For before certain men came from James, he ate with the Gentiles; but when they came he drew back and separated himself, fearing the circumcision party. And with him the rest of the Jews acted insincerely, so that even Barnabas was carried away by their insincerity. But when I saw that they were not straightforward about the truth of the gospel, I said to Cephas before them all, "If you, though a Jew, live like a Gentile and not like a Jew, how can you compel the Gentiles to live like Jews?" We ourselves, who are Jews by birth and not Gentile sinners, yet who know that a man is not justified by works of the law but through faith in Jesus Christ, even we have believed in Christ Jesus, in order to be justified by faith in Christ, and not by works of the law, because by works of the law shall no one be justified.

St. Peter had stopped following the Jewish ceremonial law while living among the Gentile Christians. St. Paul reasoned that if he, as a Jew, did not follow the Law, how could he lead the Gentiles to observe the Jewish rites? The very logic of these rites points to their fulfillment in Christ and His Church. The Sabbath was a figure of the Lord's Day. The Paschal lamb is a figure of Jesus. The kosher laws had separated Jews from all other peoples, to preserve the faith revealed to them by

God, which included the expectation of the Messiah. But after Christ had come and had commanded them to go out to the whole world, the ceremonial law was fulfilled and separation was no longer expedient.

Tensions arose and the problem came to a head, culminating in the accusation that St. Paul was a heretic. The support of James was needed, so the Council of Jerusalem was called, described in Acts 15, which authoritatively settled the issue of whether Gentile Christians were bound to follow the Mosaic ceremonial law. The answer was a decisive no, but a minimal observation was required of them for the sake of peace: they were not to eat animals killed by strangulation contrary to the kosher law, nor sacrificed to idols.

The Council of Jerusalem, however, said nothing about whether Christians from the circumcision should continue to practice the ceremonial law of Moses. Apparently this was not yet a burning issue, or one capable of resolution at that time.

It seems that it was assumed that the church in Jerusalem and Palestine would continue to observe the ceremonial law. However, St. Paul (and St. Peter appears to have agreed) thought this would not be the case (at least with regard to dietary laws) where the Christian community was composed both of Gentile and Jewish believers, for it would have the effect either of leading the Gentiles believers into adopting the ceremonial law—contrary to the decision made by the Council of Jerusalem—or of separating the community in a harmful way into two factions who could not enjoy table fellowship.

The Judeo-Christian Church of the First Three Centuries

The church in Jerusalem was governed by bishops from the circumcision until the time of the second Jewish revolt.[5] The first bishop was James, traditionally identified with the Apostle James the Less, cousin of Jesus, and author of the Epistle of James. The historian Josephus speaks about him in his work, *Antiquities of the Jews*. Although he apparently continued to follow the Jewish ceremonial law, he was nevertheless martyred by the High Priest Ananus in the year 62 AD.[6]

---

[5] Eusebius gives us a list of fifteen Hebrew-Christian bishops in his *History of the Church* 4.5.1–4, trans. G.A. Williamson (London: Penguin Books, 1989), 156.

[6] Josephus, *Antiquities of the Jews* 20.9.1, trans. William Whiston, in *Josephus: Complete Works* (Grand Rapids, MI: Kregel Publications, 1978), 423: "Ananus . . . assembled the Sanhedrin of the judges, and brought before them the brother of Jesus, who was called Christ, whose name was James, and some others, and when he had formed an accusation against them as breakers of the Law, he delivered them to be stoned." The martyrdom of James was also narrated by Hegesippus, quoted by Eusebius in *History of the Church* 2.23, pp. 99–103.

After the first revolt, Jewish life was greatly disrupted, and tension with the Romans increased. Things became radically worse after the second Jewish War under Hadrian in 132. This rebellion was led by Bar Kochba ("son of the star"), who proclaimed himself as the Messiah and was supported by leading rabbis, such as Rabbi Akiba. He was utterly defeated; Jerusalem was again destroyed and a pagan temple was constructed on the Temple mount. After the terrible disaster of this war, circumcised men were forbidden to come near to Jerusalem, and it became an exclusively non-Jewish city; the church in Jerusalem thus had only Gentile members, with Gentile bishops.

What happened to the Jewish Christians?[7] They were caught in a terrible position, suffering persecution from all sides: first from the Jews under Bar Kochba and the rabbinical authorities, and then from the Romans.

Why did this happen? It can be seen that this dual persecution was in part a bitter fruit of the Jewish Wars, and thus had a political/social dimension. In addition, after 132 AD, the church in Jerusalem was no longer a Hebrew-Christian community. This meant that the four great apostolic sees of the early Church—Jerusalem, Antioch, Rome, and Alexandria (founded by St. Mark)—were governed by Gentile Christians. The church from the circumcision lost its apostolic see, and its members (that is, those who were still practicing some Jewish rites such as circumcision) were continually diminishing, probably through assimilation.

Hebrew Christians who continued to observe the ceremonial law also suffered persecution from Gentile Christian leaders of the second century, who often denounced the continued practice of the Mosaic ceremonial law on the part of Christians, even if they were of Jewish descent. We see this, for example, in the great martyr and Father of the Church, St. Ignatius of Antioch. Several times he warns the churches of Asia Minor against the continued observance of the Jewish ceremonial law as if it remained obligatory. He was probably also concerned that the centrality of the Paschal mystery would be obscured if Hebrew Christians continued to follow the ceremonial law of Moses, as though, after the Passion of Christ, nothing fundamental had changed. The strength of his language shows that he regarded this as a significant

---

[7] For information on the Hebrew Christians of the first centuries, see Bellarmino Bagatti, *The Church from the Circumcision: History and Archaeology of the Judaeo-Christians*, trans. Eugene Hoade (Jerusalem: Franciscan Printing Press, 1984); Emmanuel Testa, *The Faith of the Mother Church: An Essay on the Theology of the Judeo-Christians* (Jerusalem: Franciscan Printing Press, 1992); Lino Randellini, *La Chiesa dei Giudeo-cristiani* (Brescia: Paideia, 1968).

pastoral problem.[8] He therefore held that Christians from the circumcision should leave aside the observance of the ceremonial law of Moses, observing Sunday instead of the Sabbath, etc. In his Letter to the Magnesians 8–10, he writes:

> For if we continue to live in accordance with Judaism, we admit that we have not received grace. . . . If, then, those who had lived according to ancient practices came to the newness of hope, no longer keeping the sabbath but living in accordance with the Lord's day, on which our life also arose through him and his death, . . . how can we possibly live without him, whom even the prophets, who were his disciples in the Spirit, were expecting as their teacher? . . . It is utterly absurd to profess Jesus Christ and to practice Judaism. For Christianity did not believe in Judaism, but Judaism in Christianity, in which every tongue believed and was brought together to God.[9]

In conformity with this attitude, it seems that the great majority of Hebrew Christians in the early Church tended to assimilate and gradually lose their specific Hebrew-Christian identity.

At this time the Talmud tells us that the Hebrew-Christian community was known as the Nazarenes. This community used the Gospel of Matthew in its original Aramaic (or Hebrew). It consisted of orthodox Catholics who maintained their Jewish identity by following Jewish law as a custom of their people. Their number steadily diminished, and they finally died out by the sixth century.

Another problem was the rise of a Hebrew-Christian heretical sect called the Ebionites. They believed in Jesus as the Messiah and continued to practice the ceremonial law, as did the Nazarenes, but they did not believe in the divinity of Christ, the Virgin Birth, nor did they recognize the authority of St. Paul and his teaching.[10] Obviously they also did not recognize the authority of the Catholic Church, nor the ecclesiological principle of communion with the universal Church. The Fathers of the Church spoke negatively of them; they were condemned by councils and eventually died out.

In summary, we can recognize three tendencies among the Church from the circumcision. The majority, it would seem, followed the practice of St. Paul and St. Peter in ceasing to observe the Mosaic ceremonial law, for the sake of communion with the Gentile Christians.

---

[8] It is probable that certain Hebrew-Christian sects separated themselves from the Gentile Christians and observed their Eucharist apart, perhaps on the Sabbath.

[9] *The Apostolic Fathers: Greek Texts and English Translations*, 207–9.

[10] See St. Irenaeus, *Against Heresies* 1.26.1-2; 4.33.4; and 5.1.3.

A second group, principally in the land of Israel, followed the example of James in continuing to observe the ceremonial law without holding it to be necessary for salvation, while remaining orthodox in faith in the divinity of Christ, accepting the teaching of St. Paul, and remaining in communion with the universal Church. A third group fell into heresy, denying the divinity of Christ and the Virgin Birth, denying the authority of the teaching of St. Paul, holding the necessity of the ceremonial law, and thus falling out of communion with the universal Church.

The result is that from about the fourth century to our own day, the visible existence of a Hebrew-Catholic community—as a manifestation of the acceptance of Christ by a significant portion of the Chosen People—has practically disappeared, to the point that awareness that the Church was Hebrew Christian at its origin has been largely lost. This loss of awareness has undoubtedly contributed to the tragic history of Christian anti-Semitism. It is not unreasonable, however, to think that things are beginning to change, if we read the signs of the times. Today the Church has called for a greater awareness of her Jewish roots,[11] and we find these three types of Hebrew Christians again represented in greater numbers.

Hebrew Catholics in Modern Times

Alphonse Ratisbonne

The last two centuries have seen a great influx of Hebrew Catholics. Alphonse Ratisbonne was one of the most dramatic cases in the nineteenth century. He had been a brazenly outspoken secular atheist Jew, of an eminent Jewish family, engaged to be married to a sixteen-year-old woman whom he loved very much. Since she was so young, it was determined the wedding should be put off for six months, during which time he could distract himself on a grand tour of Europe. His brother, who had already become a Jesuit priest, had a friend in Rome, Theodore de Bussieres, who met with Alphonse and was inspired to pray for him, even though (or perhaps because) Alphonse made his views on religion quite clear to him. He gave Alphonse a miraculous medal and challenged him to pray the *Memorare*.[12] After all, he said, it means nothing to you, so what difference does it make if you say it or

---

[11] Vatican II, *Nostra aetate* 4.

[12] Remember, O most gracious Virgin Mary, that never was it known that anyone who fled to your protection, implored your help, or sought your intercession, was left unaided. Inspired with this confidence, I fly to you, O virgin of virgins, my mother. To you I come, before you I stand, sinful and sorrowful. O mother of the Word Incarnate! Despise not my petitions, but in your mercy hear and answer them. Amen.

not? Alphonse agreed, and said it many times, almost against his will, for it would not leave his head. Other people were praying for him, one of whom died while Alphonse was still in Rome. Theodore wished to make a certain amendment to the funeral arrangements of that man, and Alphonse accompanied him to the church where the plans were to be discussed. Alphonse was left alone in the church for not more than fifteen minutes, but when Theodore returned, he found his friend kneeling in deep recollection at a side altar. He had seen Mary, in great splendor, as she appears on the miraculous medal. She had not said anything, but he said that now he understood everything and desired to be baptized as soon as possible. He also exclaimed that he knew that his conversion was due in great part to the prayers of the man who had died. Ratisbonne became a priest, and founded the Fathers of Zion and the Daughters of Zion in the Holy Land.[13]

Edith Stein

Edith Stein was one of the most famous converts of the twentieth century. She was born into an orthodox Jewish family, but lost her faith while in college and became an atheist. She was considered a very fine philosopher: she studied phenomenology with Husserl, wrote her doctorate under his direction, and became a professor of philosophy at the University of Freiburg at the age of 26.

One evening while on holiday with friends, she picked up *The Life of St. Teresa of Avila*, which she did not put down until finishing it the following morning, with the conviction that it was true. She was baptized shortly afterwards, on January 1, 1922, at the age of 30.

She was immediately drawn to the idea of becoming a Carmelite, but it was thought more prudent for her not to act so quickly. So she taught at a Dominican girls' school for ten years and familiarized herself with Catholic philosophy. In 1933 she entered the Carmelite convent in Cologne, received the habit in 1934, and was later transferred to a convent in the Netherlands to avoid the Nazi threat. However, when the public letter of the Dutch Bishops' Conference was read in all the churches of that country in July of 1942 to protest Nazi anti-Semitism, the Nazis retaliated by arresting all Jewish converts, who up to that time had not been deported.

St. Edith knew that the Jews had been carrying the Cross of Christ throughout history, without knowing it. But she knew it, and sensed a

---

[13] See *The Conversion of Ratisbonne, Narratives of Alphonse Ratisbonne and Baron Theodore de Bussieres* (Fort Collins, CO: Roman Catholic Books, 2000), and Roy Schoeman, *Honey from the Rock* (San Francisco: Ignatius Press, 2007), 1–32.

special mission to carry it with them in a more conscious way.[14] She was taken to Auschwitz and died there with her sister Rosa, also a convert, on August 9, 1942. John Paul II declared her the patroness of Europe.

Israel Zolli

Israel Zolli was the Chief Rabbi of Rome during World War II. His first encounter with Christ occurred when he was a young boy playing in the house of a Catholic friend. A crucifix was on the wall, and he did not know what it was. Why was a crucified man hanging on the wall? Had He been evil, to suffer such a punishment? He knew He couldn't be evil, because the family who possessed the crucifix was so good, and because the expression of the man showed extraordinary patience and humility. He wondered if He was the Suffering Servant prophesied by Isaiah in four separate texts, known as the canticles of the Suffering Servant (Is 42, 49, 50, and 53).

Rabbi Zolli became a great philologist and Bible scholar. His studies and prayer led him to believe in the divinity of Christ, but he was not ready to take the final step of conversion until 1944. He was leading the services for Yom Kippur when Christ appeared to him and said it would be the last time he would celebrate that event. At home that evening, his wife said to him, "Today while you were before the Ark of the Torah, it seemed to me as if the white figure of Jesus put His hands on your head as if He were blessing you." His youngest daughter then called to him from her room. She said, "You are talking about Jesus Christ. . . . You know, Papa, tonight I have been dreaming that I saw a very tall, white Jesus, but I don't remember what came next."[15] A few days later Rabbi Zolli requested to enter the Church and was baptized shortly thereafter, followed by his wife and daughter. He took the name of Eugenio, after Pope Pius XII,[16] in gratitude for all the Pope had done for the Jews during the war. The Vatican had filled its rooms and other Church properties with Jews in hiding and had spent millions of dollars to aid Jews; Rabbi Zolli himself had asked for fifteen kilos of gold to satisfy the Nazis as a ransom for his community and was granted it.

Other important Hebrew Catholics of recent generations include Herman Cohen, the Lehmann brothers, the Libermann brothers, Raissa Maritain, Karl Stern,[17] Cardinal Lustiger, archbishop of Paris, Bernard Nathanson, and many others.

---

[14] See Waltraud Herbstrith, *Edith Stein: A Biography*, 162–69.

[15] Eugenio Zolli, *Before the Dawn* (New York: Sheed and Ward, 1954), 184.

[16] The Pope's given name was Eugenio Pacelli.

[17] His conversion is beautifully recounted in his autobiographical work, *The Pillar of Fire* (New Hope, KY: The Remnant, 2000).

Messianic Judaism

In recent years, the flow of converts has vastly increased, although they mostly remain in Evangelical or non-denominational circles. Today it is estimated that there are about 150,000 Messianic Jews in the United States, and 500,000 to 1,000,000 worldwide.

The former Soviet Union also has large Messianic Jewish congregations. "Yevgeny Umedman, a secular Jew in Kiev who secretly attends Messianic meetings and advises a local Orthodox rabbi on the issue, has no doubts about the scale of the situation. 'I'd say that for every one Jew going to synagogue, there are ten going to church,' he says of Kiev's Jews."[18]

Some segments of Messianic Judaism have parallels with the heretical Hebrew-Christian sects of the early Church, such as the Ebionites. For example, a Messianic Jewish website posted a question asking whether Messianic Jews have an official position on the divinity of Christ. The answer was as follows:

> The only official view that we all agree on in Messianic Judaism is that Yeshua is the Messiah, that he was a Jew and lived as a Jew without changing or abolishing anything previously established in Torah, and therefore, we need to follow it. That's basically it. Other theories, points of view and theological subjects are subjected to debate.[19]

The End of the "Time of the Gentiles"

John Paul II put great importance on reading the signs of the times in order to understand where the world is going. Where are the opportunities of faith? Israel is now a Jewish state, and memorials of Jesus and His activity are present throughout the country. The Christian presence predisposes Jews to ask questions they prefer not to ask. They do not understand the Church, but they are beginning to be open to Jesus. Thus the signs of the times indicate that there is a greater providential opening for faith in Christ among the Jewish people. A sociological study of the perception of Jesus in present-day Israel states:

> The figure of Jesus, the Jew from Nazareth, looms large on the Israeli horizon, although not much is said about him openly and most Jews cautiously refrain from mentioning his name in public. Still he is very much in the mind of the Israeli Jews, more now

---

[18] Frank Brown, "A Cross of Two Faiths," *Moscow Times*, June 22, 2001, available at http://www.ncsj.org/AuxPages/062201Messianic.shtml.

[19] Beliefnet.com, available online at:
http://www.beliefnet.com/boards/message_list.asp?discussionID=480652.

than ever, and the awareness of his shadow in Israel is constantly growing.

In Galilee, the most beautiful and inspiring part of Israel, he is the dominating figure. Every site of antiquity and every beauty spot in Galilee bears his footprints. He is still walking by the sea of Galilee (cf. Mt 4:18); on the Sabbath day he enters the synagogue in Capernaum; in Tabgha, close to Capernaum, he performs the miracle of the loaves and the fishes. On the Mount of Beatitudes, which overlooks the waters of the lake, he utters his immortal Sermon on the Mount. Of course, Nazareth is the center of his life, and Jerusalem the scene of his last ministry. Much of the charm and magnetism of the Holy Land is due, not only to echoes of the Old Testament, but also to echoes of Jesus' life. Being confronted with Jesus in this way is a new experience for the Jew. In the Diaspora, Jesus looked alien to the Jew, an outsider, an interloper. But in Israel, he is seen as the Jew from Nazareth, a native of this country, a Sabra, with claims to the land as strong as any. He cannot be brushed aside as a foreign influence. . . .

If Israel is heir to the Second Commonwealth, is she not heir also to the most significant spiritual message of that Commonwealth? Rabbinical Judaism was the Judaism of the Diaspora. What is the Judaism of the Third Commonwealth to be? Should it not incorporate the most important message of the preceding Commonwealth?

The mystery of this simple Jew from Nazareth, who managed to conquer almost the whole world and whose spiritual power was stronger than that of the whole of Jewry is simply puzzling to the Israeli Jew. Who was he? Where lies the secret and mystery of his power? How did this Jew manage to attract the immense love and admiration of the world, while the Jews attracted only hatred and contempt? How did he manage to fulfill the task set in the Bible for the Jews to serve as "a light unto the nations," while Jewry failed? Why was it that only he managed to shape and mold the world, while the Jews played a losing game, rolling in the dust? Why has the genius of Jesus never been repeated within Jewish gates? And will it ever be repeated?[20]

Various Christian theologians also see the state of Israel as a possibility of grace, as represented in this statement by Edward Flannery, SJ:

---

[20] Ferdynand Zweig, *Israel, the Sword and the Harp: The Mystique of Violence and the Mystique of Redemption* (Rutherford: Fairleigh Dickinson Univ. Press, 1970), 219, 225–26. Quoted in Elias Friedman, *Jewish Identity* (New York: Miriam Press, 1987), 163–65.

With Congar, we may think that God wished to bring a representative cross-section of the Jewish people to the Holy Land in order to bring it face to face with the great question of the messiah. Israel's restoration to the land of the promise, even though under secular auspices, may thus be a distant preparation for her final encounter with grace.[21]

Jesus prophesied that "Jerusalem will be trampled by the Gentiles, until the time of the Gentiles are fulfilled" (Lk 21:24). The fact that Israel is a sovereign nation today is perhaps an indication that that time has indeed been fulfilled, and this finds confirmation in what could be called the great apostasy of the contemporary world.

The occurrence of an apostasy before the Second Coming of Christ can be seen in Jesus' prophecies in Matthew 24:10–12 of a falling away from the faith and a cooling of charity: "And then many will fall away, and betray one another, and hate one another. And many false prophets will arise and lead many astray. And because wickedness is multiplied, most men's love will grow cold." This falling away from the faith is also implied in Luke 18:8: "When the Son of man comes, will he find faith on earth?"

St. Paul also refers to an apostasy or rebellion against the faith as a sign of the Second Coming in 2 Thessalonians 2:1–5:

> Now concerning the coming of our Lord Jesus Christ and our assembling to meet him, we beg you, brethren, not to be quickly shaken in mind or excited, either by spirit or by word, or by letter purporting to be from us, to the effect that the day of the Lord has come. Let no one deceive you in any way; for that day will not come, unless the *rebellion* [*apostasia*] comes first, and the man of lawlessness is revealed, the son of perdition, who opposes and exalts himself against every so-called god or object of worship, so that he takes his seat in the temple of God, proclaiming himself to be God. Do you not remember that when I was still with you I told you this?

"Apostasy" is used here in the social sense and apparently means that a formerly Christian society has rejected the Catholic faith. Surely this is true of the modern world, which is increasingly referred to as a post-Christian society. The roots of this apostasy reach back to the fourteenth century, with the loss of harmony between faith and reason, and grew with the sixteenth-century Protestant rebellion against the Catholic Church. Nevertheless, it is much worse today with widespread

---

[21] Edward Flannery, S.J., *The Anguish of the Jews: Twenty-three Centuries of Anti-Semitism* (New York: Macmillan, 1965). Quoted in Friedman, *Jewish Identity*, 159.

atheism and lack of faith. Although it may continue to develop for centuries, one wonders how much longer this process can go on.

John Henry Cardinal Newman commented on the coming of the apostasy in an article on the Antichrist written in 1838 while he was still an Anglican:

> Is there no reason to fear that some Apostasy is gradually gathering, hastening on in this very day? For is there not at this very time, a special effort made almost all over the world, that is, every here and there, more or less in sight or out of sight, in this or that place, but most visibly or formidably in its most civilized and powerful parts, an effort to be without Religion? Surely there is at this day a confederacy of evil, marshaling its hosts from all parts of the world, organizing itself, taking its measure, enclosing the Church as in a net, preparing the way for a general Apostasy from it.[22]

The Conversion of the Jews before the *Parousia*

One of the signs heralding the imminence of the *parousia* will be the conversion of Jews to faith in Christ after the time of the great apostasy. This hope is based on several Biblical texts. In the Old Testament, the prophet Zechariah (12:10) alludes to the future conversion of Israel, for he prophesies that the day will come when the inhabitants of Jerusalem will weep over the Messiah whom they have pierced:

> And I will pour out on the house of David and the inhabitants of Jerusalem a spirit of compassion and supplication, so that, when they look on him whom they have pierced, they shall mourn for him, as one mourns for an only child, and weep bitterly over him, as one weeps over a firstborn.

It seems that Jesus indirectly alluded to this future conversion of Israel in Matthew 23:37–39 when He wept over Jerusalem as He came down the Mount of Olives on Palm Sunday. While looking upon the Temple from the Mount of Olives, He said that the world would not see Him again until the Jewish People accept Him as the Messiah who "comes in the name of the Lord":

> O Jerusalem, Jerusalem, killing the prophets and stoning those who are sent to you! How often would I have gathered your children together as a hen gathers her brood under her wings, and you would not! Behold, your house is forsaken and desolate. For I

---

[22] Newman, *Discussions and Arguments on Various Subjects* (New York: Longmans, Green, and Co., 1897), 59.

tell you, you will not see me again, until you say, "Blessed is he who comes in the name of the Lord."

As Cardinal Journet observed, "No sooner, then, does He reproach Jerusalem for having rejected His love than He announces the triumph of God's mercy over its unwillingness. . . . Afterwards an age will come when Israel will at last open its heart to its Messiah and will bless Him in a shout of loving welcome."[23]

St. Paul develops this theme of the future ingathering of Israel into the Church in Romans 11, as seen above,[24] in which he speaks of his anguish with regard to Israel's rejection of Christ. He recognizes that the blindness of a large part of Israel was permitted by God to help the Gentiles to come into the Church. However, he reasons that "if their rejection means the reconciliation of the world, what will their acceptance mean, but life from the dead?" (Rom 11:15).[25]

He compares ancient Israel to a cultivated olive tree. With the coming of the Messiah, some branches were lopped off because of their unbelief (a symbol of the Jews who did not believe in Christ), and other branches of wild olive trees (Gentile believers) were grafted in. But those who were engrafted can easily be removed once again, and the natural branches more easily re-inserted. The hardening that has come upon Israel is only for a time, until the "full number of the Gentiles" has come in (Rom 11:25), which indicates the proclamation of the Gospel to every nation and culture (Mt 24:14).

Drawing on this text of Romans 11, the *Catechism of the Catholic Church* 674 treats this theme of the conversion of the Jewish people in the last times:

> The glorious Messiah's coming is suspended at every moment of history until his recognition by "all Israel," for "a hardening has come upon part of Israel" in their "unbelief" toward Jesus.[26] St.

---

[23] Journet, "The Mysterious Destinies of Israel," in *The Bridge: A Yearbook of Judaeo-Christian Studies*, ed. J. Oesterreicher, 2:82.

[24] Chapter 10, pp. 170–74.

[25] See Journet, "The Mysterious Destinies of Israel," 37: "It is this love, God's fidelity, that in the end will lift from Israel the heavy weight of its resistance. There will be a day, the third epoch, when it will understand and accept the mystery of the Cross and sing hosanna, hoshi'ahnna, 'save us we pray!'; when the whole people will once again, and forever, welcome Jesus with the blessing from the ancient liturgy of thanksgiving: Blessed in the name of Yahweh be He who comes. There will be a day when the Israel of the flesh will again be one with the Israel of the spirit—the great ingathering of which the Apostle says that it will be like 'life from the dead' (Rom 11:15)."

[26] Rom 11:20–26; see Mt 23:39.

Peter says to the Jews of Jerusalem after Pentecost: "Repent therefore, and turn again, that your sins may be blotted out, that times of refreshing may come from the presence of the Lord, and that he may send the Christ appointed for you, Jesus, whom heaven must receive until the time for establishing all that God spoke by the mouth of his holy prophets from of old."[27] St. Paul echoes him: "For if their rejection means the reconciliation of the world, what will their acceptance mean but life from the dead?"[28] The "full inclusion" of the Jews in the Messiah's salvation, in the wake of "the full number of the Gentiles,"[29] will enable the People of God to achieve "the measure of the stature of the fullness of Christ," in which "God may be all in all."[30]

The future recognition of Jesus as the Messiah on the part of all Israel is foreshadowed in the Biblical story of Joseph, the son of Jacob. He can be seen as a figure of Christ, and his brothers as a figure of the Jewish people, who rejected Him, but whose sin led to the salvation of the whole world. However, the typology does not have to be seen to end at the Resurrection, but could also include the Second Coming. For when Joseph was made the distributor of all the goods of Egypt, which nourished the whole world, his brothers did not know him, nor did they recognize him when they saw him. But Joseph knew them and tried their fidelity. In the end, he revealed himself to them, and brought them to a privileged position in Egypt. Could this not be seen as an allegory of what will happen to the Jews before Christ's Second Coming? Could this be what Bl. John XXIII was referring to when he greeted a group of Jews with the words: "I am Joseph your brother"?

---

[27] Acts 3:19–21.
[28] Rom 11:15.
[29] Rom 11:12, 25; see Lk 21:24.
[30] Eph 4:13; 1 Cor 15:28.

CHAPTER 12

Mary, Daughter of Zion
and Mother of the Church

The mystery of Israel and the Church is summed up in a marvelous way in Mary, who is at once the exemplary daughter of Zion, the culmination of the faith of Israel, the most perfect disciple of Christ, and the Mother of the Church and of every human being, insofar as all are called to be members of the Church. She is the most perfect link between the Old and the New Covenants. Mary is at one and the same time the perfect summary, exemplar, and recapitulation of the faith of Israel, and the Mother of the new Israel, the Church. The fact that Mary is the Mother of the Church should be familiar to all Catholics. What is less familiar is Mary's role as the exemplary and perfect "daughter of Zion." Let us look first at Mary from the perspective of Israel and then as the Mother of the Church.

Election of Israel and Mary

We have seen that God's eternal plan was to redeem mankind from original sin and from all personal sins throughout history, through the Incarnation of God the Son in the fullness of time. The Incarnation was to be the center of history, the superabundant culmination of every just aspiration of mankind, announced at the very dawn of mankind's existence, as we see in Genesis 3:15–16. The devil and his cohorts will continually tempt the human race, but there shall be a woman whose seed will crush the head of Satan and of sin, and He shall be bruised—that is, suffer—in the process.[1]

We have also seen that God prepared for the Incarnation by calling Abraham and promising him that all nations would be blessed in his seed. God formed a people in whose bosom His Son would become incarnate, electing them gratuitously and separating them from all the peoples of the earth. He prepared them by revealing Himself through the Patriarchs, through the events of the Exodus, and through the Law

---

[1] We can assume that Adam and Eve would have taught this prophecy throughout their long lifetimes to their descendants, who in turn would have passed on this knowledge as a legacy to future generations and cultures.

191

given through Moses. This included the moral law summarized in the double commandment of love and the Ten Commandments; a divinely inspired ceremonial law regulating liturgy and worship; and a judicial law that governed civil affairs. Their preparation was continued in the Wisdom literature and the writings of the prophets. In this way, when the Messiah was born, He came not unexpected, but as the object of the noblest yearning of the sons and daughters of Israel for two millennia.

If this preparation was given to the people in whom He became incarnate, would it not have to be given in a still more special way to the daughter of Zion elected to be the Mother of God? If the people chosen to receive the Incarnate Word was the object of a special divine election, would not His Mother need to be the object of a still more special election?

Here we can see the most intimate connection between the election of Israel and the election of Mary as Mother of God, between the mystery of Israel and the mystery of the Mother of God. Both were elected for the same end: to receive the eternal Son of God into human society. As Israel was eternally elected to be the people in whom God would take flesh, so Mary was eternally elected to bring Him to birth as His Mother. A further tie between the people of Israel and Mary is their relationship to the Church, for both Israel and Mary had the privilege of bringing forth the Messiah, who is the Head of the Mystical Body of the Church. Thus Israel, Mary, and the Church are closely bound to each other. When St. Paul speaks of the Incarnation in Galatians 4:4–5, he touches on this relationship of Mary, Israel, and the Church: "But when the fullness of time came, God sent his Son, born of a woman, born under the Law, that he might redeem those who were under the Law, that we might receive the adoption of sons."[2]

St. Paul condenses into a few words the great mystery of God's plan in salvation history. In the fullness of time, the Father sends the Son of God into the web of human history, such that He is born of a woman and born under the Law. In other words, He is born into a people prepared through the magnificent gift of the Mosaic Law and through 2,000 years of salvation history; and born of a woman in the bosom of that people—the daughter of Zion par excellence—who would be the Mother of messianic Israel—the Mystical Body of her Son. Her preparation, although supremely hidden, must recapitulate that of Israel.

Contact with the Lord begets and requires holiness. The greater the contact and association with the Lord, the greater the holiness that is required for it. We can see a figure of this necessary holiness in various episodes of the Old Testament. When the Lord was to speak with

---

[2] Confraternity of Christian Doctrine translation (1958).

Moses on Mount Sinai, the people were commanded to purify themselves for three days, but not to touch the holy mountain, for any man or beast that touched it would be stoned.[3] Similarly, the Ark of the Covenant was kept holy by being separated from any profane contact, such that only the high priest could enter into the Holy of Holies once a year on Yom Kippur, prostrating himself with the blood of the sacrifices. Or again, an impressive example was given when the Ark of the Covenant was recovered from the enemies of Israel and was being carried in procession on a cart driven by oxen led by two Israelites, Uzzah and Ahio. At a certain point the oxen stumbled and Uzzah touched the Ark to steady it, and was struck dead by the Lord.[4]

The fact that the Ark of the Covenant could not be touched by unconsecrated human hands is a figure of the holiness belonging to the Ark of the New and everlasting Covenant: the Mother of the Redeemer. For Mary's womb was the Ark containing not tablets of the Law written on stone, but the Torah of God made flesh: the Son of God.

Because the people of Israel were to receive the Lord into their midst in the Incarnation, they were prepared for their mission of receiving Him worthily by means of a special holiness imparted through the gift of the Old Covenant. Far more was expected of them than of any other people because of the holiness required of them by the Incarnation. If that is true of Israel as a whole, how much more true it would have to be of Mary, in whose womb the Son of God became incarnate and through whose maternal care He grew up, was nurtured, loved, and educated. How would God prepare for the maternity of her who would give birth to His Son made flesh?

Marian Privileges

Catholic doctrine speaks of the great privileges received by Mary in her role as Mother of God. It is a general principle of theology that whenever God gives a special mission to a creature, He prepares the creature to accomplish the mission by a special gift of grace. We can apply this principle to all the saints and to each one of ourselves. Of course, the greater the mission, the greater the gifts of grace.

The greatest mission of all was that given to the Messiah, whose humanity was enriched with every possible grace, which He would then transmit to His Mystical Body, the Church. After Christ, the greatest

---

[3] See Ex 19:9–24.

[4] See 2 Sam 6:7: "The anger of the Lord was kindled against Uzzah; and God smote him there because he put forth his hand to the ark; and he died there beside the ark of God."

mission of all time was that given to His Mother, Mary most holy, for she was to be the living tabernacle of God made man in her womb.

All the other privileges and graces received by Mary were ordered to this most sublime privilege. From all eternity, Mary was chosen by God to become the Mother of the Word Incarnate. This was the greatest of all graces, utterly gratuitous and absolutely unmerited, for there is no way any creature could ever merit to give flesh to the Creator, give Him birth after bearing Him in her womb for nine months, and have the responsibility of raising Him.

The Second Person of the Most Holy Trinity chose to become incarnate of a human mother, and chose His mother. Whereas no mere creature can choose his mother and enrich her with every dignity that could be desired for her role, Christ both could and did. Because Mary was chosen to become the Mother of God, it was fitting that she be adorned with every spiritual gift that would make her more perfectly disposed for the mission that was given to her of bringing Christ into the world.

The first of these privileges was that of being conceived without any stain of sin whatsoever. This is the grace of the Immaculate Conception. Another privilege was the grace to persevere without the slightest sin, even venial sin, and even without any imperfection, throughout her life, so that she was constantly growing in fullness of grace. Through this fullness of grace, Our Lady was able to correspond perfectly to God's will in every moment of her life, thus meriting an increase of grace and charity. She is thus the perfect model of all sanctity, the perfect daughter of Zion, the perfect model of the Church, and the perfect realization of holiness, without spot, wrinkle, or blemish of any kind. For this sanctity, she is spoken of as the Spouse of the Holy Spirit. Through grace she "merited"[5] to be overshadowed by the Holy Spirit so as to participate in the greatest miracle of all creation: the Incarnation of the Son of God.

A third privilege of Mary is her perpetual virginity, which is intimately ordered to her divine maternity. Catholic theology teaches that Mary's virginity was maintained perfect and inviolate *before, during, and after* her delivery of Jesus.[6] It was fitting that the womb that was to

---

[5] "Merit" is used here in the broad sense of possessing a fitting disposition (which is the result of extraordinary grace) for a gratuitous divine election. In the strict sense, of course, no creature could ever merit being the Mother of God.

[6] See *CCC* 499–500, DS 291, 442, 1880 (D 993). The Lateran Council of 649, DS 503 (D 256) defined: "If anyone does not properly and truly confess in accord with the Holy Fathers, that the holy Mother of God and ever Virgin and immaculate Mary . . . conceived of the Holy Spirit without seed God the Word . . . and that she incorruptibly bore Him, her virginity remaining indestructible even after His birth, let him be condemned."

conceive the Word Incarnate, and thus become the Tabernacle of God, be absolutely separated from normal human relations. In this greatest of mysteries it was *fitting that God alone be the agent* in the miracle of the virginal conception that occurred at the moment of Mary's "yes" at the Annunciation.

It was also fitting that Christ Himself not injure that bodily integrity of His Mother during His birth. Thus He came forth through closed doors, much as on the day of His Resurrection He passed through the locked doors of the Cenacle. This explains why Mary did not suffer the pains of childbirth as do other mothers who are subject to the penalties of original sin.

After her womb was consecrated by the presence of Christ for nine months in the greatest of all mysteries that can be conceived, is it credible that Mary would have allowed that womb to bear other normal children? A vessel consecrated to God cannot afterwards be used for ordinary human purposes, such as normal eating and drinking. Although the Gospel mentions "brothers" of Jesus, the Catholic tradition has always understood this to refer to cousins of Jesus, for Hebrew frequently uses the word "brother" in this broader sense.

Figures of Mary in the Old Testament

It is often objected by Protestants that the Marian doctrine of the Church is unbiblical and unfounded in Scripture. In Joseph Ratzinger's beautiful little book on Mary called *Daughter Zion,* he speaks of the figures of Mary in the Old Testament, showing that she is present throughout the Bible, if one has eyes to see. The New Testament's portrait of Mary is modeled on figures in the Old Testament, which she fulfills in a far higher way.

> First, the portrait of Mary includes the likeness of the great mothers of the Old Testament: Sarah and especially Hannah, the mother of Samuel. Second, into that portrait is woven the whole theology of daughter Zion, in which, above all, the prophets announced the mystery of election and covenant, the mystery of God's love for Israel. A third strand can perhaps be identified in the Gospel of John: the figure of Eve, the "woman" par excellence, is borrowed to interpret Mary.[7]

In the chapter 6 we spoke of Mary as the new Eve. Just as Eve was created to be a helper similar to Adam, so it was fitting that the new Adam—Christ the Redeemer—be joined with a co-redemptrix associated in a most intimate way with His mission of redemption.

---

[7] Joseph Ratzinger, *Daughter Zion* (San Francisco: Ignatius Press, 1983), 12.

Daughter of Zion

Not infrequently we hear the complaint that Judaism and Catholicism are patriarchal religions with no significant place for a feminine role in worship. This, however, is quite false. It is true that God is portrayed in the Revelation to Israel in male terms as Father, King, and Lord, and there is no place for the female earth deities of the pagan religions.[8] However, Israel, the people of God, is spoken of generally as female. Man's relation to God is analogous to that of a bride to her bridegroom.

There is a great feminine strand through the Old Testament, culminating in and leading to the Mother of the Messiah. The Old Testament frequently speaks of Israel as a bride. It is God Himself who espouses Israel as His bride, taking her from her abandonment and humble origin, her fornication and prostitution, and purifying her to be His. For example, in Hosea 2:19–23, God says to Israel:

> I will betroth you to me for ever; I will betroth you to me in righteousness and in justice, in steadfast love, and in mercy. I will betroth you to me in faithfulness; and you shall know the Lord. . . .
> And I will have pity on Not-pitied, and I will say to Not-my-people, "You-are-my-people"; and he shall say "Thou art my God."

Many other texts of the Old Testament manifest the feminine strand by personifying Israel as the "daughter of Zion." Zechariah, for example, tells the "daughter of Zion" to sing and rejoice, for the Lord shall come to dwell in her midst, and when that happens, "many other nations shall join themselves to the Lord" (Zech 2:10–11).

Israel is spoken of as the daughter of Zion also in the context of sorrow. Lamentations 2:13 speaks literally of the sorrow of exile, but typologically of the sorrow of Mary: "What can I say for you, to what compare you, O daughter of Jerusalem? What can I liken to you, that I may comfort you, O virgin daughter of Zion? For vast as the sea is your ruin; who can restore you?"

In these and other similar texts,[9] the "daughter of Zion" refers to faithful Israel as a whole, awaiting her Lord and King. However, Mary is the daughter of Zion par excellence because she sums up the expectation of Israel for the Messiah. She is the perfect Virgin awaiting her Lord to come in her midst.

---

[8] Nevertheless, maternal traits are also ascribed to God, as in Is 66:13.

[9] See Zech 9:9–10, a prophecy of Christ's entry on Palm Sunday: "Rejoice greatly, O daughter of Zion! Shout aloud, O daughter of Jerusalem! Lo, your king comes to you"; Zeph 3:14–18; and Is 62:11–12: "Say to the daughter of Zion, 'Behold, your salvation comes.'"

Great Women of the Old Testament: Esther and Judith

Two interesting figures of Mary are Judith and Esther. The story of Judith relates an event in which Israel has been defeated, humiliated, and lies prostrate in the dust, but arises through the aid of a *woman of valor*, Judith, a widow, who beheaded Holofernes, the general of the Assyrians.

The liturgy of the Church applies the text of Judith 15:9–11 to Mary:

> "You are the exaltation of Jerusalem, you are the great glory of Israel, you are the great pride of our nation! You have done all this singlehanded; you have done great good to Israel, and God is well pleased with it. May the Almighty Lord bless you forever!" And all the people said, "So be it!"

Whereas Judith beheading Holofernes is a figure of Mary crushing the head of the serpent, Esther is a figure of Mary's mediation by way of *intercession*. Judith and Esther, therefore, are complementary figures, highlighting different aspects of Mary's role in salvation history. Esther is able to intercede to save her people from destruction because her beauty captivates the king who styles himself the king of kings. Mary is she whose interior beauty and total purity captivates the true King of Kings, attracting Him to enter her very womb in the Incarnation. Esther's beauty, like that of Judith, is thus a key part of the typology.

Secondly, the theme of humility is also crucial. Esther is an orphan, daughter of a persecuted people facing extermination. She thus represents mankind after the Fall, orphaned and in misery. She also represents Israel in particular, who, after the Exile, has fallen from her privileges and lost her sovereignty. Like the Beatitudes and the Magnificat, Esther exemplifies the great evangelical theme that "the first shall be last, and the last first." The hanging of Haman on the gallows he erected and the vindication of Mordecai and Esther and their persecuted people is a marvelous example of the fact that God "has put down the mighty from their thrones, and exalted those of low degree. . . . He has helped his servant Israel, in remembrance of his mercy" (Lk 1:52–54).

Ratzinger explains this theme of the personification of humbled Israel in Esther and Judith:

> Both embody the defeated Israel: Israel who has become a widow and wastes away in sorrow, Israel who has been abducted and dishonored among the nations, enslaved within their arbitrary desires. Yet both personify at the same time Israel's unconquered spiritual strength, which cannot boast as do the worldly powers and for that very reason knows how to scorn and overcome the mighty. The woman as savior, the embodiment of Israel's hope,

thereby takes her place alongside the unblessed-blessed mothers. It is significant that the woman always figures in Israel's thought and belief, not as a priestess, but as prophetess and judge-savior. . . . The infertile one, the powerless one becomes the savior because it is there that the locus for the revelation of God's power is found. After every fall into sin, the woman remains "mother of life."[10]

Ronald Knox gives a beautiful explanation of the typology of Esther:

> We value, then, this story of Mardochaeus and Esther because we find in it a type of our Lady's position in the economy of grace. How often a face or a scene arrests us, only because it bears some resemblance to a face or a scene we love! So it is with these Old Testament figures; they borrow their interest from the future. Like the people of the Jews, the Church of God has its enemies and its detractors: its peace is continually threatened by the world's hatred for its strictness of principle. And when times of trouble come upon us, we, too, would win a royal audience; we would ask redress for our grievances from the King of Kings. As the Jews could plead on their own behalf the loyal act of Mardochaeus, so we would plead before God, our one hope of pardon, the all-sufficient sacrifice of his Son. But who will plead it for us? It is not that we distrust his goodness; but, conscious of our need and of our own unworthiness, we would find some advocate who has a better claim on his attention than ourselves. Who has a better right to stand in God's royal Presence than our Blessed Lady? The law which included us all under the curse of original sin was a law made for all others, but not for her. Who else dare touch the sceptre that sways a universe? . . . We say to her, as Mardochaeus said to Esther, "Remember the days of thy low estate; and do thou speak to the king for us, and deliver us from death."[11]

Mary as the Created Wisdom

In the liturgy of the Church, Old Testament texts that speak of Wisdom, which is a word in the feminine gender in Hebrew, are often applied to Mary. These texts refer both to the uncreated Wisdom in God, and to the created wisdom that is received in the souls of the faithful.

A beautiful example of a wisdom text applied to Mary is Sirach 24. Wisdom will reside in Zion, and will be known for her beauty and grace.

---

[10] Joseph Ratzinger, *Daughter Zion*, 20–21.

[11] Ronald Knox, *A Retreat for Priests* (New York: Sheed and Ward, 1946), quoted in F. J. Sheed, ed., *The Mary Book* (New York: Sheed & Ward, 1950), 20–21.

She will also be a mother given to all God's children to bring forth virtue in them, and to lead them in the path of God to truth and life:

> Then the creator of all things commanded, and said to me: and he that made me, rested in my tabernacle, And he said to me: Let thy dwelling be in Jacob, and thy inheritance in Israel, and take root in my elect. . . . And I took root in an honourable people, and in the portion of my God his inheritance, and my abode is in the full assembly of saints. I was exalted like a cedar in Libanus, and as a cypress tree on mount Sion. . . . I am the mother of fair love, and of fear, and of knowledge, and of holy hope. In me is all grace of the way and of the truth, in me is all hope of life and of virtue. . . . They that eat me, shall yet hunger: and they that drink me, shall yet thirst. . . . They that work by me shall not sin.[12]

Mary as the Mother of the Church

Let us now consider Mary as the Mother of the Church, a title solemnly given to her by Pope Paul VI during the Second Vatican Council. Although Mary remained forever virgin and had no other children of her flesh after Jesus, *her maternity was not limited to one child.* Christ came into the world not for Himself, but for us, to be the Savior and new Head of a redeemed humanity which would be His Mystical Body. He came into our world of sin and suffering, this valley of tears, to take upon Himself the weight and guilt of our humanity, so as to give us a share in His divinity through sanctifying grace. All men are called to become living members of that Mystical Body, although not all, unfortunately, choose to do so.

Just as Christ was brought into this world through the principal action of God the Father, but with the participation and cooperation of the Blessed Virgin Mary, so too it is fitting that the members of Christ's Mystical Body also be conceived spiritually through the principal action of God, *but with the cooperation of that same Mother.*

Although we all have our own mothers according to the flesh, God willed us to have only one Mother in the order of grace, the Mother of Jesus. Why is this? Because our spiritual rebirth involves the birth of Christ in our hearts. We become living members of Christ's Mystical Body by becoming like Him, its head. This is effected by sanctifying grace and the virtues of faith, hope, and charity.

St. Pius X in his encyclical on Mary, *Ad diem illum* (1904), commemorating the fiftieth anniversary of the dogmatic definition of

---

[12] Sirach (Ecclesiasticus) 24:12–17, 24–25, 29–30 (Douay Rheims version). This corresponds to the RSV Sir 24:8–21.

the Immaculate Conception, wrote: "For is not Mary the Mother of Christ? Then she is our Mother also."

This is the great spiritual theme of Advent and Christmas. We pray during Advent for the coming of Christ *here and now* in our souls. The liturgy has us pray repeatedly: "Come, Lord Jesus, and redeem us": "*Veni Domine, et salva nos.*" Jesus already came two thousand years ago and will come again at the end of the world, but nevertheless, the mystery enacted in the liturgy also must have a *present realization*. We pray that Christ be born in us ever more fully, through the outpouring of God's grace.

But just as Christ was born in Bethlehem through Mary, *He will not be born in us again without Mary's maternity*. Of all the doctrines of the Catholic faith, this is surely one of the most consoling and moving. While Christ was shedding His blood for us, He made Mary our mother in the spiritual life by giving her to His "beloved disciple"—who represents all mankind who are called to be disciples—and the disciple to her (see Jn 19:26–27).

Just as we need a mother in our physical and natural life, so too we need a mother in our spiritual life, for the spiritual life is not less important than our natural life. On the contrary, it is infinitely more important, for all of eternity depends on whether we develop a true spiritual life.

In the natural order of human life, maternity is an exquisite jewel, which can never be appreciated enough. We can never love our mothers enough. What would human life be without the beauty of maternal love? Without all the sacrifices and solicitude of that love? It would be a barren place.

If this is true on the natural level, then it must be even more true on the supernatural level. God has willed that our spiritual life be continually nurtured through the action of a Mother as well as through His divine paternity. And who is that Mother? Who else but the Mother of the Word Incarnate, the sinless daughter of Zion?

Mary is thus the perfect link between the Old and the New Testaments. She brought the Messiah into Israel and into the world. She summed up, recapitulated, and totally fulfilled the mission of Israel, and by doing so, inaugurated the new Israel—the Church—founded by her Son. Thus she was made Mother of the Mystical Body of Christ and Mother of all the faithful and of all peoples. As Mother of all peoples, she has also been made the *Mother of her own people*, and as such will lead the Jewish people back to her Son, at the time appointed by God. Let us pray that Mary intercede with her Son to lift the veil from all Israel!

Bibliography

Ahern, Barnabas M. "The Exodus, Then and Now." *The Bridge: A Yearbook of Judaeo-Christian Studies*. Edited by John Oesterreicher. Vol. 1, 53–74. New York: Pantheon Books, 1955.

The Apostolic Fathers: Greek Texts and English Translations. Edited by Michael W. Holmes. 3rd ed. Grand Rapids, MI: Baker Academic, 2007.

Augustine. *City of God*. Translated by Henry Bettenson. New York: Penguin Books, 1972.

_____. *The Trinity*. Translated by Edmund Hill. Hyde Park, NY: New City Press, 1991.

_____. *The Works of Saint Augustine. Sermons I [1–19] on the Old Testament*. Translated by Edmund Hill. Brooklyn, NY: New City Press, 1990.

Bagatti, Bellarmino. *The Church from the Circumcision: History and Archaeology of the Judaeo-Christians*. Translated by Eugene Hoade. Jerusalem: Franciscan Printing Press, 1984.

Béchard, Dean P., ed. *The Scripture Documents: An Anthology of Official Catholic Teachings*. Collegeville, MN: The Liturgical Press, 2002.

Boguslawski, Steven C. *Thomas Aquinas on the Jews: Insights into His Commentary on Romans 9–11*. New York: Paulist Press, 2008.

Catechism of the Catholic Church. New York: Doubleday, 1994.

Compendium: Catechism of the Catholic Church. Washington DC: United States Conference of Catholic Bishops, 2006.

Chervin, Ronda. *En Route to Eternity*. New York: The Miriam Press, 1994.

Chervin, Ronda, ed. *The Ingrafting: The Conversion Stories of Ten Hebrew-Catholics*. New Hope, KY: Remnant of Israel, 1987.

_____. *Bread from Heaven: The Stories of 23 Jews Who Found the Messiah in the Catholic Church*. New Hope, KY: Remnant of Israel, 1994.

Congregation for the Doctrine of the Faith. Declaration *Dominus Jesus*. 2000.

Daniélou, Jean. *Dialogue with Israel. With a Response by Jacob B. Agus*. Translated by Joan Marie Roth. Baltimore: Helicon, 1968.

Daniélou, Jean and André Chouraqui. *The Jews: Views and Counterviews: A Dialogue between Jean Daniélou and André Chouraqui*. Westminister, MD: Newman Press, 1967.

De Lubac, Henri. *Catholicism: Christ and the Common Destiny of Man*. Translated by Lancelot Sheppard and Elizabeth Englund. San Francisco: Ignatius Press, 1988.

_____. *Medieval Exegesis*. Vols. 1–2: *The Four Senses of Scripture*. Translated by Mark Sebanc. Grand Rapids, MI: William B. Eerdmans, 1998–2000.

_____. *The Motherhood of the Church*. Translated by Sergia Englund. San Francisco: Ignatius Press, 1982.

_____. *Scripture in the Tradition*. Translated by Luke O'Neill. New York: Herder and Herder, 2000.

_____. *The Splendor of the Church*. Translated by Michael Mason. San Francisco: Ignatius Press, 1986.

Duesberg, Hilaire. "The Trial of the Messiah." *The Bridge: A Yearbook of Judaeo-Christian Studies*. Edited by John Oesterreicher. Vol. 1, 225–42. New York: Pantheon Books, 1955.

Dunn, James D. G. *The Parting of the Ways: Between Christianity and Judaism and their Significance for the Character of Christianity*. 2nd ed. London: SCM Press, 2006.

The Encyclopaedia of Judaism. Edited by Jacob Neusner, Alan J. Avery-Peck, and William Scott Green. 5 vols. New York: Continuum Publishing, 1999–2005.

Eusebius. *History of the Church*. Translated by G.A. Williamson. London: Penguin Books, 1989.

Feuillet, André. *The Priesthood of Christ and His Ministers*. Translated by Matthew J. O'Connell. Garden City, NY: Doubleday, 1975.

Friedman, Elias. *Jewish Identity*. New York: The Miriam Press, 1987.

Gaboriau, Florent. *The Conversion of Edith Stein*. Translated by Ralph McInerny. South Bend, IN: St. Augustine's Press, 2002.

Garrigou-Lagrange, Reginald. *The Three Conversions in the Spiritual Life*. Rockford, IL: TAN Books, 2002.

Glatzer, Nahum N. *Language of Faith: Selected Jewish Prayers*. New York: Schocken Books, 1947.

Graef, Hilda C. *The Scholar and the Cross: The Life and Work of Edith Stein*. Westminster, MD: Newman Press, 1955.

Greenspahn, Frederick E., ed. *The Human Condition in the Jewish and Christian Traditions*. Hoboken: Ktav Publishing House, 1986.

Greenstone, Julius H. *The Messiah Idea in Jewish History*. Philadelphia: Jewish Publication Society of America, 1943.

Hahn, Scott, ed. *Catholic Bible Dictionary*. New York: Doubleday, 2009.

Hahn, Scott. *Covenant and Communion: The Biblical Theology of Pope Benedict XVI*. Grand Rapids, MI: Brazos Press, 2009.

_____. *Hail, Holy Queen: The Mother of God in the Word of God*. New York: Image Books, 2001.

Herbstrith, Waltraud. *Edith Stein: A Biography*. Translated by Bernard Bonowitz. San Francisco: Ignatius Press, 1992.

Heschel, Abraham Joshua. *Man's Quest for God: Studies in Prayer and Symbolism*. New York: Charles Scribner's Sons, 1954.

Irenaeus. *Against Heresies*. Vol. 1, *The Ante-Nicene Fathers*. Peabody, MA: Hendrickson Publishers, 1994.

Jacobs, Louis. *Faith*. New York: Basic Books, 1968.

_____. *Hasidic Prayer.* New York: Schocken Books, 1973.

_____. *Judaism and Theology: Essays on the Jewish Religion.* London: Vallentine Mitchell, 2005.

Jerome. *Jerome's Commentary on Daniel.* Translated by Gleason L. Archer, Jr. Grand Rapids, MI: Baker Book House, 1958.

_____. *Commentary on Matthew.* Translated by Thomas Scheck. Washington, DC: Catholic University of America Press, 2008.

The Jewish Enclopedia. Edited by Isidore Singer. 12 vols. New York: Ktav Publishing House, 1964.

John Paul II. Apostolic Letter *Dies Domini.* July 5, 1998.

_____. Encyclical *Dominum et vivificantem.* May 18, 1986.

_____. Encyclical *Redemptor hominis.* March 4, 1979.

_____. *Mary: God's Yes to Man: John Paul's Encyclical Redemptoris Mater.* Introduction by Joseph Card. Ratzinger. San Francisco: Ignatius Press, 1988.

Josephus. *Complete Works.* Translated by William Whiston. Grand Rapids, MI: Kregel Publications, 1978.

Journet, Charles Cardinal. "The Mysterious Destinies of Israel." In *The Bridge: A Yearbook of Judaeo-Christian Studies.* Edited by John Oesterreicher. Vol. 2, 35–90. New York: Pantheon Books, 1956.

_____. *The Theology of the Church.* Translated by Victor Szczurek. San Francisco: Ignatius Press, 2004.

Judéo-christianisme: Recherches historiques et théologiques offertes en hommage au cardinal Jean Daniélou. Paris: Editions Beauchesne, 1972.

Justin Martyr. *First Apology.* Vol. 1, *The Ante-Nicene Fathers.* Peabody, MA: Hendrickson Publishers, 1994.

_____. *Dialogue with the Jew Trypho.* Vol. 1, *The Ante-Nicene Fathers.* Peabody, MA: Hendrickson Publishers, 1994.

Kevane, Eugene. *The Lord of History: Christocentrism and the Philosophy of History.* Boston: St. Paul Editions, 1980.

Kinzer, Mark S. *Post-Missionary Messianic Judaism: Redefining Christian Engagement with the Jewish People.* Grand Rapids, MI: Brazos Press, 2005.

Klausner, Joseph. *The Messianic Idea in Israel: From Its Beginning to the Completion of the Mishna.* Translated by W. F. Stinespring. New York: Macmillan, 1955.

Klyber, Arthur. *The One Who Is to Come: A Collection of Writings of Father Arthur B. Klyber, Hebrew Catholic Priest.* Edited by Matthew McDonald. New Hope, KY: Remnant of Israel, 2000.

Kugelman, Richard. "Hebrew, Israelite, Jew." *The Bridge: A Yearbook of Judaeo-Christian Studies.* Edited by John Oesterreicher. Vol. 1, 204–24. New York: Pantheon Books, 1955.

Lagrange, M.-J. *Saint Paul Épitre aux Romains.* Paris: Libraire Lecoffre, 1950.

Levering, Matthew. *Christ's Fulfillment of Torah and Temple: Salvation according to Thomas Aquinas.* Notre Dame, IN: University of Notre Dame Press, 2002.

_____. *Sacrifice and Community: Jewish Offering and Christian Eucharist.* Malden, MA: Blackwell Publishing, 2005.

Louis de Montfort, *True Devotion to the Blessed Virgin.* Bay Shore, NY: Montfort Publications, 1980.

Lustiger, Cardinal Jean-Marie. *The Promise.* Grand Rapids, MI: William B. Eerdmans, 2007.

Manns, Frédéric. *Les Enfants de Rébecca. Judaïsme et christianisme aux premiers siècles.* Montrèal: Éditions Médiaspaul, 2002.

_____. *Jewish Prayer in the Time of Jesus.* Jerusalem: Franciscan Printing Press, 1994.

Marshall, Taylor. *The Crucified Rabbi.* Dallas, TX: St. John Press, 2009.

Martin, Bernard. *Prayer in Judaism.* New York: Basic Books, 1968.

Midrash Rabbah. London: Soncino Press, 1961.

Neusner, Jacob, ed. *The Babylonian Talmud: A Translation and Commentary.* 22 vols. Peabody, MA: Hendrickson Publishers, 2005.

_____. *Messiah in Context: Israel's History and Destiny in Formative Judaism.* Philadelphia: Fortress Press, 1983.

_____. *The Oral Torah: The Sacred Books of Judaism: An Introduction.* San Francisco: Harper & Row, 1986.

_____. *A Rabbi Talks with Jesus.* Revised ed. Montreal: McGill-Queen's Univ. Press, 2000.

Newman, John Henry. *Discussions and Arguments on Various Subjects.* New York: Longmans, Green, and Co., 1897.

_____. *An Essay on the Development of Christian Doctrine.* Notre Dame: University of Notre Dame Press, 1989.

O'Connell, Patrick. *Science of Today and the Problems of Genesis.* Rockford, IL: TAN Books, 1993.

Odom, Robert Leo. *Israel's Preexistent Messiah.* New York: Israelite Heritage Institute, 1985.

Oesterreicher, John. "The Hasidic Movement." *The Bridge: A Yearbook of Judaeo-Christian Studies.* Vol. 3, 122–86. New York: Pantheon Books, 1958.

Oesterreicher, John, ed. *The Bridge: A Yearbook of Judaeo-Christian Studies.* 4 vols. New York: Pantheon Books, 1955–61.

Pascal, Blaise. *Pensées.* Translated by A. J. Krailsheimer. New York: Penguin Classics, 1966.

Patai, Raphael. *The Messiah Texts.* Detroit: Wayne State University Press, 1979.

Pesikta Rabbati: Discourses for Feasts, Fasts, and Special Sabbaths. Translated by William G. Braude. 2 vols. New Haven, CT: Yale Univ. Press, 1968.

Petuchowski, Jakob J. *Understanding Jewish Prayer.* New York: KTAV Publishing House, 1972.

Pius X. Encyclical *Ad diem illum:* On the Immaculate Conception. February 2, 1904.

Pius XII. Encyclical *Divino afflante spiritu:* On Promoting Biblical Studies. 1943.

_____. Encyclical *Humani generis:* Concerning Some False Opinions Threatening to Undermine the Foundations of Catholic Doctrine. 1950.

_____. Encyclical *Mystici Corporis:* On the Mystical Body of Christ. 1943.

Pontifical Biblical Commission. *The Jewish People and Their Sacred Scriptures in the Christian Bible.* May 24, 2001.

Pritz, Ray A. *Nazarene Jewish Christianity: From the End of the New Testament Period until Its Disappearance in the Fourth Century.* Jerusalem: Magnes Press, 1988.

Rahner, Hugo. *Our Lady and the Church.* Translated by Sebastian Bullough. Bethesda: Zaccheus Press, 2004.

Randellini, Lino. *La Chiesa dei Giudeo-cristiani.* Brescia: Paideia, 1968.

Ratisbonne, Alphonse and de Bussiere, Theodore. *The Conversion of Ratisbonne.* Fort Collins, CO: Roman Catholic Books, 2000.

Ratzinger, Joseph. *Daughter Zion.* Translated by John M. McDermott. San Francisco: Ignatius Press, 1983.

_____. *Jesus of Nazareth: From the Baptism in the Jordan to the Transfiguration.* Translated by Adrian J. Walker. New York: Doubleday, 2007.

_____. *Many Religions—One Covenant: Israel, the Church, and the World.* Translated by Graham Harrison. San Francisco: Ignatius Press, 1999.

Refoulé, François. *"...Et ainsi tout Israël sera sauvé": Romains 11, 25–32.* Paris: Editions du Cerf, 1984.

Schauss, Hayyim. *The Jewish Festivals: A Guide to Their History and Observance.* New York: Schocken Books, 1996.

Schoeman, Roy. *Honey from the Rock.* San Francisco: Ignatius Press, 2007.

_____. *Salvation Is from the Jews.* San Francisco: Ignatius Press, 2003.

Scholem, Gershom. *The Messianic Idea in Judaism and Other Essays on Jewish Spirituality.* New York: Schocken Books, 1995.

_____. *Major Trends in Jewish Mysticism.* New York: Schocken Books, 1961.

Sheed, F. J., ed. *The Mary Book.* New York: Sheed & Ward, 1950.

Scholl, Andrew. *Completed Jew.* East Keilor, Vic.: Cosmoda Communications, 2002.

Skarsaune, Oskar, and Reidar Hvalvik, eds. *Jewish Believers in Jesus: The Early Centuries.* Peabody, MA: Hendrickson Publishers, 2007.

Soloveitchik, Rabbi Joseph B. *Worship of the Heart: Essays on Jewish Prayer.* Edited by Shalom Carmy. Jersey City, NJ: KTAV Publishing House, 2003.

Stark, Rodney. *The Rise of Christianity: A Sociologist Reconsiders History.* Princeton, NJ: Princeton Univ. Press, 1996.

Stein, Edith. *Life in a Jewish Family: Her Unfinished Autobiographical Account.* Translated by Josephine Koeppel. Washington DC: ICS Publications, 1986.

Stern, Karl. *The Pillar of Fire.* New Hope, KY: Urbi et orbi/Remnant of Israel, 2000.

Teresa of Avila. *The Life of Teresa of Jesus: The Autobiography of St. Theresa of Avila.* Translated by Allison Peers. Garden City, NY: Image Books, 1960.

_____. *The Way of Perfection.* Translated by Kieran Kavanaugh. Washington DC: ICS Publications, 2000.

Tertullian. *Adversus Marcion.* Vol. 3, *The Ante-Nicene Fathers.* Peabody, MA: Hendrickson Publishers, 1994.

_____. *On the Flesh of Christ.* Vol. 3, *The Ante-Nicene Fathers.* Peabody, MA: Hendrickson Publishers, 1994.

Testa, Emmanuel. *The Faith of the Mother Church: An Essay on the Theology of the Judeo-Christians.* Translated by Paul Rotondi. Jerusalem: Franciscan Printing Press, 1992.

Thomas Aquinas. *The Aquinas Catechism: A Simple Explanation of the Catholic Faith by the Church's Greatest Theologian.* Manchester, NH: Sophia Institute Press, 2000.

_____. *Summa contra gentiles.* Translated by Anton Pegis, James Anderson, Vernon Bourke, and Charles O'Neil. 4 vols. Notre Dame, IN: Univ. of Notre Dame Press, 1975.

_____. *Summa theologiae of St. Thomas Aquinas.* 2nd ed. Translated by Dominican Fathers of the English Province. London: Burns, Oates, & Washbourne, 1920–1932.

_____. *Super epistolas S. Pauli lectura.* Edited by Raphael Cai. 2 vols. Turin: Marietti, 1953.

Vatican II. *The Sixteen Documents of Vatican II.* Boston, MA: Pauline Books and Media, 1999.

Wyschogrod, Michael. *The Body of Faith: Judaism as Corporeal Election.* New York: Seabury Press, 1983.

Your Word Is Fire: The Hasidic Masters on Contemplative Prayer. Edited and translated by Arthur Green and Barry W. Holtz. New York: Paulist Press, 1977.

Zolli, Eugenio. *Before the Dawn.* New York: Sheed and Ward, 1954.

_____. *The Nazarene: Studies in New Testament Exegesis.* Translated by Cyril Vollert. New Hope, KY: Urbi et Orbi/Remnant of Israel, 1999.

Zweig, Ferdynand. *Israel, the Sword and the Harp: The Mystique of Violence and the Mystique of Redemption.* Rutherford, NJ: Fairleigh Dickinson University Press, 1970.

Index

Scripture Index

Numbering follows the RSV edition.

OLD TESTAMENT

Genesis

1:1–2:4 94	6–9 97–99	27:27–29 104
1:2.......................6	12:3 ....1, 10, 20	28:13–15 21
3:4–5...................... 7, 17	18:18 ....1, 10, 20	28:14 .... 1, 10
3:15 ...8, 16–20, 23, 31, 44	22:16–18 102	37:3–4......................108
	22:18 .... 1, 10	49.......................22
3:15–16...................191	24:43 29	49:10 ......22–23, 33, 36
4:25–26.....................24	25:30–34 103	
5...............................24	26:4 ....1, 10, 21	

Exodus

3:8........................87	19:9–24...................193	23:16 116
3:14 30	20:18–19 117	34:22 116
4:22 151	21:12–21 136	34:23 110
12:3–14....................111	21:32.........................50	
19:18–19 117	23:14–17 110	

Leviticus

16:7–22...................125	23:14 130	23:31, 41 130
19:18 139	23:15–21 116	23:40–43 120
20:24 87	23:27–29 125	

Numbers

15:19–21 172	21:4–9................83–84	24:17–19 23

Deuteronomy

4:7–8........................12	6:5.......................139	18:15–19 .... 9, 24
6:1–12........................87	16:13–15 121	28:15–65 89
6:4–5........................148	16:16 110	32:6 151

1 Kings

19:16 9

1 Chronicles

22:10 27

Ezra

7............................. 35	7:12–26.......................35

Nehemiah

2................................ 36	2:7–8................. 35, 36

Tobit

2:1........................ 115

213

P. 44-45 Conversion of Chief Rabbi
of Rome

P.51 footnote
P. 99 footnote — book
P. 118 Pentecost (old + New)
P. 142 Sin + Enslavement

CPSIA information can be obtained at www.ICGtesting.com
Printed in the USA
BVOW05s2215120614

356215BV00016B/69/P